HISTORY OF THE SCANDINAVIAN LI

PT

THE SCANDINAVIAN LITERATURES

THE HISTORY OF THE SCANDINAVIAN LITERATURES

A Survey of the Literatures of Norway, Sweden, Denmark, Iceland and Finland, from their Origins to the Present Day, including Scandinavian-American Authors, and Selected Bibliographies

Based in part on the work of

GIOVANNI BACH

With additional sections by

RICHARD BECK
University of North Dakota

ADOLPH B. BENSON
Yale University

AXEL JOHAN UPPVALL
University of Pennsylvania

and others

COMPILED, TRANSLATED IN PART, AND EDITED

BY

FREDERIKA BLANKNER
Western Reserve University

KENNIKAT PRESS, INC./PORT WASHINGTON, N. Y.

DEDICATED

TO

AMERICANS

OF SCANDINAVIAN ORIGIN

FOREWORD

A need has long been felt for a concise history of the Scandinavian literatures. This book has been written to help fill that need.

No single survey of the literatures of Norway, Sweden, Denmark, Iceland, and Finland from origins to the present day has been available. The existing treatments of the subject, few of them in English, have, for one reason or another, left parts of the field untouched. The works that present the several Scandinavian literatures separately are in various languages and each work as a rule is in several volumes. Thus to date a general view of the subject has been beyond the reach of any but the special student.

A set of working bibliographies designed for the reader whose principal language is English has also been needed, and likewise a survey of the considerable productions in the field of Scandinavian-American literature.

The present volume is based in part on a history of Scandinavian literatures by Dr. Giovanni Bach, a readable survey; not, however, designed by its author for use as a work of reference. The Introduction of Dr. Bach's work and its sections on Norwegian, Swedish, and Danish literature have been translated, checked, enlarged throughout and in part re-written to form the corresponding sections of the present history, with the aim of supplying a book suitable for reference as well as one of interest to the general reader.

In further pursuit of this aim, various additional sections have been obtained from leading scholars in their respective fields; namely, the Icelandic and Finnish sections, the bibliographies, and also the chapters on Scandinavian-American literature, in order that this extension of the Scandinavian field which is generally overlooked should receive the attention it merits. Certain of these sections, for example that on Icelandic literature, do not treat material subsequent to the opening of the year 1934, since they were finished before that date.

It may be added that the surveys of modern Icelandic and modern Finnish literature by Professor Richard Beck are the most complete yet to appear in English. Because of the dearth of easily available material in these fields, somewhat more space proportionately has been allowed for the presentation of them. The section on Danish-American literature is the first review of that material, and the surveys of Finnish-American and general Icelandic-American literature are the first to be made in English.

Because of the magnitude of the subject covered, *i. e.,* the literary productions of the five Scandinavian countries during a period of over eleven centuries, the present book involves countless matters regarding which the best authorities differ in greater or less degree. Subjects of a broader nature are involved in these differences as well as details of date, spelling, nomenclature, etc. In such cases of divergence, either the fact, date, or spelling given is the one supported by what has seemed the best author-

ity or group of authorities for the point involved,
or, where it has been desirable, I have sought to be
mindful of both the diverging views. In deciding
such questions especially in the Norwegian, Swedish,
and Danish sections, I have consulted the collabora-
tors hereinafter named, for whose invaluable co-
operation I express my deep appreciation. For their
kind assistance in checking such matters throughout, I wish especially to thank Dr. Richard Beck,
Professor and Head of the Department of Scandinavian Languages and Literatures in the University
of North Dakota; Dr. Adolph B. Benson, Professor
of German and Scandinavian in Yale University;
and Dr. Axel Johan Uppvall, Professor of Scandinavian Languages and Literatures in the University
of Pennsylvania.

In addition I am greatly indebted to Professors
Beck, Benson, and Uppvall, and to Professor Einar
Haugen, Chairman of the Department of Scandinavian in the University of Wisconsin; to Professor
Johannes Knudsen, formerly in charge of the Department of Danish and Scandinavian Literature in
Grand View College, and to Mr. Georg Strandvold, Associate Editor of *Decorah-Posten,* for reading proof of the entire book, and for the important
suggestions, data, and comments they have contributed. Professor Uppvall graciously consented to
prepare the passages on Strindberg and Karlfeldt,
as well as several others including some on early
orthography and Professor Beck to make various ad-
ditions in the Norwegian section and elsewhere.

For similar courtesy in reading proofs and offering valuable suggestions, grateful acknowledgment

FOREWORD

is made to Dr. J. L. Borgerhoff, Professor and Head of the Department of Romance Languages in Flora Stone Mather College, Western Reserve University; Dr. Halldór Hermannsson, Curator of the Fiske Icelandic Collection and Professor of Scandinavian Languages in Cornell University; Mr. J. Christian Bay, Librarian of the John Crerar Library in Chicago; Miss Hanna Astrup Larsen, of the American-Scandinavian Foundation, Editor of the *American-Scandinavian Review;* and the late Mrs. Sigrid Hakstad of the Chicago Public Library.

The helpful interest shown by Dr. Winfred George Leutner, President of Western Reserve University, in various matters concerning the volume has been deeply appreciated.

Thanks are due also to Dr. Stefán Einarsson of the Johns Hopkins University for reading proof on the Danish section, as well as for making suggestions for the Danish bibliography; to Dr. John Wargelin, President of Suomi College, Hancock, Michigan, for reading proof on the Finnish and Finnish-American sections and for supplying certain dates therein; to Dr. G. N. Swan, formerly Vice-Consul of Sweden in Iowa, for several bibliographical suggestions; to Dr. Archer Taylor, Professor and Chairman of the Department of Germanic Languages in the University of Chicago, for his opinion regarding a matter of folk-lore; and to the staffs of the Libraries of Western Reserve University and the University of Chicago for assistance in obtaining works of reference.

Among the organizations and persons who have kindly contributed information concerning certain

FOREWORD

dates or the securing of dates, especially the elusive
ones of the Scandinavian-Americans, are the following: Mr. J. Leavitt, Chief of the Catalogue Division
of the Library of Congress and Mr. Jens Nyholm of
the Catalogue Division; Mr. Einar Mose, Reference
Librarian in the John Crerar Library, Chicago;
Mr. K. D. Metcalf, Chief of the Reference Department of the New York Public Library; the Consu-
late General of Finland in New York; the Albert
Bonnier Publishing House; the Finnish-Lutheran
Book Concern; Miss Dorothea Hygen; Mr. Torger
Kleiberg; Mr. V. S. Alanne; Mr. John Suominen;
Mr. Henry Puranen, and Mr. Antero Riippa.

Relative to form, it may be said that an effort
has been made to maintain consistency in orthography insofar as the variations in usage in four related
languages and many different periods make it possible. For the sake of uniformity the letter *ö* rather
than *ø* has been used throughout, even in the Danish
section, with the approval of the scholars previously
mentioned; likewise the form *ae* replaces *æ* throughout. In the Icelandic section, the symbols for Icelandic voiceless þ (pronounced like English *th* in
thin) and voiced ð (pronounced like English *th* in
bathe) have been replaced by *th* and *d* respectively
as being more appropriate for a book intended primarily for the English-speaking reader.

In the citation of all but periodical titles the
prevalent library usage is followed in the adoption
of lower-case letters throughout except where capitals would be required in ordinary prose. Danish
nouns have been capitalized in accordance with the
dominant usage.

FOREWORD

Since the bibliographies are designed for the guidance mainly of English-speaking readers, they are made to include principally books and articles in English, as well as English translations of the major works, but they list also standard historical and critical books in all languages. Feeling that it would be to the advantage of the bibliographies themselves, I have left the plan and form of each bibliography to the respective compiler. Where it has seemed advisable, certain general works have been mentioned in more than one bibliography.

It is hoped that this volume may prove useful to readers already familiar with the field, and may also attract new friends to the literary treasures of the Scandinavian North.

FREDERIKA BLANKNER

Western Reserve University,
May 8, 1937.

TABLE OF CONTENTS

[xi]

TABLE OF CONTENTS

TABLE OF CONTENTS

TABLE OF CONTENTS

THE SCANDINAVIAN LITERATURES

THE
SCANDINAVIAN LITERATURES

INTRODUCTION

D ESPITE their major importance, Scandinavian
literatures as a whole are still insufficiently
known outside of Scandinavia.

The culture of the North has, it is true, found an
important interpreter in Germany, and now France
and especially the United States boast leading Scandi-
navianists. But for many the conception not only of
the literature but also of the geography and history
of the North remains so vague and inaccurate that
greater efforts to penetrate the clouds enveloping
them are opportune.

To understand the northern literatures it is well
to bear in mind the linguistic, historical and social
diversity of the four Scandinavian peoples, which
are ordinarily grouped together when they are not
massed outright with the Germans. Among them
are to be found certain clear and precise distinc-
tions which definitely separate them one from the
other; and these are not divisions of recent date but
have their origins in the early Middle Ages. In fact
as early as the third and fourth centuries, if not
earlier, Germanic linguistic unity may be considered as having disappeared to give place to the
formation of three dialectal groups,—*i. e.* the
Gothic, of which we have a specimen in the frag-

ments of the translation of the Bible (*Codex argenteus*) made by Bishop Ulfilas; the western group (High German, Low German, Flemish-Dutch, Friesic and English); and the northern or Scandinavian group. This last group until about the year 800 used a common primitive language, of which important monuments are extant. The inscriptions are executed in the older Germanic runes. None of these inscriptions can be traced farther back than the third century.

During the period c. 800 through c. 1000 or c. 1100, known as the Viking Period, the language underwent many phonetic changes, as an accompaniment to the violent political changes that took place in the North at that time. Monuments extant (over 2000) are executed in the so-called "younger" runic alphabet of sixteen characters. About the close of the eleventh century or the beginning of the twelfth, although the differences increased later, the once common language had by gradual transformations already developed into four distinct literary dialects, Old Danish, Old Icelandic, Old Norwegian, and Old Swedish.

Later, after the union of Norway with Denmark in 1397, Danish gradually replaced Norwegian as the official written language of Norway, and strongly influenced the speech of the educated classes. The resultant mixture of Danish and Norwegian forms became the basis of the modern *riksmål*, or Dano-Norwegian. However the ancient tongue persisted in the country districts where the several dialects continued their life. About 1850 an attempt was made by Ivar Aasen to create a written language formed on the basis of the least "corrupted" of these dialects. This was to be a "New Norse" language legitimately descended from Old Norse, and genuinely Norwegian in contradistinction to Dano-Norwegian. This language, variously known in Norway and elsewhere as the *landsmål* or *nynorsk*, is officially on a par with the *riksmål* or *bokmål*, but has not yet displaced the latter as a national language.

Icelandic, in the immense solitude of its great northern island, has maintained almost uncorrupted the linguistic elements of the Old Icelandic so that the Icelanders of today can still read, without serious difficulty, the songs of the *Edda* and the various sagas.

Swedish and Danish, already differentiated, became still more definitely separated by the time of the Reformation, when political, cultural and social exigencies made necessary the adoption by each of a native dialect as the official language (*riksspråk*). Sweden adopted the dialect of the territory of Lake Mälaren, while Denmark adopted the language used in Zealand.

It was during this time, about the first half of the sixteenth century, that the four languages developed enough to enter the modern stage and be known thereafter as Modern Danish, Modern Icelandic, Modern Norwegian and Modern Swedish.

Thus, since about the twelfth century, the Scandinavian countries have had four different though closely related languages, this linguistic diversity offering the major difficulty to be overcome by the serious student of their literatures. The total present population of Scandinavia, exclusive of Finland, is

about thirteen millions, and today each of the four
languages except Icelandic is spoken by several million people, Norwegian by over two million, Danish
by over three million and Swedish by over six million. In addition there are some three hundred and
fifty thousand Finns of Swedish extraction, who
speak and write Swedish as their mother tongue.*
Icelandic is spoken by somewhat more than a hundred thousand.†

Corresponding to these four languages, diverse
although related, there are four distinct though
similar mentalities: Norway with its strong and
mighty frame, like the elk that inhabits its forests;
Sweden with its plains broad, green and fertile;
solitary and rugged Iceland; and Denmark, forming
an organic part of Europe but at the same time
projecting with its little peninsula of Jutland
toward the cold and cloudy North. Each of these
has its own individuality, easily detected in its literature.

The Norwegian, philosophically inclined, is reserved and introspective by nature, though by no
means devoid of a sense of humor. He has the ingenuous pure mind of a child. As Haukland has
said, "when the man of the North smiles, he is like a
babe in his unthinking joy. But underneath this joy
of his pulsates an infinite melancholy."

* In any consideration of Scandinavia, Finland always may or may
not be included. Some exclude it because the original Finns had no racial
connection with Scandinavia. Some include it for historical or traditional
reasons, since Finland for over six hundred years was united with Sweden
and many citizens of Swedish descent still live there.

† Icelandic is also spoken or read by a large number of Icelandic-Americans
in the United States and Canada, estimated variously as between twenty-five
to thirty-five thousand. It might be added that the number of other Americans of Scandinavian birth or extraction is estimated at about three millions.

INTRODUCTION

The Icelander is brother to the Norwegian by racial and spiritual affinity; but in his solitude uncheered by the more tender and expansive moods of nature, he has conserved something of the primitive,—something that has the quality of myth and legend.

If the Norwegian is a son of the sea and mountain, the Swede is a son of the earth. His deep blue eyes mirror the solemn peace of his fertile fields and woodlands. And this love for the virgin earth, this love for the fields furrowed by the fecundating plow may be noted more or less in the works of Strindberg, Lagerlöf and Bondeson, works in which one often breathes the resinous air of fir-woods or the free and moving atmosphere of plains open to wind and tempest.

Old in history and in traditions, the Danish people once knew the mighty joy of dominion and the bitter discouragement of defeat. A critical nation yet a light-hearted one, it is removed indeed from the mystical transports of the Swede or from the frequent seriousness of the Norwegian.

Despite these manifest differences of inclination and of character, more than one accredited Scandinavian author has attempted to bring the Scandinavian nations again into their former closer mutual relationship,—making appeal to their unity of origin and racial affinity, as during the war of Schleswig-Holstein (1848–50) and during the World War; but the efforts have never been successful and Scandinavianism * is now the subject

* On Scandinavianism see: Georg Strandvold, "The triple alliance of the North," in *Quarterly Journal of the University of North Dakota*, Grand Forks, N. Dak., 1924, pp. 111–27.

merely of some academic magazine article or of an occasional lecture for literary and scientific reunions.

The rifts between the peoples remain,—indeed, they tend to widen. For the Scandinavian countries are jealous of their individual independence. The maintenance of a sane nationalistic policy is their aim. Never in the long and sometimes turbulent history of the Scandinavian North have the four sister nations lived in such concord as at the present time. But Iceland, for example, a sovereign state since 1918, has the right to separate completely from Denmark and to found an independent republic. In 1943 this separation may take place.

Nevertheless, despite this, one can trace in the four Scandinavian literatures a single physiognomy quite clear-cut and definite: namely, a noble, thoughtful vision of life, which often imparts to them a grey and solemn tonality, brightened however by gleams of sunlight. To readers of the more southern races it appears that in the literature of the Scandinavians is mirrored the crepuscular nature of their country, serving as a responsive background for their deep sense of the elemental forces of the universe.

NORWEGIAN LITERATURE

NORWEGIAN LITERATURE

based on the treatise by
GIOVANNI BACH, Ph.D.
translated by
FREDERIKA BLANKNER, Litt.D.
Western Reserve University
and enlarged in collaboration
with contributors

ANCIENT AND MEDIAEVAL PERIOD

NORWEGIAN literature has two periods of flourishing production: the era between about 900 and the latter part of the thirteenth century, which saw the development of the rich early literature of Norway and Iceland; and the nineteenth century, the golden age of Norwegian letters. In the interval between these two periods the Norwegian language is largely lost and the literary history of Norway is almost identified with that of Denmark, although a stream of popular native poetry remains, traversing like a live and roaring brook the vast moors of Norwegian literary production.

The fundamental character of Norwegian literature is eminently dramatic, undulating between realism and spirituality, between rationalism and mysticism.

When did Norwegian literature have its beginning?

[11]

It is always difficult, if not indeed impossible, to establish the beginnings of a literature, since together with the beginnings of a language they are lost in the darkness of the centuries; nor on the other hand can one give literary value to the inscriptions in runic characters, the primitive symbols of the Germanic peoples; these inscriptions point, nevertheless, to the cultivation of oral literature among the Norwegians of old long before they appear definitely on the stage of written history. Norwegian literature proper may, on the other hand, be said to begin with Norway's share in the *Eddas*, sagas, and skaldic poetry, which flourished, although not all simultaneously, from c. 900 to c. 1250. Norway and Iceland both shared in the production of this literature. Some of the Eddic poems are of Norwegian origin, yet all of them have been preserved only in Iceland, and in the Icelandic language. Much traditional material from Norway went into the making of the Icelandic sagas, but as Professor Halldór Hermannsson has effectively phrased it: "the saga as a literary phenomenon is undeniably an Icelandic creation." The first skaldic poets on record were Norwegian, but, on the other hand, their existing poems have been preserved in Iceland, and the art of skaldic poetry was perfected and after the first half of the tenth century virtually exclusively practiced by Icelandic skalds. So this early literature will be considered under the country which has preserved, and to a great degree, at least, produced this remarkable literary legacy.

It may be added that while Norwegian traditions were woven in great abundance into the pattern of early Icelandic literature, the latter has in turn had a marked influence upon later Norwegian literature as regards both subject-matter and style.

At the end of the twelfth century and the beginning of the thirteenth the saga, which had flourished so abundantly in Iceland, was already decadent. The political and social conditions no longer lent themselves to a literary form of this nature requiring a romantic and legendary concept of life. Contacts with the western European world, contacts favored by the great king Haakon Haakonsson (1217–63), had brought Norway toward a more stable and peaceful political systematization than before. Little by little a court life of the type found in other European nations was developing and this gave rise, in 1250, to a great original work in prose, entitled *Konungsskuggsjá* (The King's mirror), a long didactic composition, in which the author gives an extensive picture of the political and court life of his time.

Religious poetry also flourished in the North throughout the thirteenth and fourteenth centuries. The most remarkable of Norwegian poems of this type is the *Draumkvaedet* (Dream vision), a work of the thirteenth century, ranking high among the vision poems of the Middle Ages and revealing admirably the spirit of the times; it bears some resemblance to the *Divine Comedy*..

In a rising rhythm, along with religious poetry, popular poetry developed, delighting in trolls (fantastic beings conceived of as giants and goblins), in fairies, mermaids, and other supernatural creatures. The place of the god Thor, who in the pagan poems used to fight against the giants with his enchanted hammer, was taken by the Saint-King Olav, who fought them with the Cross. Heroic ballads, historical ballads, ballads of chivalry, and humorous ballads also were numerous. The variety and richness of this folk-poetry becomes more impressive still when it is borne in mind that some two hundred Norwegian ballads have survived down to the present day. Besides this folk-poetry, which we might call epical-mythological, the Norwegian people possessed a rich store of folk- and fairy-tales. It is not easy to establish when they arose, which of them were indigenous and which were imported.

THE REFORMATION

When their rulers imposed the Reformation upon the Norwegian people there was a time when it seemed that poetic art, like every other art, must become extinct. The old literature in prose and in poetry was forgotten and replaced by an arid religious poetry, without light or spirit. Nevertheless the folk-tales and the popular poems continued to live in the steadfast hearts and on the lips of the peasants.

The religious struggle, aggravated by pillage and rapine, was followed by a period of great confusion, from the results of which the language did not escape. However, in Denmark during the period of the Reformation, a written language was in process of formation, which little by little penetrated also into Norway.

Nothing of the Old Norwegian remained except in the phraseology of the laws. The new written language, the Danish, passed slowly into current use in the cities, while Old Norwegian persisted only in the phraseology of the laws and in the numerous rural dialects.

The Reformation, having, as indicated, been forced upon Norway, brought there no national spiritual revival in its trail, as it had done, for instance, in Denmark; the energy of the Norwegian nation was at a low ebb, and adequate leadership was sadly lacking. As a result the period surrounding the beginning of the Reformation, the first half of the sixteenth century, is one of the most barren eras in the cultural and literary history of Norway. Fortunately, after the middle of the century, signs appear of an awakening in both Norwegian literature and culture. Life-giving streams from the humanistic movement, which in Norway, as elsewhere in the Scandinavian countries, merged largely with the Lutheran Reformation, played an important part in the increasing literary activity.

Geble Pedersson (c.1490–1557), the first Lutheran Bishop in Bergen and rector of the cathedral school of that city, was one of the leaders in the new movement. A man of broad humanistic training, endowed with genuine vision, he stimulated intellectual and creative activity and made his school a great educational centre. His pupil and adopted son, Absalon Pedersson Beyer (1528–75), became the leading Norwegian humanist of his day and a fearless spokesman of Norwegian nationalism and independence. This feeling is a strong undercurrent in his writings, notably in the book, *Concerning the Kingdom of Norway* (1567), a

[15]

historical and descriptive work. Beyer promoted dramatic performances in Bergen and he, too, probably wrote several dramas.

A younger contemporary of Beyer was the influential pastor Peder Clausson Friis (1545–1614), a vigorous and zealous humanist, who spared no effort to interpret their glorious past to his people in order to restore their faith in themselves. He has an honored place in the history of Norwegian literature for his masterful translation of Snorri Sturluson's *Heimskringla*, the sagas of the Kings of Norway, which continued to be read down to the nineteenth century. He also wrote the first natural history of Norway and an important topographical description of the country.

Christiania had its group of humanists during this period no less than Bergen, but these wrote almost exclusively in Latin and are therefore of comparatively small significance in the history of Norwegian letters.

Although the seventeenth century was in Norway an era of meagre creative literary activity, there was not lacking a characteristic figure, Petter Dass (1647–1707), who lived during the latter half of the century in Helgeland, in northern Norway. He was at the same time a preacher and a leader of men, and through the power of his strong personality and his untiring clerical labours he exerted an enormous influence not only on his farflung parish but upon his people as a whole.

In his major work *Nordlands trompet* (The trumpet of the North country, 1678–92) he describes in fluent and graphic verse northern Norway:—the landscape, the mode and conditions of life, and the character of the people. His various shorter poems, religious and secular, were on everyone's lips long before they were collected in a volume; and they are still living today after more than two centuries since the death of their author, not least among them his strikingly realistic and sonorous *The song of the dalesman* (1683).

In the fancy of the people he became with time a legendary figure, a mythic hero, exacting obedience even from Satan.

Two other authors of the period merit special mention. Dorothea Engelbretsdatter (1635–1716) was generally hailed as one of the foremost hymn-writers of the day, even Holberg referring to her as "the first poetess of the northern countries," but from the modern point of view she is definitely lacking in poetic ability. Much more gifted a writer of religious poetry was the Dane, Anders Arrebo (d. 1637), who became at an early age Bishop of Trondhjem. His translation of the *Psalms* became popular reading in Norway and he wrote an ambitious narrative-descriptive poem, *Hexaëmeron* (1661), on the creation. Composed in the Alexandrine metre, this work introduced to the northern countries a verse form which was destined to become popular and significant as the vehicle of dignified poetry.

LUDVIG HOLBERG

In the history of Norway, there is a period commonly known as "the four hundred years of uninterrupted night" (from the last years of the fourteenth century until 1814). In this period Norway found itself united to Denmark, in consequence of a marriage between the two reigning families. However, this union represented, according to the opinion of the Norwegians, a grave misfortune for Norway. For their branch of the reigning family became extinct, and the two kingdoms were inherited by German descendants, who preferred to establish their residence in Denmark. In this way all the power was centred in Copenhagen and the interests of Norway were ill-protected. Pestilences and other disasters decimated the population. It seemed as though the Norwegian people were immersed in a sort of lethargy and awaited only the end of its existence. It is natural that under such conditions art and poetry could not prosper; nevertheless this period of inactivity was not able entirely to destroy the poetic vein of the Norwegians. And the greatest Scandinavian writer of the eighteenth century, Ludvig Holberg, was born in Norway, in Bergen, in 1684.

Holberg represents a living pulsating idea in the Stygian marsh of Danish-Norwegian literature, stagnant in an abstract and empty doctrinairism. Even from boyhood, he interested himself little in the musty and conventional scholastic disputes, while all his spirit was by instinct attuned to the real life that vibrated in the streets and byways of his old Hanseatic town.

His studies in theology completed, he travelled over half of Europe, including England, and came in contact with the most representative men of the time. He was familiar with the writings of Montaigne, Montesquieu, and Bayle, and they exerted a very great influence on him. He knew Molière thoroughly and in Italy he had the opportunity to form an exact idea of the theatre of masques.

Harassed by financial necessity, he had to accept a chair of metaphysics at Copenhagen, he, the anti-metaphysician *par excellence,* and only in 1730 did he succeed in becoming a professor of history. It should be added that apart from his comedies, on which his fame was based, Holberg's output in the field of Scandinavian general and ecclesiastical history was enormous.

In 1719–20 his work entitled *Peder Paars* was published, a sort of comic epic. Paars is a brewer of Kallundborg who goes to join his *fiancée* in Jutland. The author parodies Homer and Vergil, caricaturing at the same time the defects, the pedantry and the superstitions of his time and country.

The book caused a great stir. The author was menaced with severe penalties, but the Council of the King of Denmark, meeting to decide regarding the guilt of the work, judged that *Peder Paars* was an innocent book written to amuse, at the same time however advising the author to desist and not give occasion for further protests. In 1722 Holberg wrote his first comedies and in two years he completed almost twenty.

After a second trip to Paris, made in 1725, Holberg composed a poem entitled *Metamorphosis,* wherein, contrary to Ovid, he imagines men transformed into plants and animals. From 1732 to 1740 he devoted himself to the publication of historical and philosophic writings, until in 1741 his satiric spirit burst forth again with greater vigour than before in *Niels Klim's underground journey*, which, incongruously enough for the book of an author championing a national language, was written originally in Latin (*Nicolai Klimii iter subterraneum*).

The idea for this novel is taken without doubt from *Gulliver's travels*. Holberg imagines that a Norwegian student has the idea of exploring a cavern located on the summit of a mountain. But the rope by which he is bound to four of his companions breaks and he falls into the cavern, whence he penetrates into the vitals of the earth. There he finds peoples strange and bizarre, who nevertheless in their laws and customs are quite superior to folk of the earth's surface. Holberg imagines that one of these inhabitants of the centre of the earth has made a visit to the surface and composed a sort of diary concerning this journey, which he reports. In it are found highly original observations on the political and social conditions of Europe in the eighteenth century.

This book enjoyed an unheard-of success; in a short time it was translated into seven languages. It combines imagination with spirit, and fancy with reality in such a way as to be equally amusing to adults and children.

Shortly after being elevated to the nobility and created a baronet, Holberg retired to his estates near Sorö, where he died January 28th, 1754, leaving his entire patrimony to the college there.

At the time of Holberg's death the Danes did not fully realize the loss that they had suffered; not until the nineteenth century did they adequately recognize the value of this great writer of Norwegian birth who for his highly enjoyable comedies came to be called "the Molière of the North."

His comedies, about thirty in number, are all profoundly human, interesting and extremely amusing, not only because of the subject,—the comic vein gushes from the facts themselves, from the very situations as in Molière and in Goldoni,—but because of the way in which the subject is handled.

Whether in the trio of his most important plays, *The political tinker* (1723), in which he ridicules the politician of the petty bourgeoisie, *Jeppe on the hill* (1723) and *Erasmus Montanus* (1731); whether in *Jean de France* (1723), in which he strikes at the frenzy for the French fashion, *The busy trifler* (1723), *The lying-in room* (1724), *Masquerade* (1724), *The Arabian powder* (1724), *The fortunate shipwreck* (1731), *Honest ambition* (1731), or *Don Ranudo de Colibrados* (1753),* in which he satirizes the proud and silly nobility, the art of this Norwegian writer, despite the various French, Italian and English influences, reveals itself as being original. What in general is criticized in Holberg is the absence of the feminine note, perhaps because there was lacking in him that tenderness of heart so much a part of some poets, that sweet necessity for a weakness that seduces one's strength and at the same time sustains it. In his comedies there is never a word expressing the involuntary start of delight, the spontaneous uplifting of the spirit at the sight of a woman beloved.

* The dates of the plays are those given in the first collected edition.

But though such lack in a lyric poet would be unforgivable, in a poet essentially satiric and comic like Holberg it does not constitute a fatal defect. It may be noted that this absence of tenderness in Holberg's works no doubt has some connection with the fact that he remained unmarried.

Judged according to whatever standard, his comedies will always remain masterpieces of satiric art and his heroes will never fail to interest, entertain and provoke thought.

The Danish poet Oehlenschläger said of him: "He has known how to paint the *bourgeois* life of Copenhagen of his time so faithfully that if this city were to be swallowed up and if at the end of two hundred years the comedies of Holberg were rediscovered, from them one would be able to reconstruct the epoch just as from Pompeii and from Herculaneum we know the times of ancient Rome."

THE AGE OF ENLIGHTENMENT OR RATIONALISM AND THE FIRST SIGNS OF CULTURAL INDEPENDENCE

One might say that the death of Holberg marked the beginning in Norway of the struggle between romanticism and rationalism. Not being able to boast great literary personalities who could place themselves at the head of a movement or a school, Norway lived by importing ideas, tendencies, opinions, and books from abroad. The writers about whom the struggles and the enthusiasms of the disagreeing critics centred were the Dane Ewald and the German poet Klopstock. Many, like Holberg, championed Montesquieu, Voltaire, Diderot;

others Boileau, Batteux, Lessing, and still others the French and English authors, Rousseau, Pope, Thomson, Macpherson.

Deeply influenced by English writers, and not least by Young, was Christian Baumann Tullin (1728–65), an extremely popular poet in his time, whose principal work, *May day* (1758), inaugurated a new tendency in Norwegian lyric poetry. The new element was its pronounced delight in nature and praise of rural life.

The romantic current manifested itself, as elsewhere, in a revival of the national element, in an exaltation of the native land, the native language, the native race, the essence of which found representation in the peasant, who in Norway had never been a bondsman, and had jealously conserved his ancestral traditions and customs.

The history of Norway was studied assiduously also by a number of men in various parts of the country, and their labours did much to arouse the national consciousness. Among these Gerhard Schön-ing (1722–80), for a long period head of the Trond-heim cathedral school, stands in the forefront. With his historical writings, particularly with his monumental *History of Norway* (1771–81), although left uncompleted at his death, he laid the foundation for Norwegian historical research and contributed greatly to the development of the Norwegian national feeling.

A practical consequence of these nationalistic currents was the founding of the "Norwegian Society," which arose in Copenhagen in 1772 through the efforts of Norwegian students impatient of the political and cultural dominion of Denmark. From the heart of this literary circle echoed the song which half a century later was to become the first Norwegian national hymn, *Hail! O Norway!* by Nordahl Brun. The song was banned by the Danish censors, but this did not mean that it was forgotten.

Brun (1745–1816) was a lyric and dramatic poet, and a hymnologist of note; he was also a famous polemic and orator. A pupil of the historian Schöning, one of the founders of the Norwegian Society, he inherited his teacher's scorn for pedantry and his sense of reality. In 1772 he wrote *Einar Tambeskielver*, the first historical drama in Norwegian literature, more notable, however, for its vigorous nationalism than for its literary excellence, as a consequence of which he aroused the ire of the Danish censors. After a long sojourn in Copenhagen, he returned to Norway, where he composed patriotic and religious hymns, which constituted his best work.

In 1814, Brun was the ardent champion of the independence of Norway. He died in Bergen in 1816.

Another illustrious member of the Norwegian Society was the poet Johan Herman Wessel (1742–85). Bohemian in temperament he had, however, a clear and unprejudiced mind, hostile to every affectation and to every sentimentalism. His masterpiece is *Kjaerlighed uden strömper* (Love without stockings, 1772), in which he scoffs at the imitations, then in vogue, of the French tragedies and the Italian melodramas. His tales in verse also display a comic vein of the first order, not free, however, from a pessimistic sarcasm which reveals him fundamentally as a tragic and melancholy spirit.

In this second half of the eighteenth century the interest of Norwegian literature was primarily directed to political ideals, an interest which if it at times resulted in the loss of the aesthetic element, nevertheless prepared the way for the definitive conquest of the cultural independence of Norway, which by that time had been subjected for three centuries to the yoke of Denmark.

WERGELAND AND THE CULTURAL INDEPENDENCE OF NORWAY

The long period of apparent death in the cultural and political life of Norway came to an end at the beginning of the nineteenth century. The echoes of the French Revolution had penetrated even into the North, and everywhere a new life was germinating and new hopes were being born.

Norway separated from Denmark in 1814. Christiania (now Oslo) had its own university, established in 1811, so that the Norwegian students were no longer compelled to betake themselves to Copenhagen to complete their studies, but instead remained in their own country. A band of poets arose who extolled love of liberty and country, in poems, plays, and stories, wherein they described and exalted the ancient greatness. At the same time they turned their attention to the peasant, who had always constituted and constitutes today the heart of Norway.

As has been said before, the Norwegian peasant

has never been a vassal or bound in any way to the soil, but has always enjoyed great liberties, and has made use of such liberty not only to create for himself a social position of the first order (a large number of Norwegian peasants are proprietors), but also to improve his culture, which has served him to reach eminent posts in the political life of the country.

Now it seemed that the poet could draw from the life of the peasant inexhaustible material for his own work, since throughout the period in which all activity in Norway appeared to be extinct, poetry had played a very important part in the life of the peasants.

And so there had arisen a great quantity of ballads, popular songs, and folk-tales taken from the very lips of the peasants, who had passed them down from father to son. These popular productions and peasant motifs, often accompanied by music and the dance, served as pattern for poetic compositions. Along with the kings and heroes, the peasant, too, became a protagonist of the new poetry.

The most characteristic figure of this period was Henrik Wergeland, born in Christiansand in 1808. Following in the footsteps of his father, Dean Nicolai Wergeland, a prominent clergyman, author of the pamphlet *The political crimes of Denmark against Norway,* he was the greatest political agitator of the country, a fervid admirer of the principles of the French Revolution.

Wergeland wrote a large number of plays, or satirical sketches, most of which have been completely forgotten. Nevertheless his name is known to everyone in Norway, not so much for his literary production, as for his fervid apostleship of Norwegian independence. His fantasy was ardent and youthful but chaotic, as appears from his trilogy entitled *Skabelsen, Mennesket og Messias* (Creation, Man and Messiah, 1830).

Wergeland's love for liberty and justice induced him in addition to champion the cause of the Hebrews who at that time did not have the right of entrance into his country. With fire and eloquence he dedicated himself to the Jewish cause. And thus came about the creation of two beautiful and delicate poems, *Jöden* (The Jew, 1842) and *Jödinden* (The Jewess, 1844), among his few poetic productions that are read with pleasure even today. These poems are said to have induced the Norwegian government to concede to the Jews the same right as to other foreigners. For this work of his the Norwegian Hebrews raised a monument on Wergeland's tomb.

Among the other finest poems of this versatile author must be cited that in prose entitled *Jan van Huysums blomsterstykke* (Jan van Huysum's floral painting, 1840), the graceful little poem called *Et gammelnorskt herresaede* (An old Norwegian manor, 1835), and the one he wrote on his deathbed, *Til min gyldenlak* (To my gilly-flower, 1845).

As in his poetry Wergeland sowed seed for freedom of the spirit, for tolerance and justice, in the same way he sowed seed (in the literal sense of the word) among his beloved people. Often in fact he travelled about, carrying vegetable and flower seeds in his pocket for distribution among the poor and he gave advice on how to raise the most useful and beautiful plants. "My life," he used to say, "must be a faithful comment on my poetry."

He was persecuted and despised by the rich, but idolized by the poor and the humble.

He died July 14th, 1845. His statue is now in Oslo and he occupies a post of honour among the immortals of the Norwegian Parnassus.*

A battling spirit like Wergeland could not but arouse strong hatreds, sympathies, rancours, and enthusiasms. In fact, already during his lifetime two currents arose in Norway, two parties, one made up of his adherents, called "patriots,"—convinced and tenacious champions of the political and cultural independence of Norway,—and the other composed of the friends of Denmark, who did not wish to break the bonds which for so many centuries had held the two peoples together and served to direct Norwegian literature into the great channel of European culture.

Among the latter was the poet Johan Sebastian Welhaven, born in Bergen in 1807. His sympathy for Denmark originated also from the fact that he was related to Danes and that his poetic taste owed much to the works of the great Danish poets of his time. Unlike Wergeland, who was a true viking by temperament, violent, exuberant, instinctive, Welhaven was highly critical, refined, and of classical taste; hence adverse to fanaticism. If the form of Wergeland was careless and unadorned, Welhaven was instead a master of poetic

* In 1908 a monument was erected to Wergeland by his fellow-countrymen in North Dakota.

art and all his poems are pervaded by a tender and graceful romanticism.

Also in the political field he opposed Wergeland, whose declamatory and demagogic tone he did not approve, and in whom he believed he detected dilettantism.

In 1836 he was in France and Germany, in 1840 he was nominated by the king to be Lecturer on Philosophy at the University of Christiania, and in 1858 he went to Italy to study archeology. He died in October, 1873.

Wergeland and Welhaven, each in his own field, had completed a work that was purely poetic, yet they had not interested themselves actively in the treasures of popular poetry hidden here and there in the valleys of Norway. They did nothing to unearth them and put them into circulation in the great cultural current of the country. To this task the two writers Peter Christian Asbjörnsen (1812–85) and Jörgen Moe (1813–82) dedicated themselves, collecting all the copious store of folk-tales which were found scattered in the various regions of Norway. Thus in a few years, from 1841 to 1844, four volumes of Norwegian folk-tales were published; an augmented second edition appeared in 1851; and in 1871 Asbjörnsen brought out a larger collection, all of which contributed greatly to the development of the narrative style.

In 1845–48 Asbjörnsen alone published a collection of folk-tales which he titled *Norske huldre eventyr og folkesagn* (Norwegian fairy- and folk-tales). Moe also, in 1851, published a collection of tales in prose for children, *I brönden og i tjaernet* (In the well and in the tarn), and in 1860 *En liden julegave* (A little Christmas gift).

In all of these collections the writers display a narrative style that is simple but very effective, because it is in keeping, in so far as possible, with the peasant language. The erudite, accustomed to the correct and elegant phraseology of the Danish authors, were scandalized at such a style, which they found offensive to literary good taste; but later the salutary effects of it were noted in Norwegian narrative prose.

The unearthing of the popular folk-tales contributed also to the unearthing of the old Norwegian language, still traceable in the various dialects that were spoken in the valleys of Norway. To this study Ivar Aasen (1813–96) dedicated himself with zeal and enthusiasm; it was he who created the so-called *landsmål*, or New Norse, the language of the countryside, which he distinguished from the official language, the Dano-Norwegian, to which much later the term *riksmål* was applied.

In the *landsmål* Ivar Aasen wrote a large number of poems that were simple and devoid of ornament, but at the same time immediate and spontaneous in sentiment and imagery. One feels in these the peasant folk who suffer and rejoice, who think and speak without rhetorical frills but with instinctive naturalness. The finest collection of these lyrics is entitled *Symra* (The anemone, 1863).

Aasen wrote plays also, but his immortal glory is contained in the lyrics.

Nor was the rich store of Norwegian folk-songs neglected. Jörgen Moe had already, in 1840, published a small collection of these; but the first great collector and editor of Norwegian folk-songs was the pastor Magnus Brostrup Landstad (1802–80), whose important and extensive collection appeared in 1853 and established for him a prominent place in the history of Norwegian folk literature. Several noted collectors and editors have since his day carried on this work. Landstad was also an especially gifted hymn-writer. With the noted *landsmål*-poet Professor Elias Blix (1836–1902) he ranks as Norway's leading hymnologist.

This romantic-nationalistic period constituted the period of preparation for the great golden age of Norwegian literature. The political struggles were allayed if not ended. Political and cultural independence was attained. The writers of this period were certainly not figures of the first importance who could rank as peers with the great European authors of other nations, but they nevertheless sowed a seed that was to germinate and bear fruit.

The struggle between the various tendencies that was characteristic of this period is summed up in the two names Wergeland and Welhaven, in the "patriot" and the "Scandinavian." But now that many of the dissensions and hostilities were quieted or forgotten, a man arose who would gather the two tendencies into himself and surpass them in a superior ideal; the ideal of a literature human and universal, transcending, while recognizing, the limits that previous writers had imposed upon themselves.

HENRIK IBSEN

Really to understand the thought of Ibsen it is necessary to recall one of the greatest philosophers Scandinavia can boast of up to the present, the Dane Sören Kierkegaard (1813–55), whose fundamental work *Enten-eller* (Either-or, 1843) is without doubt the one whose echo is most felt in the earlier plays of Ibsen, above all in *Brand*.

The first part of this work *(Enten)* treats of the aesthetic conception of existence. As a certain critic says, it could constitute a philosophic *summa* of the life of pleasure, a sort of breviary of the *enfant de volupté*. All the personages who appear in this first part are incarnations of the epicurean ideal.

The second part *(Eller)* is instead a crushing confutation of the first, a sledge-hammer blow, under which the arguments expounded in *Enten* are reduced to dust and fragments. The apology for a life of pleasure gives way to a eulogy of altruism, sacrifice, and temperance. The aesthetic life is supplanted by the ethical, which in its turn is no more than a stepping-stone, since above it rises a still greater ideal, a sublime one, the religious life, that of the ascetic.

In *Brand*, the drama that expresses the thought of Ibsen most clearly, we find this dialogue:

Brand: I will not compromise in my demands. I want all or nothing. The slightest evidence of weakness, and you forfeit your life. Do not hope for any concession. You must not shrink from sacrifice. The demand is unconditional: faithfulness even unto death.

Einar (*turning to Agnes*): Flee! Escape this cruel game. Leave him. He is heartless to propose an inaccessible goal. I offer you a life of pleasure.

Brand: Very well. Choose! It is here the ways divide.

Einar: Choose between strife and peace, between joy and torment, yearning and contentment, life and death. Choose!

Agnes (*following Brand*): Beyond the night and mortal anguish, I see the dawn breaking on the horizon.

Anyone can see the spiritual affinity between the philosopher and the playwright, a spiritual affinity which has led some to consider *Brand* and other Ibsen plays dramatized comments on the thought of Kierkegaard. In fact, Ibsen's attacks against official Christianity, his point of view regarding the question of matrimony, his scorn for the various Peer Gynts,—half-characters which ought to be melted down again in the crucible of the button-moulder,—all are motifs frequently found in the works of the great Danish philosopher.

Kierkegaard is the true spiritual brother of Ibsen. But Rousseau and Kant also, and Paludan-Müller, Danish writer of the first half of the nineteenth century, author of a great pessimistic epic entitled *Adam Homo;* and Welhaven, too, contributed to give form and content to his art.

Together with these ideas of moral and religious rigidity which predominated in all of northern Europe in the first half of the nineteenth century one must take into consideration the unhappy events that left profound and indelible traces in the entire life of the tragic Norwegian.

Ibsen was born March 20th, 1828, in Skien, a small

and melancholy port of southern Norway. His father, a sociable and vivacious individual who was in the lumber business, had attained a fairly comfortable income which permitted him to provide his numerous family with all they needed. His mother, Marichen Altenburg, of German descent, was a retiring and reserved person, but extremely devoted to her children and her home; in her later years she withdrew more and more into herself, "and in this aversion to self-revelation," observes Professor Halvdan Koht, "we can recognize one of her son's traits." It also appears that Ibsen may, in a degree, have inherited his art interest from his mother, who seems to have possessed some artistic talent. As a boy Ibsen lived much to himself, taking small part in the play of other children but occupying himself with reading and drawing, and with his own thoughts. An unusual youth indeed!

In 1836 a grave misfortune befell his home. His father was compelled to declare himself bankrupt. Everything was sold; it was necessary to abandon the old house in town and to find refuge in the country, at Venstöp. Not until seven or eight years later was his family able to return to Skien. But Henrik, who was the eldest of the family, had to think how to provide for his own existence. It was thus that in 1844 he went to Grimstad, as a pharmacist's apprentice. In 1848 the echoes of the revolutions which had burst forth in various states of Europe reached Norway and the spirit of Ibsen became inflamed with indignation and enthusiasm. He wrote an ode on the subject, glorifying the Hungarians, and a cycle of sonnets in which he urged the Scandinavians to reunite and struggle against being overpowered by the Germans.

While he was preparing for his entrance examination to the University, Ibsen read with passionate attention the histories of Sallust and the Catiline orations of Cicero; the figure of Catiline interested him exceedingly, and so it was that he wrote his first play (1850), which carries the name of the great conspirator. The work, launched with difficulty and only with the assistance of a friend, had no success; it is immature, but not without promise, and anticipates the future dramatist. In 1850 Ibsen left Grimstad and went to Christiania. He succeeded, in September of that year, in getting a new play of his produced, *The warrior's barrow*, a romantic drama, which appealed to the popular taste. But the profits were paltry and often the poet could not manage to have both dinner and supper the same day. He was already on the point of abandoning himself to the deepest desperation, when Ole Bull, the Paganini of the North, whose interest and affection for the young dramatist had been aroused, offered him the post of *régisseur* and stage poet in the theatre of Bergen, which he had founded just two years before.

For Ibsen this was a stroke of fortune, which carried him suddenly from misery to a modest but certain livelihood. He remained in this position five years, from 1852 to 1857, and he had the opportunity to produce several of his plays, national and historical in theme, among which were: *St. John's* *night* (1853), *Lady Inger of Östrat* (1855), *The feast at Solhaug* (1856) and *Olaf Liljekrans* (1857).*

In the summer of 1857 he left the direction of the theatre of Bergen for that of Christiania. A year later he married the woman who was his faithful companion during all his life, in the days of unhappiness as in those of happiness.

In Christiania he had one of his historical dramas produced, *The vikings at Helgeland* (1858), an excellent play which enjoyed, however, at the time, only a moderate success on the stage, and caused a celebrated controversy between its author and the Christiania Theatre. In Christiania Ibsen had the opportunity also to strengthen the bonds of friendship which had long attached him to Björnson and Vinje.

After a parenthesis in the series of historical dramas, furnished by *Love's comedy* (1862), a satirical play in which he attacked with pitiless sarcasm the social lies regarding the most sublime of human sentiments, Ibsen wrote two other historical plays: *The pretenders* (1864), a masterful piece of dramatic art, which takes us back to the thirteenth century to the epoch of Haakon Haakonsson, and *Emperor and Galilean* (1873), in which already one finds a new concern, that of the philosophy of history. This drama, which tells of the greatest social transformation in history, marks also a total change in the art of Ibsen. After this play, Ibsen ent red resolutely on the way most adapted to his genius; he initiated the series of his satirical-

* These are dates of first performance.

social dramas, of which he had already given a suggestion in *Love's comedy*.

In April, 1864, filled with disillusionment over the failure of his nation to come to the aid of Denmark, Ibsen, thanks to the assistance of the Government, was able to go to Italy and Germany, where he remained for a number of years.

One of his most beautiful lyrics well characterizes Ibsen's state of mind in the act of leaving his country:

The Eider-Duck

The eider's home is in Norroway;
He dwells by the fiord that is leaden-grey.

He plucks the soft, soft down from his breast,
And warm and cosy he builds his nest.

But the cruel fisherman does not spare;
He plunders the nest till all is bare.

The fisher is hard, but the bird holds true;
He strips his own warm bosom anew;

And robbed once more, he will yet make rich
Once more his nest in a secret niche.

But steal this treasure, his third, his last—
One night he spreads his wings to the blast;

With bleeding bosom the sea-fog dun
He cleaves, to the South, to the South and sun! *

* Translated by F. E. Garrett.

Mid the orange-groves and under the burning sun of Italy were born the most Norwegian of the Ibsen plays: *Brand* (1866) and *Peer Gynt* (1867).

Brand, as already stated, is the drama of absolute intransigence in support of the religious life as opposed to the hedonistic one. The motto of Brand is "All or nothing"; he does not admit compromises nor expedients, but goes directly to his goal, overriding affections, memories, traditions. The conventional God is a God too spineless, weak, and antiquated, a God who contents himself with fragments of human hearts, and who finds it sufficient that man, fortified by the Christian doctrine of redemption, offers Him homage every seven days.

Upon this petty and vulgar conception of religion the young Norwegian pastor declares war to the death. Better, according to him, to live in utter impiety, better to live like a libertine than to accommodate oneself to the practice of such a false and lying life. "Either everything or nothing." If there is a God, one should dedicate oneself to Him completely, without dissimulation and without defections. In conformance to this ideal of his, Brand refuses to leave his parish although the climate threatens the life of his wife and child and later they die; he denies the sacrament to his aged dying mother, because she will not consent to give away all her riches. Contrary to Zarathustra, who from the mountain descends into the valley to be among men, Brand painfully climbs to the summit in order to be nearer to his God. But an avalanche descends upon him. Dying he asks of the Eternal if the little grain of human will has any weight in the scale of redemption. In the midst of the crash of the avalanche the answer comes to him: "God is love!" With such an answer the tragic Norwegian arrives at a more humane and generous conclusion than the philosopher Kierkegaard, whose life has some points of similarity with that of the cleric Brand.

In 1867 Ibsen wrote *Peer Gynt,* which some call "the most Norwegian of his plays." In *Brand* Ibsen had challenged his countrymen with the impressive picture of an uncompromising crusader, who was willing to sacrifice all in achieving what he considered to be his God-given call in life. Here was portrayed with white-hot anger the very antithesis of that lack of vision, that half-heartedness and readiness to compromise, which Ibsen had found so prevalent among his contemporary compatriots.

In *Peer Gynt* the dramatist presents the exact reverse of Brand; Ibsen's anger having been replaced by scorn, he bitterly and brilliantly ridicules his countrymen by holding up before them the true embodiment of their most fundamental shortcomings. Peer Gynt is the spirit of compromise incarnate; unable to face life squarely he steadfastly obeys the command, "Go round about," and shrinks from every moral responsibility, finding refuge in lies and idle dreams. Because he has lived so utterly to himself, he fails to realize his true self and to find his calling in life; for, according to Ibsen, "to be oneself is to slay oneself." At last, on the brink of ultimate destruction, his death drawing near, Peer is saved through Solveig's unselfish and ennobling love, which kindles the latent spark of divinity within him, enabling him for once to face life unflinchingly and thereby to find himself.

Peer Gynt, besides being in the intention of the poet a satire on the Norwegian nation, is no less universal in its application and appeal. Nor are the moral implications of this drama, though fundamental and challenging, its greatest attraction. Here is more variety, dash, caprice alternating with profundity,—greater flight of fancy, in a word, richer poetry than in any of Ibsen's other works.

After *The league of youth* (1869), he began his series of great social and psychological dramas: *A doll's house* (1879), *Ghosts* (1881), *The wild duck* (1884), *The lady from the sea* (1888), *Hedda Gabler* (1890), *The master builder* (1892), *Little Eyolf* (1894) and *John Gabriel Borkman* (1896).

As in *Brand*, *Peer Gynt*, *Emperor and Galilean*, and in the plays just cited, Ibsen proclaims the individualistic gospel of the domination of the ego. "Let humanity," he says, "finally discover Beauty in Liberty, let it refuse to be subject to certain truths which have ceased to be true, and through its spirit let it return to nature."

This is the ideal longed for also by the French encyclopaedists, by the *Stürmer und Dränger* and by the entire innumerable band of German romanticists. In the name of this ideal, Ibsen assails the life of the family, the relationship between man and woman (*Hedda Gabler*, *The lady from the sea*, *A doll's house*), between parents and children, in the form it has taken in our social life, relationships which constitute only an impediment to the development of the true force and joy of living; and the relationship between the individual and society (*An enemy of the people*, 1882).

But against this ideal, dark forces are encamped, inflexible as destiny. The individual knows that he is subjected to countless miseries, which are his through heredity (*Ghosts*), that he is the victim of a physiological determinism, from which, however willing he may be, he is unable to free himself. "He remains," says a French critic, "until death a slave to this physical ego that is opposed to his intellectual and moral ego."

But what then can one substitute for this violent negation?

To such a question Ibsen gives an answer, although without emphasis, in two of his most moving dramas: in *The wild duck* (1884) and in *Rosmersholm* (1886). One must will and act according to the measure of one's own forces, and not desire more than it is possible to accomplish: for in this way both desire and capability are fully realized. The need for the ideal must be banished, since this weakens the will and hinders the realization of what is actually within one's power.

In the last drama written by him, *When we dead awaken* (1899), Ibsen puts the question whether all his aspirations, all his renunciations for the love of art have been worthy of the sacrifice. The question was a painful one for the old poet, whose life had been a daily struggle against falsehood. Perhaps the answer that his noble and honest conscience must have given him made tranquil and happy the last days of his troubled existence.

He had plans for additional works, but grave illness darkened his last years until death overtook him on May 23rd, 1906.

BJÖRNSON AND VINJE

If Ibsen is an intellectual, who demonstrates, deduces, and arrives at conclusions that are precise and axiomatic, Björnson is a sentimentalist, who probes, divines, and grows enthusiastic over his revelations.

He was born in 1832 in one of the most solitary districts of Dovrefjeld. His father was pastor of the parish of Kvikne, a place lost in the heart of Norway. He received his first impressions in this wild Alpine setting, over which during a good part of the year shadows lie gloomy and implacable.

At Romsdal on the west coast, with its widely varied scenery, where his father had been transferred, Björnson began to attend school. Later he went to Christiania where he passed the entrance examination to the University. From Christiania he went, in turn, to Copenhagen, and there he published (1857) the first of the Norwegian peasant tales which made him known throughout the North. In Rome, where he stayed from 1860 to 1863, he wrote *Sigurd Slembe,* a dramatic trilogy taken from the history of Norway and one of his outstanding dramas. Returned to his own country, he was appointed director of the Norwegian Theatre in Christiania, a position Ibsen had held before. Attracted anew by the fascination of Rome, he returned there in 1873 and like Ibsen before him at Naples and Sorrento, he wrote two of his best plays in the Eternal City, *The editor* (1875) and *A bankruptcy* (1875); upon which followed later when he returned home *The king* (1877), *A gauntlet* (1883), *Beyond human power* (first part 1883, second part 1895), considered by most as his dramatic masterpiece, *Paul Lange and Tora Parsberg* (1898) and *When the new vine blooms* (1909).

In 1880 he went to the United States where he lectured in the East and West and remained until April, 1881.

In 1903 he received the Nobel Prize for literature.

He died in Paris in 1910.

Björnson's best works are not his plays, but his stories: *Synnöve Solbakken* (1857), *Arne* (1858), and *The fisher maiden* (1868).

Synnöve Solbakken expresses Björnson's sympathy for the Norwegian man of the people, combative and brutal but at the same time generous and proud. Ibsen in *Peer Gynt* describes him as he sees him through his pessimism. Björnson rehabilitates him, and though recognizing all his defects, brings into evidence his fundamental virtues. If in Synnöve Solbakken Thorbjörn incarnates the bellicose Norwegian, Arne incarnates an opposite aspect of the national character. Arne is the Norwegian full of fancies and dreams.

Both *Synnöve Solbakken* and *Arne* are love stories, rural idylls, in which there are traces of the spirit of Gessner, rendered, however, more alive and effective by a pervasive lyrical pathos. There are pages delicious and exuberant with poetry, in which the nature of Norway, now harsh and wild, now gentle and serene, offers a perfect frame for the characters, simple and instinctive, dominated by love or hatred.

The fisher maiden already gives evidence of the seductive fascination of the theatre.

The novels of Björnson have, on the other hand, less literary value, whether it be *The heritage of the Kurts* (1884), in which the cause of so-called scientific morality is defended, or the ambitious *In God's way* (1889), wherein it is sought to reconcile science and religion.

Of the plays, too, few will be spared by time. Among these there are some that are *bourgeois*, some that are political, and some that are social. *Beyond human power* is in a class by itself.

The best *bourgeois* plays are *A bankruptcy* (1875) and *Daglannet* (1904) in which the revolt of children against their parents is dramatized, the fatal struggle of two consecutive generations, wherein Björnson decidedly takes the part of the young. Politics predominates in *The editor*, in *The king*, and in *Paul Lange and Tora Parsberg*. Yet, strictly speaking, these are hardly plays, since everything in them takes place through discussions or declamations, while the action is almost nil.

The social group comprises: *Leonarda* (1879), *The new system* (1879) and *A gauntlet* (1883).

Beyond human power (1883) is a tragedy of faith. The drama revolves about the figure of pastor Sang, a sort of Brand, but a Brand of action, no longer a Brand of inflexible and tormenting asceticism.

He has an unshakable faith in the effects of

prayer, by means of which every sort of illness is healed. A sense of the Divinity pervades his being to the most hidden recesses of his soul, and like a god he is strong, pure and generous. From him irradiates a splendour which illuminates thousands and thousands of the faithful in all the surrounding country.

It is only his invalid wife Clara that he cannot heal, because she is lacking in faith. His children also, Elias and Rachel, have lost their faith while living in distant foreign cities.

But the good pastor perseveres constantly in his prayer. In the village church, he shouts his prayer to God, certain that his fervid hope will be granted. And then he goes from the church to his home. He appears upon the threshold, while the sun encircles his head with a golden halo. Clara comes toward him and seems healed, but it is only imagination. She reels, makes an effort to keep erect, but she barely manages to say: "You shone . . . as you entered . . . O my beloved . . ." when she falls senseless to the ground, dead. Sang leans over her body and places his hand upon her heart; he murmurs a few words and then he, too, falls lifeless, beside his wife.

Beyond human power is indeed a drama of faith. Sang believed he could touch God with his own hands; and then, at his moment of triumph, he sees his wife fall dead at his feet. His prayer has failed in its purpose, his faith has been deluded. His way of belief cannot be right. Now, suddenly, in an instant, his soul becomes empty, without content, and this empty soul cannot endure.

The blind faith which the God of the Christians exacts is, then, beyond the powers and the limits of reason. One must seek elsewhere the solution of the problem of life.

The second part of the play, which is bound to the first by a tenuous thread of idea, develops the struggle between employers and workmen. Acts of violence are succeeded by anarchy, whence it follows that the new religion, that of revolution, as well as the old, exceeds human power. Only the reforms that are practical, systematic and continuous will resolve the social question.

Björnson's last work is the drama entitled *When the new vine blooms* (1909) wherein he holds up to ridicule the exasperated individualism of the Scandinavian women.

Björnson's lyric poems, *Poems and songs* (1870), fill only a slender volume, but their worth is beyond estimation. They,—not least the patriotic ones,—have had tremendous influence in Norway where they are known and loved by everyone; they have literally sung themselves into the hearts of Norwegians everywhere. His epic-lyric poem *Arnljot Gelline* (1870), all things considered perhaps his greatest literary masterpiece, combines penetrating characterization with epic grandeur and lyric beauty.

Ibsen and Björnson are continually being paired like Goethe and Schiller, but they are two natures profoundly diverse, indeed opposite.

If Ibsen is individualist even to excess, Björnson places at least the family above the individual. If Ibsen is an enemy of the people, Björnson is a man of the masses. Ibsen is a cosmopolite, while Björnson is a full-blooded Norwegian. Ibsen is a pessimist, while Björnson believes in social progress and the perfecting of humanity. Ibsen elaborates his works in the strictest solitude, he is taciturn and uncommunicative, whereas Björnson is the born orator who holds and sways an audience with the impetuosity of his eloquence.

In any case these two men represent two characteristics typical of the Norwegian people: one the tendency to conciliate theory and practice in a union violent and almost never happy, an inclination which is an intrinsic part of the mental build of the people of the North; and the other the tendency to a rushing impetuosity of sentiment, an impetuousity which recalls the violent but always heroic deeds of the ancient vikings.

Beside the solemn and imposing figures of Ibsen and Björnson rises the satyr-like figure of Aasmund Vinje (1818–70).

Like the greater part of the Norwegian writers, from Ibsen to Hamsun, from Björnson to Haukland, Vinje is a self-made man. After being a shepherd he became an elementary school teacher, then a brandy distiller, a shoemaker, a student, a journalist, and a lawyer, but none of these trades or professions provided him with an assured and lucrative position.

Irony is Vinje's main strength. Confronted by it, even Björnson's peasant stories and Ibsen's *Brand* are overshadowed. This tendency of his found a valid medium in the *landsmål* in which he wrote his greatest work, *Ferdaminni frå sumaren 1860*

(Memories of the summer of 1860, published 1861), memories of a journey which has many points of contact with the *Reisebilder* of Heinrich Heine.

The finest part of this work is that in which the author is exalted before the ever-new spectacle of nature. Then irony is silent, and not infrequently one detects on Vinje's faunish mask the intense emotion of the dreamer and the poet.

Another major work of his is the epic-lyric poem *Storegut* (Big boy, 1866), a vivid account of life in the author's romantic native district, Telemarken, into which numerous experiences are woven.

Journalism became, however, Vinje's principal literary interest; in the course of his turbulent career he was associated with several papers, but his most significant journalistic venture was his own paper *Dölen* (The Dalesman), where in his inimitable, ironic-lyric style he wrote on the most varied subjects. Nevertheless, his genius finds its fullest expression in his lyric poems, not a few of which are among the finest in Norwegian literature. "No poet in the whole field of Norwegian literature surpasses Vinje in the lyric expression of beauty gathered around Norway's snowcapped peaks" (Jorgenson).

OTHER AUTHORS OF THE NINETEENTH CENTURY— REALISTS AND NATURALISTS *

Camilla Collett (1813–95), a sister of the poet Henrik Wergeland, occupies a unique position in the history of Norwegian letters. The foremost

* The section on the modern period of Norwegian literature embodies various passages prepared by Professor Richard Beck.

Norwegian woman writer of the last century, she was the precursor of the Norwegian realists and the pioneer novelist of modern Norway. Her first and principal work, *The Governor's daughters* (1854), a strikingly realistic picture of life among the upper classes, is a passionate indictment of the unjust position of woman in society and marriage, a relentless attack upon the social inequality of men and women. Fearlessly the author demands full freedom and self-determination for her sex. This book of hers has profoundly influenced later Norwegian literature.

Other important writers of the period are Lie, Kielland, and Garborg.

Jonas Lie was born at Eker near Drammen in 1833 and died at Fredriksvern in 1908. His first work *The visionary* (1870), a beautiful and touching love story with impressive and romantic Nordland as background, immediately brought him fame as a great writer. His second Nordland novel *The barque "Future"* (1872) is inferior, but with *The pilot and his wife* (1874), which combines a colourful description of the life of the seamen with a penetrating study of marriage, he scored another great success. *Rutland* (1880) and *Onward* (1882) are vigorous and masterfully told stories of the sea, the former being as well a story of married life.

Lie is much concerned about the problems and the conflicts of the home, notably in his novels *The family at Gilje* (1883), generally considered his best work, in *The Commandant's daughters* (1886), and *A marriage* (1887). Written more directly in the spirit of realism are *The life convict*

(1883) and *Maisa Jons* (1888), graphic and sympathetic accounts of the step-children of life.

Although in a number of his works Lie is a follower of realism, he indulges in it more in order to keep in with the trend of the times than through a spontaneous inclination of his temperament. When realism had run its course he gave full rein to his fancy and mysticism in his two collections of unusual tales, *Trolls* (1891–92), many of which are little masterpieces, and in his novels *Evil powers* (1890) and *Dyre Rein* (1896), wherein he probes the depths of the subconscious mind. Lie's novels constitute a landmark in the development of impressionistic style.

Alexander Kielland (born at Stavanger in 1849, died at Bergen in 1906) was an ardent champion of naturalism which provided the inspiration of almost all his novels and stories. In *Else* (1881), in *Poison* (1883), in *Fortuna* (1884), in *Snow* (1886), and in *Midsummer festival* (1887), he combated the current false morality, the State Church, the conservatism of the university professors, and social injustice in various forms.

His best novels are *Garman & Worse* (1880) and *Skipper Worse* (1882), in which he describes the business and everyday life of his native town. Here his art is more objective, his character-portrayal more penetrating (especially in *Skipper Worse*) than in his other novels. His style is ever impeccable, dignified and poetic, veined throughout with a light and subtle irony that flows from a profound, bitter pessimism.

Arne Garborg, born at Time on Jaeren in 1851, is

an ironist. Pessimist and philologist, this Norwegian writer has been by some compared with Amiel. Starting from his original severe pietism he is plunged into doubt, to take refuge later in modern mysticism. His first significant work was the story *A freethinker* (1881), but he won his first great victory with the novel *Peasant students* (1883), a challenging picture of the cultural turmoil of the day. Endowed with a powerful capacity for analysis, in his two novels *Weary souls* (1891) and *Peace* (1892), he cries out his intellectual desperation. In these pages is gathered all the weariness felt by the nineteenth century which broke and ruined so many idols. There is that intellectual and sentimental indisposition which, allayed toward 1840, reappeared in other forms toward the end of the last century.

How is one to face this torment, this mental dissipation that obstructs all action?

One must not will nor think, but instead permit oneself to be dragged by the irresistible current toward an unknown goal, remaining rigid in a passivity that is perhaps humiliating but certainly comfortable. This is the only repose that it is permitted us to enjoy. It is the thesis that Garborg develops in *Menfolk* (1886).

Other works of Garborg include: *The lost father* (1899), *Jesus Messiah* (1906), *The son come home* (1908),—all taken from Biblical incidents.

The first named, written in lyric prose, vibrates with intense feeling and abounds in pure poetic beauty,—a work ranking with the finest in Norwegian letters.

Garborg was, however, far more than a gifted novelist, who entered profoundly into the inner life of his characters. He was also a brilliant and extremely productive journalist and pamphleteer; and he takes high rank as a lyric poet. Here his chief works are his poem-cycles *Haugtussa* (The shepherdess, 1895) and its sequel *In Helheim* (Realm of death, 1901), whose protagonist is a shepherdess endowed with second sight. The first part is notable, alike for its magnificent descriptive passages and psychological depth. In these poems Garborg's neoromanticism finds a vigorous expression in contrast with his naturalism in his novels. He rendered Norwegian literature a distinct service also with his excellent translation of the *Odyssey*.

In the mountainous solitude of Österdal Garborg wrote *Kolbotn letters* (1890), highly personal documents, pervaded by a melancholy humour and containing vivid descriptions of nature; and at Jaeren on the sea-coast *Knudahei letters* (1904), which offer, among other things, brilliant observations on Norwegian life in general.

Garborg died at Asker in January, 1924. A richly endowed literary genius, he is no less important in the history of the Norwegian language than in Norwegian letters. Throughout his life a strict adherent and a fearless spokesman of the *landsmål*, he contributed immeasurably to its development and prestige with his work in the field of journalism and literature, writing in the *landsmål* nearly all his works.

With these two last-mentioned writers Norway embraced both realism and naturalism, which reached its extremes with the novel of Hans Jaeger (1854–1910) entitled *From the Christiania Bohême* (1885) and in the story of the famous painter Christian Krohg (1852–1925) called *Albertine* (1886); both books were suppressed. A less violent representative of the same literary tendency was Kristian Elster, the elder (1841–81), whose most significant work is the highly critical novel *Dangerous people* (1881), which depicts the conflict between the spirit of progress and reaction in a small Norwegian town. His shorter stories are characterized by genuine feeling, deep insight, and varied narrative art. His untimely death deprived Norway of a highly gifted writer.

Amalie Skram (1847–1905), a pessimist of the pessimists, was, however, the most consistent adherent of naturalism among the Norwegian writers of the period. Her best known and greatest work is the four-volume novel series entitled *The people of Hellemyr* (1887–98), a graphic family history told in the spirit and according to the accepted method of naturalism, wherein heredity and its influence play a fundamental part. Skram's negative view of life and her morbid genius repel many readers, but her honesty is refreshing and her style is intense and vigorous.

Other writers who carried on the tradition of naturalism are Theodor Madsen (b. 1858), a brilliant psychologist, whose chief work is *Under the tree of knowledge* (1897); Gabriel Finne (1866–99), whose defiant spirit and despair are most forcefully expressed in *Doctor Wang's children* (1890) and the strange drama, *The owl* (1893);

and Arne Dybfest (1868–92), in whose works, *Ira* (1891) and *Two novelettes* (1892), morbid anarchism is a key-note.

But these philosophic and literary currents imported from abroad were ill-suited to the native temperament, in which the subjective nature is dominant; in fact such currents were only superficial and did not succeed in penetrating deeply into the hearts of the people. Moreover, if one observes closely, this objective naturalism of the last two decades of the nineteenth century conceals an ardent subjectivism, a constant aspiration toward the liberty of the individual, a sincere hatred of every constraint. The city is considered as a narrow prison, there is longing for the fields, for the mountains, for the sea. Painting with Edvard Munch, sculpture with Gustav Vigeland marvellously represent this tendency, this ardent desire of liberty enjoyed in the infinite and luminous realm of nature.

In the field of letters new figures begin to arise who will give to Norwegian literature a more spontaneous character, better in keeping with the dreaming and profound mind of the people of the North.

NEO-ROMANTICISM AND NEO-REALISM

In literature as in every cultural manifestation which takes place in the field of the spirit, it is difficult to mark clear-cut limits and to establish with mathematical precision where a given movement has its beginning and where another has its end. Classifications, divisions, sortings are all arbitrary, though of service to the student in orienting himself in his researches and investigations. And so in this period of Norwegian literary history, a period which we shall refer to as neo-romanticism and neo-realism, we find figures of transition, writers who still in part sympathize with the nineteenth century, having its tastes and tendencies, but who already let us glimpse something new, buds that later in the works of greater authors will burst into abundant flower.

Thus Gunnar Heiberg (1857–1929) still has many points of contact with the ideas current in the final decade of the nineteenth century, but on the other hand he already represents the new generation. He is the greatest Norwegian dramatist after Ibsen; he wrote social plays and political comedies, wherein a tenuous vein of humour meanders across the clear mirror of the dialogue.

His first play was the comedy *Aunt Ulrikke* (1884), notable no less for its excellent dramatic technique than for its brilliant political satire, certainly one of the author's best works. His satirical and controversial spirit expresses itself equally vigorously in *King Midas* (1890) and in half a score of later dramas, relentless in their exposure of the flaws of the social structure and national life, biting in their mockery. A more attractive, more human side of Heiberg is seen in his sparkling psychological love dramas, mostly lyric and impressionistic in tone. *The balcony* (1894) and *The tragedy of love* (1904) rank greatest among these and constitute the highwater-mark of the author's production. A worshipper of beauty, a devotee of the theory "art for art's sake," Heiberg was also a remarkable essayist, a master of scintillating style.

Nils Collett Vogt (b. 1864), Tryggve Andersen (1866–1920), Thomas P. Krag (1868–1913), Hjalmar Christensen (b. 1869), Nils Kjaer (1870–1924), Vilhelm Krag (b. 1871), and Sigurd Mathiesen (b. 1871) are in varying degrees representatives of the neo-romantic movement. Vogt has written novels and dramas, but is primarily a lyric poet, with several notable collections of verse to his credit. His poems are virile, impassioned, challenging; they breathe a genuine love for his people and his native land, in particular his jubilee cantata of 1914. Andersen's greatest work is his excellent historical novel (or rather a series of closely related shorter stories), *In the days of the chancery councillor* (1897); he was a master of lucid, beautiful prose. Thomas Krag, who enjoyed a high reputation in his day, wrote a number of novels, of which *Gunvor Kjeld* (1904) is the most successful. Christensen has earned his place in the literature of his country with a series of novels which interpret graphically and excellently the development of Norwegian culture from the end of the eighteenth century to the beginning of the twentieth; of these *The old community* (1913) and *The new community* (1914) rank highest. Kjaer, a satirist and controversialist, is the author of significant plays such as *The day of reckoning* (1902) and *The fortunate election* (1914). Also an essayist, his prose is polished. Vilhelm Krag, who scored a great victory with his *Poems* (1891), has written a number of volumes of charming verse; he is at his best in descriptions of southern Norway. Mathiesen's ablest works, such as his short stories and the earlier novels *Hide Unas* (1903) and *Grudge* (1906), are characterized by marked literary artistry; first of all he is a stylist of rare ability and charm.

But above this gifted group of writers rises the pallid, evanescent figure of Sigbjörn Obstfelder (1866–1900), a melancholy and solitary dreamer, whose mind is tormented by the gnawing moth of thought. In his works, which are few in number, all is dissolved in a phantasmagoria of images, tenuous, filiform, impalpable, which weave about his words like a fine and gilded tracery. Throughout his writings runs a deep undercurrent of wonderment regarding life, a spirit of questioning and of restless yearning. The stories *Life* (1895), *The plain* (1895), and especially *The Cross* (1896), overflow with a doleful pessimism such as it is possible to find in few writers. His poems likewise have the oppressive perfume of the fragile and melancholy flowers in a cemetery. His characteristically symbolic form was original, his style fascinating in its rhythmical melodiousness.

It is Knut Hamsun who brings the neo-romantic art to a point of balance. Knut Hamsun was born August 4th, 1859, at Lom in Gudbrandsdal. He is the son of a tailor and his right name is Knud Pedersen Hamsund, which through an editor's mistake became Knut Hamsun, a name the writer appropriated, since it seemed to him more convenient and fitting for entrance into the literary field.

His life is like a novel. In youth he lived in the Lofoten Islands, early shifting for himself. After a period during which he worked at various trades, for the most part of the humblest sort, he went to Christiania with the intention of devoting himself to writing, but he did not accomplish this object. Twice he tried his fortune in America,—where he was a farm hand in North Dakota and a street-car conductor in Chicago,—but without success. He had very early decided to become a writer. His first printed efforts were a short love story (1877), a narrative poem (1878), and the story *Björger* (1879), the most ambitious of the three, in which the influence of Björnson is strongly felt. His first novel, *Hunger* (1890), made Hamsun known throughout the literary world.

Hunger is the painful experience of his years of vagabondage. It concerns a young writer, struggling with poverty, who does not succeed in allaying the aching pangs of hunger. Day by day is described the torment of this man who tries every means to place his articles with some newspaper but is never successful; he has recourse to the pawnbroker's, there to pledge among his last possessions his glasses, his overcoat, everything he can get rid of in order to appease his hunger and to keep on living even though hardly able to stand on legs that have been weakened by long fasting.

The entire story centres in this one character who moves about like some madman or somnambulist through the streets of the Norwegian capital. There are pages of a heartbreaking sadness, in which the art of Hamsun, an art entirely introspective, at times reaches the lofty peaks touched only by certain Russian authors.

In 1892, he published *Mysteries,* notable for its lyric qualities of style and psychological insight.

In 1893, two other volumes appeared, *Ny jord* (Shallow soil) and *Editor Lynge.* With these two works Hamsun passed at one leap from themes of solitude to subjects involving the centres of life and culture in Christiania.

Editor Lynge treats of the manoeuvres, the intrigues and the political controversies which preceded the separation of the two sister nations. *Shallow soil* is a lively painting of the academic literary and artistic youth of the capital, arrogant and unscrupulous.

In 1894 *Pan* appeared, perhaps the widest known work by Hamsun. Otto Weininger, the author of *Sex and character,* says that *Pan* is the most beautiful story ever written. Here also the principal interest is concentrated in a single personage. Lieutenant Glahn, possessed by a pantheistic admiration for the nature which surrounds him, retires into a hut, where he lives in isolation with his dog Aesop. A girl, Edvarda, comes to disturb the solemn and idyllic peace to which the young officer has given himself, and he seeks to escape the sentiment that penetrates into his heart by embarking for India. But here also, despite the adventurous life he leads, he does not succeed in forgetting the fair blonde vision.

Understanding by this time that forgetfulness is impossible, he provokes his companion, one day while out hunting, until the latter kills him.

In *Pan* is found one of those battles between the sexes, as in the comedies of Marivaux, with the difference that Hamsun locates the struggle in the region of the heart and Marivaux in the region of the head. *Pan* might almost be called a prose-poem, such wealth is there of pure poetry. It is a book "full of lyric outbursts," an eloquent hymn in praise of nature, and a glorification of life lived close to the bosom of mother earth.

Victoria (1898) is a delicate and graceful idyll, in which nature is in perfect sympathy with the love of men.

After a trip in the Caucasus, Hamsun wrote *In fairyland* (1903), impressions derived from his long wandering in that mountainous territory.

Between 1903 and 1912 a number of wanderer-books followed, praising, once more, a life close to nature, and contrasting the natural man with the city-dweller. Akin to these are his novels descriptive of northern Norway, *Benoni* (1908) and *Rosa* (1908).

Hamsun's social philosophy is, however, expressed much more directly and vigorously in *The children of the age* (1913) and *Segelfoss town* (1915) wherein he describes in strong colours the commercialized culture of village and city in contrast to the more wholesome and solid culture of the rural districts. Modern mechanization finds small favour with Hamsun.

In 1917 appeared the work generally regarded as his greatest accomplishment, *Growth of the soil*, which won him world fame, and deservedly, for it is a profound and a powerful book—"the great epic of the pioneer-farmer," the story of man's conquest of the soil down through the ages. The author's message to his generation is here revealed forcefully and highly artistically:—faithful labour in close union with nature. After the publication of this novel he was awarded the Nobel Prize (1920).

Optimism and constructive thought characterized *Growth of the soil;* the opposite is true of Hamsun's next two books, *The women at the pump* (1920) and *Chapter the last* (1923), pessimistic and bitter in their attack upon society.

In his recent novels, *Vagabonds* (1927), *August* (1930) and *The road leads on* (1933), he returns to the wanderer-theme and proves himself as before a master of delightful narrative. The vagabonds in these three books serve as symbols of our restless age in contrast to the home-keeping tillers of the earth praised in *Growth of the soil.*

Hamsun has published a volume of short stories, *Siesta* (1897), in which, however, are rarely found pages comparable to those of his novels. His lyric poems, on the other hand, rank very high, because of their sincerity, originality of thought, and masterly form.

He has tried his hand also at the drama; his dramatic trilogy, *At the gates of the kingdom* (1895), *The game of life* (1896), *Sunset* (1898), is well known. But Hamsun is not a dramatist; in these plays he arranges situations one beside another, but he does not know how to coördinate them and the characters lack dramatic essence. Someone has rightly called these plays dialogued novels, in fact the true art of Hamsun is all in the novel. His art is, as we have said, introspective; it turns its back on the externalities of the world to submerge completely in the labyrinth of the inner life. Naturalism wishes to see things in the full light of the sun; the new art instead immerses them in the crepuscular light of the soul.

This art marks the literary life of Norway with a pathway wherein the new generation will march, more or less compactly.

The neo-romantic current at the same time also revived interest in the soil and in the Norwegian people. Evidence of this is found in the works of Hans Ernst Kinck (1865–1926), and among these principally in *A young people* (1893), *Bats' wings* (1895), *Sighing wind* (1896), *Emigrants* (1904), *The avalanche* (1918–19), *Herman Ek* (1923), and *The drover* (1908), in which the character of the Norwegian peasant is admirably described,— simple and violent, dreaming and brutal. If Björnson has idealized the peasant of the northern valleys, framing him in a sort of snowy Arcadia, Kinck, like Ibsen in *Peer Gynt*, has depicted his true physiognomy.

Kinck also visited long in Italy, where he was interested principally in two figures of the Renaissance, Aretino and Machiavelli. From this visit were born the essays, *Italians* (1904), and the plays, *Agilulf the wise* (1906), *The last guest* (1910), *The wedding at Genoa* (1911), and *Toward carnival* (1915).

As a literary artist Kinck is at his best in his short stories; here his power of concentration, his ability to portray vividly and colourfully a single situation is seen at its height. The short-story collection, *Bats' wings*, together with a number of later ones, reveal him as a master craftsman, who deals equally effectively with a wide variety of themes, ranging from impressive nature descriptions to broadly humorous pictures of peasant life. His novels are less successful artistically, frequently suffering from a lack of unity and excessive argumentation. Most significant are *Emigrants, The avalanche,* and *Herman Ek,* which deal penetratingly, in one form or another, with Kinck's chief problems, the relationship of the individual to the group and to his background, as well as the clash between old and new cultural currents. Here the brilliant race and folk psychologist is no less evident than the gifted and highly imaginative poet.

Kinck's rich art and vigorous personality nowhere find, however, a more memorable expression than in the dramatic poem, *The drover,* in which the Norwegian national character is profoundly analysed; the verse form is also strikingly original. Here as in the author's books on Norwegian life the conflicting cultural tendencies are the central interest.

In addition to being a master of the short story, a gifted novelist and dramatist, Kinck was a brilliant essayist. His language is forceful and realistic; he excels as a painter in words. Though not nearly so widely known as his leading contemporaries in the realm of Norwegian letters, he ranks among the greatest because of his many-sided and original genius.

A number of writers, differing widely in their literary tendencies, have dealt with contemporary rural life in various parts of Norway or found their

inspiration in the historical past of certain locali-
ties; as in the works of Kinck the interest in the soil
is here a dominant note.

Jacob Breda Bull (1853–1930) and Jakob Hil-
ditch (1864–1930) have effectively pictured folk
life in Österdal and eastern Norway respectively,
whereas Hans Aanrud (b. 1863) has written excellent stories descriptive of life in his native
Gudbrandsdal. Bernt Lie (1868–1916) has written
popular Nordland descriptions, and Ole Lie Sing-
dahlsen (b. 1876) has interpreted rural life in Hal-
lingdal truthfully and artistically. Matti Aikio
(1872–1929) and Carl Schöyen (b. 1877) have ably
portrayed the life of the Lapps in northern Norway;
especially successful because of their genuineness
and their vividness are the stories on this theme by
Aikio, himself a Lapp by birth and rearing. Olaf
Benneche (1883–1931), whose most important
work is the historical trilogy, *The man at Rygne-
stad*, *The Knight Mundius*, and *The farmers of the
Raa district* (1911–13), recounts vividly life in
Setesdal during the second half of the sixteenth century. In the *landsmål* Jens Tvedt (b. 1857), Anders Hovden (b. 1860), primarily a gifted lyric
poet, Rasmus Löland (1861–1907), Hans Seland
(b. 1867), and Sven Moren (b. 1871) have written
graphic and able stories of country life. Three other
noted *landsmål* writers, although differing from the
preceding in themes and artistic form, may be mentioned here: Per Sivle (1857–1904), the author of
excellent short stories, but best known for his vigorous patriotic poems; Ivar Mortensson-Egnund
(1857–1934), an admirable translator and author

of a powerful saga-drama, *The outlaw* (1901); and Vetle Vislie (b. 1858), a versatile writer whose most significant work is the prose poem *Solstice* (1897).

In the new century a neo-realistic current also arose, which had for one of its principal representatives the noted novelist Johan Bojer (b. 1872). Bojer like Hamsun had to fight against poverty in his youth, and like Hamsun he came off victorious.

With Bojer, social, ethical and cultural questions again became the fashion. His first literary success was the novel *A public procession* (1896), a gloomy picture of the baneful influence of politics on the Norwegian peasant. Bojer the moralist and controversialist had already found himself, and his narrative talent is already evident. In 1903 with *The power of a lie* (the true title of which, to be exact, is *The power of believing, Troens makt*) he acquired world fame. In this novel is described in an admirable way how a lie can become truth in the mind of a man. In the years following he published *A mother* (1894), *A pilgrimage* (1902), *Our kingdom* (1908), *Life* (1911), *The prisoner who sang* (1913), *The great hunger* (1916), *Dyrendal* (1919), *The last of the vikings* (1921), *The emigrants* (1924), *The new temple* (1927) and *The everlasting struggle* (*Folk ved sjöen*, 1927), all novels ably constructed although padded here and there with prolix discussions on moral and sentimental problems. *The great hunger,* in particular, is a deeply felt story with a compelling message, told simply and directly. Much higher artistically ranks *The last of the vikings,* a powerful and colourful picture of life among the Lofoten fishermen. Here Bojer's unusual narrative talent is seen in its true light, unhampered by direct moralizing. The same is true of *The everlasting struggle,* an impressive, straightforward story of those who are left at home by the adventurous fishermen; this is a highly realistic account, told with insight and unfailing artistry.

Bojer was attracted also by the theatre and has written, among others, the following dramas: *Saint Olaf* (1897), *Theodora* (1902), *Brutus* (1904), and *Sigurd Braa* (1916), his best play.

Other writers who belong to this neo-realistic current are Andreas Haukland (1873–1933), Gabriel Scott (b. 1874), Olav Duun (b. 1876), Kristofer Uppdal (b. 1878), Johan Falkberget (b. 1879), and Oscar Braaten (b. 1881).

Haukland has written effective stories of forests and of pioneer life, and a significant novel of saga times, *The Norns are spinning* (1923). Scott's principal work is the two-volume historical novel *Ordeal by fire* (1915–17); his story *The fountain* (1918) is a charming idyll, told in a prose of rare beauty. Uppdal, who is one of the leading *landsmål* writers, has produced several noteworthy books of verse, but his major work is the series of novels, *The dance through the world of shadows* (1911–24), which portrays vividly and realistically the life and the struggles of Norwegian mine and railway workers, one of whose number the author himself once was. Falkberget, a product of the Röraas mining district, has also written challenging novels dealing with the labouring class, particularly the mine workers. His literary artistry is still more evident in *Lisbet of Jarnfjeld* (1915), a penetrating study of married life, and in his splendid historical novel *The fourth night watch* (1923). Braaten is the interpreter of the Oslo labouring class. His most important works are the two-volume novel *The wolves' lair* (1919), *Mathilde* (1920), and his monumental three-volume novel *Christianus Sextus* (1927–35), which has established him throughout Scandinavia.

The most eminent dramatist of the group is Peter Egge (b. 1869), who has to his credit some most noteworthy plays and novels, besides such successful works as *The heart* (1907), a profound story of marriage, and *Hansine Solstad* (1925), an excellent and delicately wrought peasant novel which has been translated into several languages.

Olav Duun, the greatest of the many gifted *landsmål* authors and one of the most profound and vigorous writers of present-day Norway, is a native of Namdal in the Trondheim region, and here is laid the scene of his novels, overflowing with a strong sense of life and of nature. Among his earlier works the novels *Three friends* (1914) and *The good conscience* (1916) stand out, notably the latter, a penetrating psychological study which traces the influence of conscience on three generations.

This interesting and challenging novel definitely anticipates Duun's major work, the six-volume series *The Juvikings* (1918–23), which tells the story of a leading peasant family over a period of some two hundred years down to our day. Here is indeed a large canvas and a whole gallery of life-like, unforgettable characters, differing to be sure in stature, but frequently of a truly heroic mould. The author's narrative power and unusual psychological penetration are seen in this series in all their glory. Not only does he interpret his characters with profound understanding, he portrays them equally masterfully in their relationship to their historical background and their natural surroundings.

In their restraint and taciturn style, their "eloquent silences" and epic quality *The Juvikings* recalls the Icelandic sagas. In this monumental work Duun has interpreted to his people their innermost self with insight and literary mastery rarely equalled. His later works, although of great merit, are not on a level with his mighty historical cycle; nor is that to be expected.

WOMEN AUTHORS

Among the woman writers Sigrid Undset (b. 1882) towers highest and unquestionably belongs with the greatest creative writers of the day. Her earlier works *Fru Marta Oulie* (1907), *The happy age* (1908), *Jenny* (1911), and *Springtime* (1914) treated admirably of the erotic problem and of the condition of woman in modern society. There followed several collections of short stories on similar themes marked by sincerity and effective character-portrayal. Undset's great triumph came, however, with the publication of the monumental three-volume series *Kristin Lavransdatter* (1920–22), in which the brilliant authoress interprets Norway of mediaeval days. *Master of Hest-·v·iken* (1925–27) is a historical novel like the preceding. Undset's later novels *The wild orchid* (1929) and *The burning bush* (1930) deal with contemporary life, telling of a young Norwegian who is converted to Catholicism, a faith which the authoress herself had formally embraced in 1924. In her latest work, *Ida Elisabeth* (1932), Undset returns to her first theme, woman in marriage, and searchingly interprets the life of her heroine.

But, penetrating and engrossing as Undset's novels of modern life are, particularly the later ones, she owes her high place in present-day literature to her historical novels, especially *Kristin Lavransdatter*, indeed a very remarkable book. Here was a theme which appealed to the writer's taste and sympathies and brought her genius to a full flowering. The absorbing tragedy of Kristin (although by no means a story of defeat) is not only a most discerning study of human relationships, but no less the history of the evolution of a human soul. Here is much to admire. The geographical and the essential historical accuracy are amazing; Undset not only pictures the Norwegian scene truthfully and vividly; what is more she makes the civilization of the distant period which she describes live again. Clearly and accurately as she pictures the geographical and the historical background, Undset is, nevertheless, primarily interested in her human beings and their destiny; and what gives to her work its strongest general appeal and modernity is her rare power of revealing the fundamental and universal humanity of her men and women; although they live and breathe in a spiritual atmosphere different from our own, we fully recognize their kinship to ourselves and share their fate. Because of this

rich literary excellence and magnitude of conception, *Kristin Lavransdatter* takes its place with the
greatest literary achievements of our time.

Other women of the Norwegian Parnassus are:
Hulda Garborg (b. 1862), Regine Normann
(b. 1867), Barbra Ring (b. 1870), Nini Roll
Anker (b. 1873), Ragnhild Jölsen (1875–1908),
and Cora Sandel (b. 1882), all of whom have written noteworthy fiction aside from other works of
merit. Jölsen, endowed with exceptionally keen
psychological insight, was probably the most gifted
of the group. Sandel's novel *Alberta and Jacob*
(1926) is an uncommonly brilliant piece of writing. And still other Norwegian women writers
might be mentioned, such as Ingeborg Refling
Hagen (b. 1895) who has written prose and verse
of a high order and Sigrid Boo (b. 1898), whose
richly humorous novel *Servants' entrance* (1930)
has become a popular favourite even outside of Norway.

THE YOUNG GENERATION

The tendencies, the aspirations, the tastes of the
young generation are various and are difficult to
define within precise boundaries.

As everywhere else, one observes also in recent
Norwegian literature a certain dispersion and dis-
orientation, although, in addition to the great
figures living on from the last century, distinguished personalities are not lacking among the
young, but these are not such as to be able to give a
rhythm or a dominant tone to the new literature.

Alf Harbitz (b. 1880), Kristian Elster, the

younger (b. 1881), Hans Lyche (b. 1885), Theodore Dahl (b. 1886), Eilert Bjerke (b. 1887),
Johan Ellefsen (1888–1921), Sigurd Hoel
(b. 1890), Sigurd Christiansen (b. 1891), Axel
Krogh (b. 1892), Finn Halvorsen (b. 1893), and
Mikkjel Fönhus (b. 1894), are all recent writers
who have tried their hands at various forms of prose
with more or less success. With his brilliant psychological novel *Two living and one dead* (1931)
Christiansen won the international Gyldendal novel
competition in 1931, with writers from all the
Scandinavian countries taking part. Second prize in
the same competition was won by Hoel with his
novel, *A day in October* (1931). Fönhus occupies
a place by himself in Norwegian letters; he is the
master interpreter of animal life in the wilds of
his country. There is not lacking among these
younger Norwegian writers even a great author of
detective stories, Sven Elvestad (1884–1934), who,
according to some, has points of superiority to the
classic Conan Doyle. Kristmann Gudmundsson
(b. 1902), a young Icelander who writes in Norwegian, has already, with his novels and short
stories, made a name for himself even outside the
northern countries, but he will be dealt with under
Icelandic literature.

Four poets of distinguished talent are Herman
Wildenvey (b. 1886), Olaf Bull (1882–1933),
Arnulf Överland (b. 1889) and Johan Nordahl
Grieg (b. 1902), a young recruit of the Norwegian
Parnassus.

The first-mentioned is the true type of trouba-
dour, of the poet *bohémien,* whose poems light,

sensuous, musical, are the delight of the young. As a master of verse he has few equals; his love poems are especially noteworthy for their melodiousness and freshness.

Olaf Bull is the opposite. His poems reveal a masculine power and a forceful affirmation of his own individuality, notwithstanding the pessimism that often envelopes them like a voluminous thick black veil. His poetry is deeply felt, rich in imaginative and intellectual quality.

Överland is the poet of renunciation and of solitude. He has tried his hand also at the writing of short stories and the drama. Profoundly earnest, he is the fearless spokesman of modern Norwegian socialism.

Grieg's poems are intense and vigorous, vibrating with strong love for his native Norway. He has also proved himself an able novelist and an uncommonly gifted journalist.

Other noteworthy lyric poets who write in the *riksmål* are Charles Kent (b. 1880), Alf Larsen (b. 1885), who excels in poems of the sea and the coast, Rolf Hiorth Schöyen (1887-1932), and Gunnar Reiss-Andersen (b. 1896).

Two highly gifted poets, whose medium is the *landsmål*, are Olav Aukrust (1883-1929) and Tore Örjasaeter (b. 1886). The former is the author of the impressive, if uneven, poem *The heavenly beacon* (1916), which interprets the struggle between good and evil; while the latter has written splendid nature poetry and a notable narrative poem.

The leading younger dramatists writing in the

riksmål are Helge Krog (b. 1889) and Ronald Fangen (b. 1895). Far apart in their literary preferences, both have produced significant dramas and distinguished themselves in other branches of literature, Krog as an essayist, Fangen as a novelist. Of a number of dramatists who write in the *landsmål* Sigurd Eldegard (b. 1866) and Olav Hoprekstad (b. 1875) are the most outstanding.

Round about these greater poets there are many other minor ones, who have given homage to the extreme forms of literary anarchy (futurism, cubism, dadaism), and others still, who have indulged in the mystical currents originating in Sweden; but it is needless to mention their names since they have exerted no notable influence on the country's literature.

The principal characteristic of all the Norwegian literature, from the poetry of the skalds to that of the moderns, remains always individualism, the powerful affirmation of the ego which asserts itself forcefully even where it makes its appearance covered by social and religious superstructures.

NORWEGIAN-AMERICAN LITERATURE

by

RICHARD BECK, PH.D.
*Professor and Head of the Department of
Scandinavian Languages and Literatures
in the
University of North Dakota*

LITERARY interest, so characteristic of the Norwegians in their native land, has been equally dominant among them and their descendants in America. Fiction in one form or another has had many representatives. In his *History of the Norwegian people in America* (1925) Dr. O. M. Norlie points out that it would not be difficult to list at least a hundred names of Norwegian-Americans who have published works of fiction, and he goes on to name fifty such writers. In the realm of lyric poetry the productiveness has been even more amazing as seen in the hundreds upon hundreds of poems scattered over the pages of the numerous Norwegian-American newspapers. Dr. Norlie, in his work mentioned, lists fifty lyric poets who have published one or more volumes of poetry. There is, to be sure, some overlapping between these and the writers of fiction, as many of the authors in question have cultivated both prose and poetry. The quality of this extensive literary production is, of course, not by any means commensurate with the quantity; nevertheless, here are to be found a number of poems, stories, and novels of genuine literary merit. The bulk of this literature, as well as its most important contribution, falls within the last fifty years, since the pioneer settlers naturally were too occupied with home building to find time or opportunity for sustained literary efforts.

The pioneer Norwegian-American poet was Ole A. Buslett (1855–1924), frequently referred to as the father of Norwegian-American literature. His first book, the story *Fram* (Onward), appeared in 1882. This was followed by a number of works in verse and prose, in which he vigorously championed Norwegian traditions and the highest ideals in Norwegian-American life. He was the forerunner of a long line of gifted Norwegian-American poets, including Ole S. Sneve (1846–1913), Knut M. Teigen (1854–1914), Wilhelm Pettersen (1860–1933), Johannes O. Saeter (b. 1860), John Benson (b. 1862), D. G. Ristad (b. 1863), Gustav Melby (b. 1865), Olav Böhmer (b. 1869), Julius B. Baumann (1870–1923), Sigurd Folkestad (b. 1877), and Jon Norstog (b. 1877). They differ indeed in literary artistry, selection and treatment of themes, no less than in productiveness; but they have all written poetry deserving of attention; and several more names could justifiably be added to the list.

By far the most productive of the group and in many respects the most remarkable is Norstog, who has to his credit a number of Biblical dramas and epics, conceived on a grand scale; uneven and frequently obscure to be sure, but revealing at the

same time high flight of the imagination, originality and penetration. He has also written a three-
volume novel, *Exodus* (1928–31), a number of
short stories, and several collections of lyric poems;
many of the latter are exquisitely beautiful. In
Norway Norstog ranks high as a lyric poet; among
his countrymen in America his books have not been
so widely read as they deserve, largely because he
writes in the *landsmål,* primarily in the dialect of his
native Telemarken. An unusual and most interesting
circumstance about this poet-farmer of the North
Dakota prairie is the fact that he not only writes
his books, but also prints them and binds them.
Deeply religious and concerned about moral values,
Norstog frequently appears as the merciless chas-
tiser of his people.

These Norwegian-American lyric poets have
written almost exclusively in the Norwegian language. Melby, alone among them, favors the English as his medium of expression and has published,
in that tongue, the following collections of poems:
The seamless robe and other poems (1914), *The
lost chimes and other poems* (1918), *Twilight*
(1921), *Blue haze* (1925), *Light and shade*
(1931), and *King Saint Olaf* (1916), a drama in
verse. His works have found their way into many
homes and won much praise from Norwegians and
non-Norwegians.

The first Norwegian-American to devote himself to the writing of fiction and gain a wide
hearing was Hjalmar Hjorth Boyesen (1848–95),
whose story *Gunnar* (1873) was the first novel
written in the English language by a Norwegian;

he continued in that language with a number of
novels, of which the earlier ones rank highest,
dealing, like *Gunnar,* with life in Norway where
the author was on thoroughly familiar ground.

In the matter of language Norwegian-American
writers of fiction have not, however, followed the
example of Boyesen, having down to the immediate present, with hardly an exception, chosen
to write in Norwegian; foremost among them are
the following: Waldemar Ager (b. 1869), O. E.
Rölvaag (1876–1931), Olai Aslagsson (b. 1885),
H. A. Foss (1851–1929), Simon Johnson (b. 1874),
N. N. Rönning (b. 1870), Peer O. Strömme
(1856–1921), and Johannes B. Wist (1864–1923).

Aslagsson's book *Under vestens himmel* (Under
western skies), which was published in America
in the original Norwegian in 1918 and in the
English translation in 1923, as well as being published in Norway under the title *Under praeriens
himmel* (1918) in an edition preferable as far as
language is concerned, is American in theme and
belongs properly to Norwegian-American letters;
it is a collection of excellent American animal
stories and nature descriptions.

Foss, who has been called the Norwegian-American Björnson, won deserved popularity especially
with his story *Husmandsgutten* (The cotter's boy,
1889). His book *Den amerikanske saloon* (The
American saloon, 1887), translated two years later
into English under the title *Tobias, a story of the
Northwest,* also takes high rank among his literary
productions. Another well-told, interesting story
of his, which became popular reading, was *Kristine*

Valdersdatter (1886), of which a motion picture was shown throughout Norwegian-America in 1933.

Johnson, an able journalist and lyrist, has also made a noteworthy contribution to Norwegian-American fiction with his masterful short stories and his well-written realistic novels dealing with Norwegian pioneer life in the Northwest. His novel *I et nyt rige* (In a new kingdom, 1914), translated into English as *From fjord to prairie* (1916), is a book distinctly worth reading. His extensive novel *Fallitten paa Braastad* (The bankruptcy at Braastad, 1922) presents a vivid picture of pioneer life, an account where realism and romanticism frequently mingle happily. Its sequel *Frihetens hjem* (The home of freedom, 1925) is also a graphic story of life on the western prairies during more recent years. He has written lyric poetry of real merit.

Rönning, known, too, for his successful journalistic work, is the author of several stories in Norwegian and English, frequently religious in theme, but marked by narrative excellence and charming simplicity. His *Lars Lee* (1928) and *The boy from Telemarken* (1933) contain splendid characterizations and descriptive passages.

Strömme, an unusually many-sided individual, characterized as "the most colorful Norwegian-American figure of this period," was primarily a highly gifted and prolific journalist, but he is also remembered for his story *Hvorledes Halvor blev prest* (How Halvor became a preacher, 1893), an excellent account of life in an early Norwegian settlement, enlivened by the author's characteristic humor. He also wrote good poetry.

Wist made his contribution principally as an influential editor and publisher, but has left, under the penname "Arnljot," a literary and cultural-historical work worthy of consideration in his trilogy of Norwegian immigrant life: *Nykommer-billeder* (Pictures from immigrant life, 1920), *Hjemmet paa praerien* (The home on the prairie, 1921), and *Jonasville—et kulturbillede* (Jonasville —a cultural sketch, 1922).

In literary interest and significance the production of the foregoing Norwegian-American writers of fiction, as well as of those to be named below, is over-shadowed by the works of Waldemar Ager and O. E. Rölvaag.

Ager, an eminently successful and productive journalist, who has been all his life an uncompromising and influential champion of the temperance movement, a movement by the way which has interested and influenced a number of Norwegian-American authors, is also a creative writer of rare ability. Even his temperance stories have considerable literary value; this is particularly true of his *Fortaellinger for Eyvind* (Stories for Eyvind, 1906), which appeared in an English translation a year later. Here, as often elsewhere, the author proves himself a master of the short story. Of his novels the most important are *Kristus for Pilatus* (Christ before Pilate, 1910), the first novel by a Norwegian-American to be published in Norway, and *Hundeöine* (Dog-eyes, 1929), which was pub-

lished in English in 1931 under the title *I sit alone*.
The former is a penetrating interpretation of the
life of a struggling idealist, told forcefully and
sympathetically, where many other life-like characters also people the stage. The latter, a study of a
sensitive, suffering soul, reveals in a marked degree the same qualities, Ager's kindly sympathy,
his delightful sense of humour, and his ability to
enter profoundly into the spiritual life of the immigrant; he realizes that human beings cannot
be torn loose from their native environment without damage to the fibres of their soul.

The untimely death of Rölvaag in November,
1931, deprived Norwegian-Americans of their best
known and in some respects their most effective
spokesman. American and Norwegian literature
especially, and the literary world generally, lost in
him a great literary artist. Through translations
of his works into a number of languages he is
known internationally as an interpreter of immigrant life, and as such he will be remembered by
coming generations.

Without underestimating the importance of
Rölvaag's other novels, such as *To tullinger* (Two
fools, 1920), published under the English title of
Pure gold (1930), a challenging portrayal of
greed, and *The boat of longing* (1921), rich in
lyric and poetic quality, his literary fame rests on
his trilogy dealing with Norwegian immigrant life
in America. The first of these, *Giants in the earth*
(1924–25), may be said already to have become a
classic. Deservedly, it is generally recognized as the
author's masterpiece, for here pioneer life is inter-

preted with deep understanding and consummate art; it is forsooth an epic of pioneering. The second book in the series, *Peder Victorious* (1928), describes, with penetrating psychological insight, the conflict between the first and second generation, and is a significant contribution to the literature and the cultural history of the Middle West. In the third volume, *Their fathers' God* (1931), the central problem is that of mixed marriage; it is a frank and realistic account, but human and sincere, a powerful social document.

In common with nearly all of his fellow Norwegian-American writers of fiction, Rölvaag wrote his books in Norwegian; and he was deeply attached to his race and its traditions. The preservation of Norwegian culture in America was to him a matter of great concern. At the same time there is in his books on Norwegian immigrant life a breadth of view, a universality, which makes them appeal equally to thinking people of all races, in particular to any immigrant group or to descendants of immigrants.

Though their works are far below the standard set by Ager and Rölvaag, mention may be made of two Norwegian-Americans who have written novels in English, James A. Peterson (b. 1859) who has to his credit the two stories *Hjalmar, or the immigrant's son* (1922) and *Solstad: the old and the new* (1923); and Anthony Rud (b. 1893), author of the novel *The second generation* (1923); despite their flaws these stories possess interest and literary merit.

Kristian Prestgard (b. 1865), a gifted journalist,

editor-in-chief of the widely read semi-weekly *Decorah-Posten* and the compiler of a collection of Norwegian poetry, has written excellent sketches and essays. His extensive travel book, *En sommer i Norge* (A summer in Norway, 1928), is an extremely interesting account, rich in poetic descriptive passages and told in a fluent, charming style.

Several women also have contributed to Norwegian-American letters works worthy of note. Agnes M. Wergeland (1857–1914) has a prominent place among the lyric poets. Ulrikka F. Bruun (b. 1854) has made a name for herself with her poems and her stories in the interest of the temperance movement. Antonette Tovsen (b. 1857) and Ruth L. Fjeldsaa (b. 1880), who writes under the pen name "Jutta," have contributed numerous widely read longer and shorter stories to Norwegian-American publications. Dorthea Dahl (b. 1881) is well known in Norwegian-American circles for her collections of well-told short stories, in Norwegian and English, of everyday happenings, *Hverdagslivet* (Everyday life, 1915) and *Returning home* (1920). Her novel *Byen paa bjerget* (The town on the bluff, 1925) is a faithful account of life in Dakota territorial days. She further holds the distinction of being the first Norwegian-American woman to write fiction in English as well as in Norwegian.

Mrs. Belle Hagen Winslow who, on the other hand, writes entirely in English, has written two readable love stories, *White dawn* (1920) and *Where man is king* (1921). Much more important quantitatively and artistically is the work of

Martha Ostenso (b. 1900), no doubt the most widely known of Norwegian-American authoresses.

Like Mrs. Winslow, Ostenso was born in Norway, but was brought to America as a child; the greater part of her life has been spent in Canada where she has been a teacher in a rural school. She, too, writes exclusively in English. Her first novel, *Wild geese* (1925), which won a large literary prize, immediately established her as a writer of great gifts. It is a grim, but vigorous story of life in a farming community of the Northwest, strong in characterization, and still remains her best work, without denying considerable literary merit to her later novels such as *Dark dawn* (1926) and *The mad Carews* (1927). Ostenso's books have not only been very widely read in America, but have, in Norwegian translation, enjoyed great popularity in Norway.

The numerous Norwegian-American newspapers, of which a considerable number are still in existence and widely read, have also, by continually publishing poems, stories, and essays, kept alive and strengthened literary interest among their readers. Of Norwegian-American literary and cultural periodicals two deserve special mention, *Symra* (1905–14), established by Kristian Prestgard and J. B. Wist, and the annual *Jul i Vesterheimen* (Christmas in the western world), edited since 1911 by A. M. Sundheim.*

* For Norwegian-American papers and periodicals, see especially: Carl Hansen and J. B. Wist, "Den Norsk-Amerikanske Presse," in *Norsk-Amerikanernes Festskrift*, Decorah, Iowa, 1914; also O. M. Norlie, *History of the Norwegian people in America*, Minneapolis, 1925, and Julius E. Olson, "Literature and the press," in *Norwegian immigrant contributions to America's making*, New York, 1921.

Norwegian-American literature, although uneven in quality and largely regional, is therefore a significant and interesting chapter in the literary history both of Norway and of America; and generally speaking even more important in the cultural history of this continent. For here is clearly recorded the contribution of Norwegian immigrants to the making of America. It is to be regretted that, for the general public, much of the best efforts of Norwegian-American writers "lies frozen in the ice of a foreign tongue."

SWEDISH LITERATURE

SWEDISH LITERATURE

based on the treatise by
GIOVANNI BACH, Ph.D.
translated by
FREDERIKA BLANKNER, Litt.D.
Western Reserve University
and enlarged in collaboration
with contributors

ORIGINS

IN Sweden, as in the other Scandinavian countries,
a rich literature flourished before the Christian
era, a literature for which the deeds of the gods, the
exploits of the heroes and the expeditions of the
vikings in far-off lands furnished an abundant
variety of subjects. Also the struggles between the
Geatas, a people of southern Sweden, and the
Svear, dwelling north of Lake Mälaren, struggles
which terminated in the victory of the latter,
gave material for poetic narratives which centre
about the heroic and legendary figure of Beowulf.
Religious poetry also must have had a large place in
the first literary compositions of Sweden. The
centre of paganism was Uppsala, where rose the famous temple of Frey, the god of fruitfulness, to
whom human sacrifices were made. Hymns and
prayers were regularly offered to this god by the
priests and the people who flocked in devoted pil-

grimage to the chief temple of the Svear, which on certain days of the year must have presented a fantastic appearance, to judge from the description given us by Adam of Bremen in his *History of the Church of Hamburg* (c.1075).

A copious fount for the first cultural manifestations are the runic inscriptions, more so in Sweden than in the other Scandinavian countries. In fact nine-tenths of these—among them the famous stone of Rök, which has authentic literary value—derive from Sweden. None of the runic inscriptions antedate the third century after Christ.

It was in the thirteenth century that Christianity penetrated completely into Sweden. While Christianity affirmed itself peacefully in Iceland and Norway, in Sweden it brought about a struggle of three centuries, a struggle that was bloody but terminated with the complete victory of the new religion. The temples of Odin, Frey and Thor were razed to the ground and upon them the Cross was erected.

With the introduction of Christianity came the adoption also of the Latin alphabet, with which actual written literature has its beginning. At first this was used for the codification of the existing laws, of which the oldest monument is the fragment of law from the territory of Västergötland, dating from the first half of the thirteenth century (there is a complete manuscript dating from 1281). Whoever follows the various legal formulas can note with the passing of time a radical change in their conception and form, a change due to the infiltration of Roman and ecclesiastical law into the structure of the Swedish codes. In place of a vivacious, almost dramatic exposition, at times in poetic form, one finds being gradually substituted the smooth, monumental style of the Latin legislation. The Swedish territory that first elaborated a single codification of the law in force was the territory of Västergötland, just referred to.

With the introduction of the Latin alphabet, religious style also underwent considerable development, reaching its greatest splendour in the *Revelations* (first published 1492) of Saint Birgitta (1303–73), whose order became the centre of religious studies in the heart of Sweden. From Norway the epic was imported into Sweden, and from Denmark the historico-political song and the ballad, which was to become in time the most diffused type of popular composition, destined to assume literary form later in the romantic period.

THE REFORMATION

In Sweden the Reformation took on a character of bitter and austere intransigence, of rancorous and combative Biblical exegesis, so that while elsewhere it brought about the flowering of hymns and songs, in Sweden it gave rise to a great quantity of polemical writings which at times were harsh and violent. The most notable figure of the Swedish Reformation is Olaus Petri (1493–1552), who lived in the epoch of the great king and liberator of Sweden, Gustavus Vasa, founder of the dynasty of the same name.

Olaus Petri was present, as a student at Wittenberg, at the first skirmishes of Luther against the

Church of Rome. Full of these impressions, he returned home to Sweden where he occupied various religious posts. His writings on dogmatic and liturgical questions, which then interested all of central Europe, were numerous, and in such writings he was the true creator of the modern Swedish language, as Luther was of German. His principal works were a translation of the New Testament (1526), a *Catechism* (1529), *Collection of hymns* (oldest edition, 1530), *Homilies* (1530), and *The Swedish Mass* (1531). Later works are a translation of the Old Testament (*Biblia*, 1541) and *Tobiae commedia* (1550). *De domare reglor* (Rules for judges), a work which heads the code of laws for 1734 and is still prefixed as an introduction to Swedish law-codes, is also attributed to him.

Olaus Petri was also an historian. His *Svenska krönika* (Swedish chronicle c.1538), is a work of great merit. It was published in 1818 in *Scriptores rerum suecicorum medii aevi* (Writers on matters pertaining to mediaeval Sweden) and in 1860 by G. E. Klemming under the title *Olai Petri svenska krönika*. Olaus Petri also wrote an essay on the subject of the runes.

What is lacking in Olaus Petri is that lyrical pathos, that religious passion which animates the writings of the great German reformer. Even his prayers have a moralistic and intellectual intonation rather than the polemic ardour and the oratorical emphasis of the sermons of Luther.

Two historians of merit were the brothers Olaus (1490–1557) and Johannes Magnus (1488–1544), the latter being the last Catholic archbishop of

Sweden. Persecuted for their religious ideas, they went to Italy, where, though they did not abandon their historical studies, they devoted themselves with passionate interest to antiquarianism.

Johannes Messenius (1579–1636) is the name of another historian, who sought to dramatize Swedish history in the style of the Biblical dramas and of the student comedies. The entire cycle was to include fifty pieces, of which, however, only six were brought to completion by the author and produced. The most important element in these dramas is nationalistic, clearly distinguishing them from the Biblical dramas that had been in great vogue up to that time.

Lars Wivallius (1605–69) may be considered as the first modern Swedish lyrist. His poems already suggest those of Carl Michael Bellman, the highly popular poet of the eighteenth century.

The period during which he wrote was that of Gustavus Adolphus (1594–1632), conqueror of the Russians and the Poles, organizer of commerce, industry and navigation, protector of the sciences and of national education, and creator of the great Swedish nation.

The Swedish victories resulted in an atmosphere of excessive nationalism, which had vast and deep resonance in the work of Lars Wivallius. The nationalism concerned is not, however, exclusive and xenophobic; quite the contrary it is a nationalism open to every superior form of foreign culture.

Christina, the extraordinary daughter of Gustavus Adolphus, sought to transplant to the far North the pretentious and elegant forms of the

Italian Renaissance; she corresponded with the greatest men of the time, among them Chemnitz, Pufendorf and Descartes, whom she invited to come to the Swedish capital. She, herself, removed her residence to Rome, but the culture she had imported into Sweden continued to develop in every field. Many learned Swedes who had travelled to Italy returned laden with classical memories, impressions and experiences. Interest in the history of their country arose, not only for its civil, but also for its philological, religious and artistic development. Scholars delved into the soil and brought forth ancient relics, runic writings and tombstones. The old Icelandic parchments were thoroughly and passionately studied in the desire to recreate the period of origins, the adventurous age of the vikings and the skalds.

A fanatic scholar, Olof Rudbeck (1630–1702), in his work *Atland* (1679–1702) imagined that Atlantis, of which Plato speaks, and all the lands of happiness conceived by the ancients were none other than Sweden, the primitive abode of man.

Many authors of this time received their inspiration from the Italian Renaissance, and their works show marked signs of the taste and the style of its great authors, especially of the fourteenth and sixteenth centuries.

Gustaf Rosenhane (1619–84) published in 1680 a cycle of sonnets called *Wenerid,* sonnets resembling those written by Petrarch for Laura.

Georg Stiernhielm (1598–1672), together with Rudbeck, is the encyclopaedic and universal man of this Swedish Renaissance. He is a mathematician, philosopher, jurist, naturalist and archeologist, and furthermore he is considered as the father of modern Swedish poetry.

With his *Hercules* (written in 1647 and published in 1658) he created a poetic masterpiece of the first order. Later he edited *Västgötalagen* (The laws of Västergötland, 1663) and the Bible of Ulfilas (1671). In 1668 he published a collection of minor poems. He conceived furthermore a great dictionary of the Swedish language, which, however, did not get beyond the letter A. The work of Stiernhielm was indubitably ample and fecund. The figure of this great author dominates all Swedish literature of the seventeenth century.

Italian Marinism found in Sweden an admirer and an enthusiastic imitator in Gunno Eurelius Dahlstierna (1661–1709) who translated *Il pastor fido* of Guarini. In his panegyric on the death of Charles XI (1697) one frequently comes upon forms and images which recall the *Adone* of Marini.

But the Italian *Seicentismo* could not flourish long in Sweden, nor could it adapt itself to northern tastes. Already at the dawn of the following century the first reactions against this inflated and high-sounding literature are noted, and the need for simplicity and clearness makes itself felt. The attention of Swedish men of letters shifts from Italy to France.

As elsewhere in Europe the influence of Boileau began to predominate, and with it the Enlightenment triumphantly entered.

THE AGE OF ENLIGHTENMENT OR RATIONALISM

With the death of Charles XII (1718), the great king who merited a biography by Voltaire, the power of Sweden ended likewise. The tragic events connected with his death concentrated the attention of the nation on the naked and sad reality of things which demanded immediate reform at any cost. All scientific interest was therefore directed toward utilitarian ends; political economy and the natural sciences predominated and it was then that the great figures of Linnaeus and Scheele arose, the former celebrated for his studies in botany, the latter for his discoveries in the field of chemistry.

This atmosphere, saturated with practical and materialistic aspirations, favoured the introduction and development of rationalism, which, radiating from England, had diffused itself throughout central and western Europe. The use of reason seemed more adapted for matters that otherwise would be governed by blind instinct and the simple authority of faith. The needs of religious sentiment found outlets in pietism, in freemasonry, and in the mania for visions. Typical of this last-mentioned aspect is the figure of Emanuel Swedenborg (1688–1772), the great saint of the North, in whose visions the mystic impulse is merged with a vigorous sense of reality.

The excessive faith in scientific procedure gave rise to an exaggerated optimism, which Voltaire satirized in his *Candide* and which changed into the blackest pessimism after the bloody experiment of the French Revolution.

The most notable representative of rationalism in Swedish literature is Olof von Dalin (1708–63), who has a marked affinity with the contemporary French and English writers. Like Addison and Steele in England, he published in Sweden a periodical, *The Swedish Argus,* which mirrored the rationalistic ideas of the time, above all those deriving from France and England. In his political allegories one feels the strong influence of Dryden and Swift, but there are to be noted also the superficialities of his moral, social and religious conventions, whence his influence on the Swedish literature of the time is wholly formal; his merit consists in the development that took place, thanks to his work, in the style of Swedish prose.

Admitted to the court as tutor of the Crown Prince, the future Gustavus III, he found in Queen Louisa Ulrica, sister of Frederick the Great, a great admirer of French rationalism. These were the best years of this Swedish author. Becoming involved later in a court intrigue, he was forced to retire to private life; it was then he gave the finishing touches to his historical work on Sweden.

Mme. Hedvig Charlotta Nordenflycht (1718–63), Count Gustav Philip Creutz (1731–85), who in 1783 concluded a treaty of friendship and commerce between America and Sweden, and Gustaf Fredrik Gyllenborg (1731–1808) are the three principal representatives of that wave of pessimism which followed upon the rationalistic optimism of

Dalin. The collection of poems entitled *The mourning turtle-dove* (1743) of Mme. Nordenflycht exhibits an exaggerated, almost morbid, sentimentality. It is a poetry mild and delicate, pervaded throughout by a dolorous lyric pathos.

Philip Creutz is the representative of an aesthetic pessimism which is revealed in his pastoral *Atis and Camilla* (1761), a work proclaiming the naturalistic gospel of Rousseau.

With Gustaf Fredrik Gyllenborg the pessimism becomes stoic. In his two poems *Human joys* and *Human misery* (both 1762) he recognizes the inconsistency not only of human joy but also of knowledge and science. The only means of salvation lies in "tending patiently and with closed eyes toward an unknown goal." A sad and distressing fatalism, which is to become extinguished with his generation.

The height of French influence in Sweden was reached at the time of Gustavus III, nephew of Frederick the Great. These years marked a happy revival in the field of letters and art, and the period during which he was on the throne (1771–92),—sometimes extended to include also that of his successor Gustavus IV Adolphus (1792–1809),—came to be called the "Gustavian Age."

Gustavus III favoured artists and scientists, founded the Musical Academy, the National Theatre, the Academy of Fine Arts, the Swedish Academy, and gave a vigorous impulse to journalism, which was still in an embryonic state. He was a fluent orator and an esteemed author of elegies and plays. An admirer of France and of French rationalism, he went to France several times, officially or incognito, and he was in correspondence with its most representative persons, above all with Mme. de Staël. He journeyed also to Rome, where he obtained from the Pope the permission to open a Lutheran chapel in the immediate vicinity of the Vatican.

Of the writers who flourished during the Gustavian age there was a considerable group which coöperated actively and in an advisory capacity in the work of the great king.

Karl Gustaf af Leopold (1756–1829) wrote verbose and prosy dramas which, however, because of their frequent political allusions procured for him a temporary fame.

Johan Henrik Kellgren (1751–95) diligently assisted the king in his literary work; he in fact elaborated the plot of the drama, *Gustavus Vasa*, submitted to him by his great patron. Thoroughly saturated as he was with French culture, Kellgren displays a poetic style which is simple, limpid and clear. In 1778 he founded a newspaper, *Stockholmsposten*, in which with the cutting weapon of satire he fought every manifestation of ignorance, crudeness, and prejudice. His lyric poetry, at first soft and sensuous, reminding one of the paintings of Watteau or of Fragonard, gradually became spiritual, chiefly as the result of a more intimate observation of nature derived from the reading of Danish and English poets.

In his last work entitled *The new creation* (1790), one already finds hints of the great romantic movement.

Another rationalist is Johan Gabriel Oxenstierna (1750–1818), likewise an unreserved admirer of French culture, as were more or less all those who belonged to the Gustavian generation.

The only one to resist the Gallic influence was Thomas Thorild (1759–1808), who was an ardent follower of Rousseau, of the first English romanticists and of the German *Stürmer und Dränger*. Thorild pointed out the close connection between the Swedes and the Germanic peoples, the natural sympathy of tradition, character, and tastes existing between them, and he urged that, instead of following France, the Swedes should cultivate closer adherence to the culture of Germany and England. Like the *Stürmer und Dränger,* he demanded a boundless liberty of the spirit and naturally also of artistic form; whence he warmly pleaded the cause of blank verse, of which he gave an example in his own poem entitled *The passions* (1785).

The Gustavians violently attacked this misfit poet, who at the height of the period of French rationalism dared to take another path and follow other aesthetic ideals. On the other hand, Thorild, even if endowed with great critical acumen, was not the type of man capable of enduring the struggle successfully; hence his voice was lost in the clamour of the voices opposing him.

The other *Stürmer und Dränger,* Bengt Lidner (1757–93), who, however, had a poetic temperament very superior to that of Thorild, was likewise too weak and sentimental a character to make his authority felt. *The death of Countess Spastara* (1783) and *The last judgment* (1788), even though

[98]

they have verses of exquisite workmanship, passed almost unobserved and were soon forgotten.

One of the most important poets of the period was a woman, Anna Maria Lenngren (1755–1817). Early in life she gave evidence of her literary talent, and by the close of the 'seventies she had established a reputation for herself not only as a writer of Swedish verse but also as a translator of modern drama and classical poetry.

She contributed poems mainly to *Stockholmsposten*, of which her husband was one of the editors. These poems were published anonymously and especially those written during her golden age (1795–1800) were attributed to leading poets, to Kellgren, Leopold and others, so distinguished was their literary quality. In due time her identity was revealed, and the Swedish Academy paid her its homage through Gyllenborg who read an ode in her honour.

No collection of her works appeared in her lifetime. In 1819 her *Skaldeförsök* (Attempts at writing poetry) were published and have since then seen numerous editions.

Her work is deeply cherished in the hearts of the Swedish people, and all Swedish literary critics and historians have paid her glowing tribute, especially for her achievements in the fields of the idyll, the satire and the epigram. Her writing is marked by realism, common sense, and humour. Simple and unadorned in its language, it has a natural charm which often joins company with the satirical element and creates the truly unique atmosphere found in the most noteworthy of her poems.

Her resting place in the Klara cemetery in Stockholm is indicated by a memorial raised by the Swedish Academy.

Among this band of poets, of whom we have recalled only the most notable ones, there stands out a most original figure, that of Carl Michael Bellman (1740–95), who does not seem at all influenced by the ideas and by the literary and philosophic currents of the time.

The poetry of Bellman is pervaded throughout by a melodic vein so limpid and pure that his verses of themselves alone constitute a delicious fount of music. The characters which he as a rule elects to treat, the watchmaker Fredman and the winsome nymph Ulla Winblad, have been by some likened to the characters in the comedies of Shakespeare, so spontaneous and original is their humorous value. His figures of wandering clerics, of jesters, of drinkers, are drawn with such skill that they make one think of naturalism, but of a naturalism corrected and refined by the grace of the rococo.

The poems of Bellman are not written to be read, but are intended to be sung, and in this consists their principal fascination. In fact some of them were set to music by Bellman himself; for others he adapted popular motifs and even melodies of classical composers such as Pergolesi.

Even today the Swedish people, at festivals and reunions, delight in singing the songs of Bellman, and every year on the 26th of July, *Bellmansdagen*, and at the reopening of the university courses, the students at Stockholm gather around his statue, sprinkling it abundantly with wine.

With this poet who sought in wine inebriation
and perhaps the forgetfulness of earthly cares, with
this extravagant, charming dreamer, bohemian as he
was, and inexhaustible improvisor of music and
poetry, the eighteenth century came to a close, a
century of enlightened realism, which in Sweden
had been only an artificial superstructure, composed
of materials derived from abroad. After its close the
wave of romanticism, which had invaded all of Europe, broke also over Sweden, to find, awaiting it
there, a natural basin into which it poured and
settled.

ROMANTICISM

As says de Boor in his compendium of Swedish
literature, the pistol shot which on March 15th,
1792, found the heart of Gustavus III, put to death
also an entire era. The great rationalist King, confirmed champion of French culture, died tragically
at a masked ball, the victim of a conspiracy among
the nobles, and with him tottered in Sweden all that
scaffolding in the style of Louis XV and XVI built
by patient, tenacious and battling authors, who,
though it be granted that they had imported into
their own land new germs of art and literature,
had in some ways deviated along paths not con-
forming to the spirit of the country.

Everywhere there is a seething and fermenting
of new ideas and new ideals; everywhere resounds
the voice of the philosopher of Königsberg, which
drowns out that of the English philosopher Locke,
the dominant influence up to that time.

The first to sustain the ideas of Kant was Benjamin Höijer, who founded a sort of club which he called "Junta," in which secret literary meetings were held. These meetings were not free from political discussions, which invariably concluded with open demonstrations of applause for the French Revolution. This resulted in the closing of the club and Höijer lost his standing. He travelled in various parts of Europe, and in Germany renounced his Kantian faith to follow Fichte and later Hegel.

In Sweden, in the meantime, the ideas of romanticism ever continued to make headway. The centre of studies was shifted from rationalist Stockholm, seat of the academies opposed to the new spirit of innovation, to Uppsala, which thus became the stronghold of Swedish romanticism.

A characteristic figure of this period of transition is Frans Michael Franzén (1772–1847), bishop of Hernösand, who having held himself aloof from the pseudo-classicism of the Gustavian age, imitated in his poems the English and German poets.

Authentic types of *Stürmer und Dränger* are Lorenzo Hammarskjöld (1785–1827) and Claes Livijn (1781–1844). The former made known to the Swedes the work of Tieck and Novalis and together with the latter founded a magazine which he called *Polyfem, i. e.,* a critical-satirical review, in which was published periodically a rubric "Notes of Captain Baggfot," which held up to ridicule the rigidly conservative attitude of the Swedish academicians.

From Hammarskjöld's group a small body of young men detached itself and formed the left wing of the romantic movement. These, contrary to

Hammarskjöld, assumed a positive attitude toward the tendencies and problems of the new epoch.

They also founded a magazine, *Phosphoros,* which presented itself to its readers with a prologue of mystical intonation, in which the speculative philosophy of Schelling was openly professed. *Phosphoros* was to symbolize the new light arisen with romanticism; indeed in order always to maintain the luministic symbolism, the group was called also the "Group of the Dawn."

At the head of this little body of the extreme left was the poet, then twenty years of age, Per Daniel A. Atterbom (1790–1855). Full of the theories of Tieck, Werner, Novalis and Schelling, he wanted to give to poetry the indeterminateness of music, without at the same time neglecting naturalistic and philosophic implications, and for this purpose he and his friends created a new terminology, of symbolic character, which served them to express the concepts drawn from German poets and philosophers. This terminology, however, if it brought to poetry an influx of new ideas and ideals, ended by deforming and obscuring the thought, whence it is not rare that the verses of Atterbom become difficult for the most attentive reader to understand, though they are always pervaded by a musical quality so full and sustained that the reading of them transports us to an elevated sphere, where it seems unreality and dream reign alone. *The isle of bliss* (1824–27), a fairy-tale play taken from a mediaeval story, is considered to be one of the best productions of romanticism.

Among the other Phosphorists worthy of note is

Erik Sjöberg (pseudonym Vitalis, 1794–1828),
who, however, mixed much water in the romantic
wine of his illustrious master.

Little by little, beside the group of the Phosphorists, another group was forming, the so-called
"Gothic Society," the proclaimer of a romanticism
somewhat diverse, of a romanticism which re-
valuated the national element, unstressed by the
Phosphorists. Through the work of this new group
an interest is reborn in folk-lore, in the legends, the
fables, and the folk-songs. The Middle Ages, which
rationalism had despised, reassumes with the members of the Gothic Society its place of honour. As
in the time of Rudbeck, studies of the age of the
vikings are again resumed, the most ancient deeds
of the heroes are unearthed and the country's soil
is excavated to wrest from it treasures which it still
holds hidden. This group likewise had its magazine,
Iduna, named from the Scandinavian goddess of
youth.

Two great figures, having many points of contact, are members of the group: Erik Gustaf Geijer
and Esaias Tegnér.

Erik Gustaf Geijer (1783–1847) is the greatest
historian of Sweden. Taking first as his basis the
philosophy of Schelling he proceeded from the concept that the family, kindred, the clan and not the
individual were at the beginning of human development. With such assertion he reinstated the
validity of the mediaeval concept of corporation-
ism at the expense of individualism, exalted by
Rousseau and his followers, and he recognized at the
same time that it is not the equality of individuals as

proclaimed by rationalism, but their inequality that is the true essence of all human organization.

As a lyric poet, Geijer is one of the greatest of Sweden. For the perfect interpenetration of the ideal with the real, he has been compared by some even to Goethe.

He has above all glorified the two figures most characteristic of Sweden: the peasant and the seaman, upon whose labour rests the economic structure of the country. *Odalbonden* (The peasant freeholder) and *Vikingen* (both 1811) are the titles of two of his poems that are among the fairest pearls of Swedish lyric poetry.

Besides his history and his poetry, Geijer cultivated music as well and composed many songs which are sung by the people even today.

His contemporary, Esaias Tegnér (1782–1846), gave his country its great epic with the *Frithiof's saga* (published in *Iduna* 1820–22; published entire in twenty-four cantos, 1825).

Frithiof, young hero, son of a rich peasant of Norway, in which the peasant class is as old as the nobility, and Ingeborg, daughter of King Bele, have been educated together. King Bele has promised Ingeborg to Frithiof as his wife. Bele dies; his sons, Helge and Halfdan, who succeed him, refuse to keep the promise; they refuse as well to give the hand of their sister to King Ring, who declares war on them. After having in vain asked the help of Frithiof,—angered as was Achilles after the disgrace he suffered at the hands of Agamemnon,—they depart. Ingeborg has been left in the temple of Balder, under the custody of the god. Frithiof comes to

make her a secret visit, but he is discovered and
punished by temporary banishment. Upon his return the sons of the king have burned his property.
He plans revenge, and as a result of his plan the temple of Balder, in which they have gathered with the
people for a sacred ceremony, is burned; then he
goes again into exile and visits incognito the court
of King Ring, who has obtained the hand of Ingeborg. The old man recognizes the hero, and after
having tested his honour, sacrifices himself to the god
Odin, leaving his wife and his kingdom to Frithiof.
Frithiof returns home to his country, where finally
he marries Ingeborg.

This is the plot of the legend, upon which
Tegnér has laid the rich colours of his palette. Epical
recitations, dramatic scenes, lyric songs, all are
found here. In the development of his subject he
has given attention so far as choice of form is concerned only to the movement of the action and to
the various passions of the characters.

"The hero of Tegnér," says a French critic,
Léouzon-Leduc, "is not simply an individual type,
he is a national type. He is the great Scandinavian
nation with all its vast thoughts, its noble sentiments, its indomitable passions, and its infinite aspirations. It is true that Frithiof is the son of these
kings of the sea who look upon the world as their
possession, and who, of all things fearful, fear but
one alone, and that is to see heaven fall upon their
heads; but at the same time this hero has a heart
subject to emotion and compassion; he insults the
gods, burns their temples, dreams blood and death,
and directly becomes calm again, repents, weeps,

has no peace until he is reconciled with those whom he has stricken with his anger: a living image of the Nature that after its tempests, roaring across the dark fir of the mountains, follows with the timid sighs of the breeze and the plaintive rustlings of the melancholy birches."

Frithiof's saga is the favourite poem of the Swedes, the work of their great national poet that up to the present time is without peer. After this composition, the one they prefer is the little poem of the *First communion* (1820), which Tegnér has invested with all the fascination of his sacred character as Bishop of the Lutheran church.

Axel (1822) is a poem on King Charles XII, who by that time had attained in popular imagination the heights of the mythical; or, to be more exact, it is a poem about his favorite squire, Axel. Axel, charged with taking a message to Sweden, carries out his mission, not at all frightened by the length of the journey across the desert plains of Russia. Discovered by enemies, he is wounded; while he is lying on the ground already awaiting death, he is aided by a woman, Mary the Amazon, daughter of the desert, mistress of the Muscovite solitudes. She cares for him; nurses him back to health. From gratitude love is born. But he must be on his way to carry out the mission entrusted to him by his king. Mary awaits him, but time passes and he does not return. Finally he comes and seeks his beloved, whom he finds fatally wounded on the field of battle.

"Alas, yes, it is she. She forces herself to dominate her suffering, and with weakened voice she speaks:

'Axel my beloved, our greeting is farewell, for death is already in my heart. Do not ask what has brought me here. Love alone has been my guide. Ah, when this long night begins, when man knocks on the portals of the tomb, with what different eyes he looks on life and the vain cares of it! A love beautiful like ours,—behold the only treasure that takes us to heaven! I have yearned to know the vow that you have made; now I go to ask it of the stars, where I shall see your innocence pure as their splendor. I have not acted wisely I know. I know too that you will sincerely mourn me. Forgive every tear in the name of our love, every tear you will shed upon my ashes. I have neither brothers, nor father, nor mother; you were all to me. Axel, in this supreme hour of death, swear that you have loved me. Swear it! . . . Life has told me the most beautiful part of its saga. May not your maiden die then upon your heart? Cannot her ashes rest peacefully in a country that you have defended? See, Axel, a cloud is passing over the moon; when it passes, I shall be dead; and my soul transfigured will rest on the other shore, where it will pray for your happiness, and from which it will look upon you with all the eyes of heaven. Plant a foreign rose on my tomb, and when this daughter of the sun perishes buried under the snow, think of your beloved who sleeps like the rose under the snow of the north. The days of blossoming have been brief. See, Axel, the cloud is gone. Farewell! Farewell!' " Mary sighs, presses the hand of her lover and expires.

Axel does not kill himself on the tomb of his beloved. It is not death that rises for him "from the streams of the abyss, but its younger brother, pallid madness. His disheveled hair is bestrewn with the poppies of the fields; his haunted eyes fix now the sky, now the depths of the earth; a smile contracts his lips; tears shine in his half-blind eyes. Madness touches Axel's forehead, and from then on, the unhappy fellow goes wandering ceaselessly about the tomb of Mary, as in the ancient sagas the dead about their buried treasures, and the river resounds day and night from his tortures and laments. . . . Axel mourns on the rock of Sota. He is there when the sun rises, he is still there when night falls; always in the same place, always weeping. One morning he is found dead on the shores of the sea: his hands are joined as in prayer, the breeze of the morning has almost congealed his tears, and his blind eyes are still fixed on the tomb of his beloved."

This is the subject of the poem *Axel,* one of the finest poetic monuments of the Swedish language.

Preserved also are Tegnér's lectures and the sermons which he gave in his capacity of bishop; the former serve to demonstrate with what zeal and profundity he was dedicated to the bettering of teaching in Sweden; they are masterpieces of oratorical art, notable contributions to the science of pedagogy. The sermons are unsurpassed examples of Protestant religious oratory.

With Tegnér, a temperament idyllic and sentimental, is contrasted the figure of Erik Johan Stagnelius (1793–1823), for whom the opposition between ideal and real assumes tragic proportions. Such a contrast is not for him, as for others, a

poetical-philosophical problem, but a problem intimately lived and never resolved, and precisely for
that reason dramatic. Such inclination of his to a
tragic conception of life was aggravated by the
condition of his health and by an unhappy love
affair.

The collection of his poems entitled: *The lilies of
Sharon* (1821–22) is full of metaphysical lucubra-
tions, permeated by neo-Platonism, as is his play entitled, *The bacchantes* (1822).

The fisherman Thorsten and *The martyrs* (found
and published posthumously, 1824–26) are other
plays of his, which betray, however, a marked
tendency toward realism.

The principal merit of Stagnelius lies in his style,
vibrant with sentiment and elevated in inspiration,
but it is lacking in virility and force, poorly
adapted therefore to the drama, so that the tragedies
of Stagnelius have been considered by some as his
most beautiful lyrics.

With Stagnelius the period of the great romanticists closes and that of their imitators begins, but in
addition, across the meanderings of romanticism a
new current from abroad gains power, that of
realism.

TRANSITION

With the exhaustion of romanticism, the materialistic and radical ideas of the French Revolution returned to make headway, sustained and encouraged by the researches and discoveries in the
field of the exact sciences. The cultural centre of
Uppsala was losing its authority, while Stockholm

in which new political ideas were germinating was reacquiring it. The daily press was always gaining in power and the voice of command passed from the professors to the journalists.

This approach to French culture coincided with the ascension of the throne by Bernadotte (1818), under whom Sweden seemed to regain the pinnacles attained with Charles XII. In fact Bernadotte studied all questions which interested the well-being and prosperity of the country, and he worked ardently to heal the wounds inflicted on Sweden by the blind temerity and deplorable obstinacy of the preceding government.

In a short time Sweden, stricken and discouraged, rose again under the sagacious and energetic guidance of the foreign-born king. While he was working to assure the progress of manufacturing and agricultural commerce and industry, Bernadotte was at the same time in every way encouraging public instruction, the arts and the sciences. Writers and scientists at the beginning of their careers obtained from the liberality of the King the necessary means to travel to foreign lands and acquire new experiences and new knowledge.

The literary form most in vogue in this period of reborn realism is the novel, in place of poetry, which was the style during the romantic period. And this was natural since reflective thought, which arises from direct observation of the external world, opens better into the broad limitless basin of prose than into the narrow metrical channels of the lyric. Examples are found in the historical novels by Magnus Jakob Crusenstolpe (1795-1865), author with a rich, oratorical style, famous for his revelations of life behind the scenes at court.

Another characteristic of the period is the appearance of the feminine element in the literary field. Among the writers who, one might say, initiate the modern novel in Sweden the foremost is Fredrika Bremer (1801–65), authoress of numerous novels and travel books that mirror a sensitive delicate soul and a heart open to all the sorrows and all the joys of life. In her novels the serenity of her spirit lights with luminous reflection the scenes she brings before our eyes and one inhales the breath of a sane morality and a sound virtue. The principal gift of Fredrika Bremer lies in having imparted to her characters together with grace and fineness of detail a life that is actual and sincere. Today her most readable work is *The homes of the new world* (1853–54), a series of letters describing her sojourn in America in the early fifties.

Another authoress who was much read at that time is Emilie Flygare-Carlén (1807–92), whose novels, localized among the Swedish skerries, retain a certain popular appeal to this day.

The typical representative of the transition from romanticism to realism is Karl Jonas Love Almquist (1793–1866). He opened his literary career with some stories of pure romantic savour, but these were followed by others more realistic, treating various important problems of his period; the same is true of the *Folk-tales* (1832–51) wherein, however, there are also elements that make us think of the impressionism of our own time.

One of the problems which most interested

Almquist was that of matrimony. Already at the age of twenty-three he wrote an essay entitled *What is love?* and in it are found the following reflections:

"The world condemns to death one who counterfeits bank-notes, but not one who counterfeits love. But to unite in matrimony for a thousand other motives and not for love, creating a family without any ideal basis, is it not perhaps a crime, of which the consequences for the present and the future are more horrible and unhappy than the falsification of millions of bank-notes? Too often moral and physical degeneration has been produced by loveless parents who have given life to poor unhappy creatures."

Almquist had married a peasant woman, with whom for a time he lived happily, in the country, in the heart of nature, but after two years he grew annoyed with that life and wanted to return to the city.

Between 1832 and 1851 he published a work in a number of volumes, *The book of the brier rose,* a sort of scrap-book in which he tells of music, colours, perfumes, tears, smiles, poetry, religion, philosophy—an encyclopaedic work, wherein essays and delightful tales are interwoven: the whole turning about the central figure of Richard Furumo, the type of the ideal Swede as Almquist understood him.

In 1839 he published a work, *Sara Videbeck,* in which once again he breaks a lance in favour of free love. He holds that matrimony, as it is arranged in modern society, is immoral because founded on base motives. The woman gives herself to the man for materialistic interests. Instead the woman should work like the man; she must make an independent place for herself, because only then will she be in a position to marry for love. Woman, he says, must not believe in those who consider her inferior to man, nor must she believe that she loses her fascination when she is independent and self-sufficient. Woman loses her fascination only when she marries without love. No man will be happy with a woman who does not love him. For that reason he must take care to marry none but a woman who earns her own living, for then he can be sure that he is loved. The day in which she unites her life with that of the man who has won her love, he can cry jubilantly: "I am loved!"

Extreme and perilous theories earned for Almquist endless and increasing enmities and abuse, especially when *Amorina* (1839) came out, wherein Almquist, anticipating by many years the positivist school, sustains that one can kill and still remain innocent, since there are cases in which, owing to atavistic inclinations to evil and to crime, one can act without responsibility.

This theory formulated in a country intimately pietistic and rigidly Puritan like Sweden, aroused the scorn and wrath of all intellectual Swedish society, which called Almquist an Antichrist and corrupter of youth.

This uproar of contumely, accusations, and insults robbed the author of all desire to continue in his literary work. He wrote to gain his daily bread, but not succeeding in his purpose, he had to have recourse to usurers. In June, 1851, there was launched against him the accusation of having attempted to poison an aged usurer. Threatened with arrest, Almquist had to flee to America, where he lived for fifteen years, until homesickness brought him back to the threshold of his country at Bremen; and there he died.

Even for many years after his death, Almquist was held in the same consideration as during his lifetime; only in the final decade of the last century was his work recognized and united with that of the great writers of the period.

Beside the somewhat enigmatic and paradoxical figure of Almquist, rises that of Johan Ludvig Runeberg (1804–77). Although born in Finland, he is considered a Swede, especially since at that time Finland, taken from Sweden by Russia in 1809, was regarded by the Swedes as a land of irredentism.

The childhood of Runeberg was passed among the woods and lakes of his native land. As a youth he attended the schools of Åbo, entered the university and was, very young, appointed professor at Helsingfors. But notwithstanding this placid and carefree existence, how many ardent passions, how many sweet dreams stirred the soul of the poet in his tranquil abode, how often the interminable series of figures that he evoked from the shade of myth and legend came to life before his eyes!

But what pleases above all in the works of Runeberg is their authentic local colour, wholly northern and Finnish. The first of them to attract attention to the young Swedish-Finnish author was *The tomb in Perrho* (1831), the story of six brothers, who alone assail a troup of brigands. Five of them die from wounds suffered in combat. The aged father arrives when the struggle is at its end, and not seeing among the corpses the body of Thomas, his favourite son, he fears that he may have fled, cowardly abandoning his brothers. But Thomas was absent when the struggle began. He arrived too late to give help to his brothers, and, finding all of them bathed in their blood, he hurled himself like a furious lion in pursuit of the brigands, reached them, and massacred them one after the other, beheading their chief. Then he returns, covered with wounds, to throw himself at the feet of his father, who dies like a Spartan embracing his noble son.

The Swedish Academy awarded a gold medal to this poem and Runeberg continued in the treatment of Finnish subjects.

Between 1832 and 1836 he published two idylls, *The elk-hunters* and *Hanna,* which describe for us sincerely and unaffectedly the nature of Finland, the life and customs of her peasants.

A short epic poem, *Christmas eve* (1841), recalls the war of 1809. In a cycle of ballads entitled *The songs of Ensign Stål* (1848), Runeberg sings the heroic deeds and immortal glory of Swedish and Finnish arms in the war that tore Finland from Sweden. It is from this cycle of ballads that one of the Swedish national hymns has been taken.

His attempt at the drama, *The Kings of Salamis* (1863), in which he sought to evoke the feeling of destiny, was not successful. Like Tegnér, Runeberg had a temperament too lyric, too subjective, to adapt itself to the exigencies of the drama. But while the lyric poetry of Tegnér often holds a rhetorical pathos, that of Runeberg is reserved and almost virginal; it is full of the melancholy atmosphere of fir-woods, of solitary lakes, of cloudy skies. All his verses have a mood of suffering and of dolorous resignation. He expresses his grief in elegies more exalted than those of Young, sadder than those of Kirk White; then after this cry of desolation, we find him returning to himself, seeking to dominate his own spirit, and imposing upon himself the sorrowing calm of resignation.

The style of Runeberg offers neither the richness of images found in Tegnér, nor the studied shadings that characterize Atterbom, but is notable for its elegant simplicity.

Pupil and imitator of Runeberg was Zachris Topelius (1818–98), novelist, poet and historian, he also a Finlander by birth. His works, like those of Runeberg, though showing strong influence from the mother country, are all written in the Swedish language.

Carl Snoilsky (1841–1903) brings to the Swedish poetry of this period a luminous happy note. Even at the age of twenty he had penetrated as with a ray of sunlight the vast and nebulous panorama of Swedish literature.

The diplomatic career to which he dedicated himself gave him the opportunity to travel throughout Europe; but the country that he cared for above all others was Italy, where he lived uninterruptedly for a number of years, becoming thoroughly acquainted with its history, traditions, and customs. In Rome he met Ibsen, and the two poets became bound by a strong tie of friendship which was never broken, and to Ibsen he dedicated his poem entitled *The golden house of Nero* in his *Italienska bilder* (Pictures of Italy, 1864) which, like many of his works, among them the poem *Savonarola* (1883), is inspired by Italy.

The Slavonic origin on his father's side, his continual foreign travel and his own open and receptive temperament made of him a cosmopolitan character, capable of assimilating the literature of every country, though remaining strongly rooted in his native land, of which a considerable part of his works treats.

The poetry of Snoilsky sometimes presents the legendary figures of his country which he brings back to life with touches of rare mastery, as in *The funeral rites of Herr Johan Banér* (Johan Banér, victor of Wittstock and of Chemnitz was an ancestor of Snoilsky himself) and in *The messenger of Stenbock,* in which he describes the horrible consequences suffered by Sweden as a result of the defeat at Poltava and the flight of Charles XII to Turkey, both included in his *Svenska bilder* (Pictures of Sweden, 1886 and later); sometimes it is the northern landscapes that serve as framework for his pictures glistening with lights and colours. But if his poetry is clear and serene one must not believe that he deviates from the genius of Scandinavia; the subjects taken from Swedish history, to which he dedicated a large part of his poetic activity, testify to this, as seen in his *Svenska bilder* which are true hymns to his fatherland. For the mellow quality and the harmony of his verse Snoilsky by some critics is preferred to Tegnér himself.

Inseparable from the figure of Snoilsky is the author Viktor Rydberg (1828–95), he, too, a representative of the moribund romantic idealism.

In his novel *Singoalla* (1858) he sings "the last free song of romanticism." All the events of this famous novel are poised between reality and dream, between the real and the fantastic. The double life of the cavalier Erland, Christian and husband of the blonde Elena by day, pagan by night and lover of the beautiful gypsy Singoalla, is an ultraromantic motif, which brings to mind some of the tales of Hoffmann or of Théophile Gautier.

The interest of Rydberg in philosophic and religious studies induced him to write a study on the doctrine of the New Testament (*Bibelns lära om Kristus,* 1862), a book which caused a great stir in Sweden and anticipated ideas and concepts of the positivist school.

In *The last Athenian* (1859), Rydberg takes us back to the time of struggle between paganism and Christianity. The figures which he presents to us are purely symbolic, standing for ideas and tendencies dear or displeasing to the author. Thus the Athenian Chrisantheus impersonates the neo-Platonic doctrine, in the priest Theodorus one can see a standard-bearer of Luther, while Hermione, his daughter, realizes the union of what is best in the Christian ideal and in the pagan.

In *Roman emperors in marble* (1875–76) Rydberg's tendency to the democratic spirit is brought out, as well as his aversion to the invading aestheticism.

Final followers of romanticism were Carl Vilhelm Böttiger (1807–78), a sentimental poet facile and melodic, imitator of Tegnér, whose daughter he married; Bernhard Elis Malmström (1816–65), poet and literary critic; and Carl Vilhelm August Strandberg (pseudonym Talis Qualis, 1818–77), whose collection of lyrics entitled *Wild roses* (1845) is pervaded by sweetness and delicacy.

With the death of Rydberg, the last ideal barrier against invading realism falls. The names of Brandes, the great Danish critic, of Ibsen, Zola, and Björnson become banners which symbolize the new ideals and tendencies.

IMPRESSIONISM AND NATURALISM

The advent of Johan August Strindberg (1849–1912) in the literary arena marks the beginning of a new era in the literary and cultural annals of Sweden. The life of this author was a *via crucis*, an odyssey of torments, to which only death could make an end.

Born in Stockholm, January 22nd, 1849, he knew only briefly the tender affection of the mother whom he lost in 1862. He was entrusted, together with several brothers and sisters, to the care of a housekeeper whom his father subsequently married. Within this family he did not find the love and the tenderness of which his spirit had so great a need. In his autobiography, *The son of a servant,* he tells us that his first recollections were those of fear and hunger. "He was afraid of darkness, of being beaten, of offending people, of falling down, of knocking against things, of being in the way, of the fists of his brothers, of his father's and mother's chastisements." No wonder that from his earliest years he became introspective, embittering his spirit which called for air and light, but which grief, rancour and the morbid and precocious tendency to meditation constrained to remain among shadows and torments.

After having graduated from the gymnasium in 1867, he matriculated at the University of Uppsala in the autumn, but remained there only one term, partly because of his lack of means and partly because of the pedantic methods which were distasteful to his impatient, neurotic nature.

Returning to the capital, he secured a position in one of the public schools. After one term of teaching he was convinced of having missed his calling. For a while he engaged in private tutoring in the family of a prominent physician and became interested in medicine to such a degree that he went to Uppsala in due time and attempted a qualifying examination in chemistry. Having failed, he turned to histrionic arts in the spring of 1869. He made his *début* with one solitary line in Björnson's *Maria Stuart*. A couple of months later he had his second, more pretentious tryout. Failure attended it and he went home and swallowed an opium tablet, which in its turn failed to harm him. In the spring of 1870 he was once more in Uppsala where he organized the literary society "Runa." By this time he had writ-

ten his first classical drama *The declining Hellas*
(1869), later called *Hermione*, for which he received favourable mention by the Swedish Academy. Under the influence of Byron, Schiller,
Oehlenschläger, Björnson, Ibsen, Georg Brandes
and the Danish philosopher Sören Kierkegaard, he
now turned to the drama in earnest, producing *In
Rome* (1870), which was accepted by the Dramatic Theatre, *The freethinker* (1870), and in
1871 *The outlaw*, his first drama so far of any consequence. It was performed at the Dramatic Theatre
in the fall of 1871 and, while attracting but moderate attention, it won a friend and supporter for
the author in the person of King Charles XV.

For several reasons—chief among which were
poor health and the withdrawal of the king's sti-
pends—Strindberg left Uppsala early in the spring
of 1872. For a few months he gleaned a living from
newspaper work. But his creative impulse left him
no rest. Finally he bought a few quires of paper
and started for Kymmendö, a small island in the
Stockholm archipelago. Here he wrote his first
truly great drama, *Master Olof* (published 1880).
It was refused by the theatrical authorities. A verse
edition of the drama was completed in 1876 and
published in 1878.*

In 1873 we find young Strindberg at the head of
Svensk Försäkringstidning. Later in the year he
was attached as telegraph operator to a station in
the skerries. In 1874 fortune smiled upon him. He
received an appointment as amanuensis in the

* For a critical analysis of this drama, fundamental for the understanding of Strindberg and his dramatic art, see Martin Lamm, *Strind-
bergs dramer*, Stockholm, 1924.

Royal Library, where he delved into the study of the Chinese language. In the midst of this new life of his he met Siri von Essen, the charming young wife of a captain of the Royal Guard, Gustav Wrangel. The romance of this courtship—he married her in December of 1877 after her divorce—has been set forth in their letters, *He and she* (1875–76).

This change in Strindberg's life revived in him the creative impulse so that when he left Sweden for the continent in 1883 he had over a score of recognized works to his credit.

To this period belong such significant works as *Cultural historical studies* (1881); *The red room* (1879) in which he attacked with considerable vehemence the "follies and vanities" of the society in which he lived; the romantic dramas, *The secret of the guild* (1880), *Sir Bengt's wife* (1882) and the charming fairy play, *The journey of Lucky Peter* (1881); *The Swedish people* (1881–82), in which time-worn and honoured traditions were trampled under foot; *Swedish destinies and adventures* (1882–83) which is a collection of stories in historical setting, abounding in humour and pathos. In the same year (1882) appeared *The new kingdom* which promptly took its place in the limelight of contemporary satirical writings. "An affinity with Max Nordau," says Lind af Hageby in her *August Strindberg, the spirit of revolt* "is noticeable in certain chapters, but" the author adds, "Strindberg's exposure of conventional hypocrisy and social humbug is achieved by a tempestuous outburst, compared with which Nordau's strictures seem a discursive and spiritless sermon."

If the time-segment 1868–79 was a period of orientation and searching after truth in the life of Strindberg, that of 1880–90 was one of persistent criticism of the social *status quo*. Orthodox religious belief was gradually replaced by an attachment to nature (Rousseau) which finally developed into atheism. Politically speaking, his democratic radicalism yielded to the Nietzschean theory of the superman. His stand against the emancipation of women earned him the epithet of misogynist. Realism and naturalism dominated his literary output.

Upon arrival in France, Strindberg, Mrs. Strindberg and the children, Karin and Greta, joined the group of artists at Grez par Nemours. Between the years 1883 and 1889 the family resided in turn in Switzerland, where a third child, Hans, was born, in Bavaria and Denmark. During these years Strindberg wrote under the influence of various thinkers (Edward von Hartmann, Thomas Buckle, Darwin, Rousseau, Feuerbach, Nordau, Spencer, John Stuart Mill, Zola, Poe, and the French neuro-pathologist, Jean Martin Charcot) and with an ever-increasing interest in mesmerism, hypnotism and telepathy, a series of works of which the following deserve special mention.

Married (I–II, 1884–86) is a collection of stories depicting the imaginary raptures and shattered idylls of married life. The first volume of this work, which the author characterizes as "a defence and glorification of marriage, home, mother and child," was confiscated by the Crown, and Strindberg was obliged to return to Sweden in 1884 to stand trial before the court.* He was acquitted and left for the Continent, a broken man. His bitterness towards woman is hereafter trebled and quadrupled. Serious students of Strindberg, among them Martin Lamm, hold that the above-mentioned trial constituted the inception of the critical period in the life of the author, known as the "Inferno crisis."

The next work of special significance is his autobiography: *The son of a servant* (1886); *The time of fermentation* (1886); *In the red room* (1886); *He and she* (written during the years 1875–76, published Stockholm, Bonnier, 1919); *The author* (written 1886, published Stockholm, Bonnier, 1909). Other works, to be commented upon later, which also form part of his autobiography are: *The fool's confession, Inferno, Legends, The second story of the quarantine master* (in *Fairhaven and Foulstrand*), and *Alone.*

These works, without an understanding of which there is no approach to Strindberg, inform us in minute detail of early influences and of his childhood, youth, adolescence and manhood. Here there are pages in which the author with a sadistic pleasure reveals to us his soul in all its nudity, free of gilding and pretences. One feels as though one were attending a tragic, painful autovivisection in which bones and nerves, denuded of the tissues that enwrap them, are being probed throughout all their ramifications.

We follow this supersensitive, suffering soul from

* See *Kvarstadsresan* (The impoundage journey); first published in *Budkaflen*, Jan. 23–April 17, 1885. See also August Strindberg, *Samlade skrifter*, Vol. XVII, Stockholm, 1913.

the nursery into life, at school and college. We observe his religious complex with the attendant traditional millstone of guilt around his neck. We follow him to the university where his rebel spirit stands between him and a degree. We follow him through his youthful storm and stress, through heavy literary labours to repeated defeats; through poverty and failing health, marriage and voluntary exile, serious family troubles and divorce.

During the period from September, 1887, through March, 1888, Strindberg wrote what is now known in English as *The fool's confession* (published in a cheap German edition in 1894; a French edition *Le plaidoyer d'un fou*, Paris, 1895; a pirated newspaper serial in Sweden, 1893–94; first authorized Swedish edition *En dåres försvarstal*, Stockholm, Bonnier, 1914).

The first part of *The fool's confession* ends at Katrineholm railway station whither he had accompanied his future wife on her way to Copenhagen—the Reno of Scandinavia—in her quest for a divorce from her husband preparatory to marrying Strindberg. The short journey had been attended by serious quarrelling. He writes: "Her last embrace has brought me back to God, and under the influence of her last tears, of which there are still traces in my beard, I renounce the new faith which stands for the evolution of mankind. The first halting place on the downward path of a man has been reached; the others will follow naturally even to insensibility, to the verge of madness."

The remainder of *The fool's confession* is the

story of the first ten years of his married life. No sooner was he legally joined in wedlock to this woman than he began to suspect her of faithlessness. This mania of his continued until he was separated from her in 1892.

His anti-feminism and his own marital unhappiness reverberate in *The father* (1887), a tragedy in three acts, which represents a heart-rending struggle between a man and a woman for the possession of the soul of a child. Laura, the wife, administers the poison which unbalances the husband's mind. She suggests that he (the Captain) is not the father of the child. The thought becomes an obsession with him. Finally, when all, save the old nurse, have deserted him, he dies in a strait-jacket during a paroxysm of despair. The drama in question is simply another *Fool's confession* in dramatic form.

Other naturalistic plays of this period are: *Comrades* (1886); *Miss Julia* (1888); *Creditors* (1888); *Pariah* (1888–89), *The stronger* and *Simoon* (both of 1889). Both *Pariah* and *Simoon* are pervaded by an atmosphere of psychic intensity, of the mystical and the supernatural, thus tending strongly away from naturalism.

With the publication of *I havsbandet* (At the edge of the sea, 1890), Strindberg rejected the Nietzschean gospel. The author admitted that this novel was written under the influence of Nietzsche, adding that "the individual succumbs in the struggle for absolute individualism." Seeing the impossibility of explaining human events as a simple succession of facts, he changes the word "destiny" into that of Providence, *i. e.,* to a conscious and personal being who directs our life.

In April, 1889, Strindberg returned to Sweden, more celebrated, more hated and unhappy than he had been up to that time. He seems to have moved about freely in the vicinity of Stockholm and to have lived alone here and there most of the time. Where his wife and children had their abode between 1889 and 1892 is not explicitly stated.

During these years Strindberg wrote *The keys of the Kingdom of Heaven* (1892). The hero of the play is a blacksmith in his fifties who goes in search of his lost happiness. After long wanderings and many vicissitudes he finally locates the object of his search, the keys of the Kingdom of Heaven, within the ruins of the Tower of Babylon. At the suggestion of his guide, Dr. Omniscient, the blacksmith mounts a ladder raised against a wall, and looking through an opening he discovers an old, familiar smithy, a dingy little room and his three children fast asleep in their beds.

Mother-love and *The link* (both of 1892, or 1893) are touchingly autobiographical, particularly the last-mentioned, which presents a divorce-court scene. The applicants are willing to compromise for the sake of the link—the child of their affection. But the judge's question as to the reasons for dissension causes the parents to rise in arms against each other, thus forcing self-condemnation upon their own heads.

In the autumn of 1892 Strindberg left Sweden and settled down in Berlin. There he met, in January, 1893, Frida Uhl, whom he married on the island of Heligoland in May of the same year.

After an unpleasant honeymoon-journey to England, so well described in *The second story of the quarantine master*, found in *Fairhaven and Foulstrand* (1902), and after having played hide-and-seek with his wife between Mondsee and Rügen, the unhappy bride and groom settled down for a while in Ardagger on the Danube. From there they moved to Paris in 1894, leaving their baby girl with the grandmother.

Strindberg was at this time heading fast for the climax of his mental crisis. It came after he had sent his wife back to Ardagger, and it lasted until in the late summer of 1896, when he returned to Sweden. This crisis is fully described in the book called *The Inferno* (1897).

Strindberg's state of mind during the so-called Inferno crisis has been investigated by several psycho-pathologists. Dr. W. Hirsch pronounced Strindberg's malady *paranoia simplex chronica;* Karl Jaspers has dealt with it in *Arbeiten zur ange-wandten Psychiatrie.** Dr. S. Rahmer defined the case as *melancholia daemomaniaca*. All of these definitions have been pronounced inadequate. But most men who know something about the human mind will agree that the crisis, regardless of the name, represents a psychic catharsis which saved the patient's life. Freudian scholars will also maintain that the mental disturbance was a more or less conscious defence-mechanism: a flight into neurosis, indi-

* Vol. V, Bern, 1921. See also *Strindberg und van Gogh,* by the same author, Heidelberg, 1926.

cated by all its real or apparent torments, such
as insomnia, hallucinations, persecutional mania,
thoughts of suicide, anguish, and an overwhelming
sense of guilt. Full of the Inferno atmosphere and
neuropathic activities is the trilogy *On to Damascus* (I–III, 1898–1904). It stands in the same
relation to the Inferno crisis as does *The father* to
The fool's confession. The biographical work called
Legends was written in 1897–98 and published in
the latter year.

Like the bird phoenix rising out of its own ashes,
so Strindberg rose to a higher life and to greater
achievements after having weathered the one great
storm of his life.

After a practically blank period of four years,
the resurrected dramatist produced a torrent of
works—twelve great historical plays, emulating
Shakespeare and Goethe—a series of non-historical
dramas including such masterpieces of sunshine
and shadow, of hope and despair, as *Easter* (1900),
Midsummer (1901), *The dance of death* (I–II,
1901)—the year in which he married Harriet
Bosse, from whom he was divorced in 1904—*The
dream-play* (1902), for which no adequate stage
has as yet been built, *Swanwhite* (1902); chamber
plays, such as *Storm, The burned lot, The spook
sonata, The pelican* (all of 1907); and in addition
to these a volume of poems: *Word-play and handicraft* (1905); sagas and autobiography, *e. g., Alone*
(1903); polemical works like *Black flags* (1904);
Historical miniatures (1905); works on philology,
speeches to the Swedish nation, short stories; *The
blue books* (I–IV, 1907–12), being the synthetic

philosophy of his life; and finally, the drama entitled *The great highway* (1909) which constituted
his farewell, a swan song, in which, as Hjalmar Kotas
says, he reached the highest and purest summits of
faith.

With this drama the ideal cycle of Strindberg
was closed. Having begun with religious mysticism,
he returned to it by way of prostrating crises of
conscience, from which he lifted himself, ever to
reach new goals. The two problems which tormented his spirit most were those of religion and
sex, the problem of God and the problem of
woman. An unspeakable torment, a satanic hatred
invaded Strindberg whenever he drew near these
two beings, but a hatred that had its roots in love,
a torment expressed from a bitter desire for voluptuousness and for suffering. In *The dance of death*,
this voluptuousness transformed itself into a deso-
lating orgy, transcending all human imagination.
In Strindberg, who from infancy had felt the
ardent need of love and tenderness, of moral and
spiritual elevation through the wedding of the
sexes and constant aspiration to divinity, God and
woman were through his personal experiences and
through his morbid spiritual sensibility founts of
unutterable joys and torments.

Like Martial he could have said: "Nec tecum nec
sine te vivere possum," and his spirit sought continually to free itself from the fascination of these
two beings, but they ever found him out once
more, to drag him down into the whirlpool of their
magical seductions.

On the occasion of his 63rd birthday, January

22nd, 1912, Strindberg was honoured as no Swedish man of letters before him. He was formally over-whelmed with letters, flowers, laurel wreaths and telegrams. Four thousand Swedish-Americans sent him felicitations. A deputation of outstanding citizens paid him their tribute. Hundreds of thou-sands marched in a torch-light procession by his residence. Cheers reverberated in the streets: "Long live Strindberg!" The sum of forty-five thousand crowns, collected throughout the kingdom, was handed over to him. Most of this money he gave immediately to public charities.

Less than four months after this event, the 14th of May, 1912, his eyes closed in death. He was buried at Solna. A cross marks his resting-place. It bears his name and the Latin inscription:

O CRUX AVE SPES UNICA.

Besides Strindberg one of the greatest Swedish writers of the realist school was Gustaf af Geijerstam (1858–1909). In his early works, stories and the two novels *Erik Grane* (1885) and *Pastor Hallin* (1887), is evident a tendency to polemic and the absence of a fine and delicate psychology. Such defects one finds still, though lessened, in his later works, *Medusa's head* (1895) and *The outermost reef* (1898).

But his two best novels are *The book about little brother* (1900) and *Woman power* (1901), which, however, are not free from sentimentality.

Another confirmed realist was Tor Hedberg (1862–1931) as his novel *Judas* (1886) testifies, a book in which the author inquires into the psychological motives of the betrayal by Iscariot. From the novel Hedberg, influenced by the style of Ibsen, passes to the drama and he tries his hand also at the lyric, in which, however, one finds more of intellectual effort than of lyrical inspiration.

Foremost among the women of the realist group was Victoria Benedictsson (1850–88), whose works draw liberally from the life of the Swedish people. She was interested also in treating the problem of marriage, taking a decisive position in favour of the indissolubility of the matrimonial bond.

Among the lyrists of realistic tendency, the most noteworthy are Albert Ulrik Bååth (1853–1912) and Ola Hansson (1860–1925), who is also a writer of stories, strongly influenced by Strindberg.

NEO-ROMANTICISM AND NEO-REALISM

In the decade 1890-1900 the violent reaction against realism began in Sweden, fostered by the tendency of the Swedish people to a lyrical conception of nature. The cult of poetry, against which realism had been opposing its prejudices, returned vigorously, and the Swedish language, a language sweet and melodic, if little adapted to objective narration, could once more in poetry show to advantage all its beauties and many excellences.

A group of eminent lyrists arose on the literary horizon, lyrists such as Verner von Heidenstam, Oscar Levertin and Gustaf Fröding.

Verner von Heidenstam (b. 1859), reacting against the turbid realistic pessimism, opened his literary career with some poems, *Years of pilgrimage and vagabondage* (1888), glorifying the joy of living. Also his novel *Hans Alienus* (1892) is wholly pervaded by this new spirit; one breathes in it an atmosphere saturated with Hellenism.

With his *Poems* (1895), Verner von Heidenstam is distracted from his vision of classic imitation to turn himself wholly to the cult of traditions of the fatherland. He begins also the series of his historical romances, in which the great figures of Swedish history are idealized by him. *The Charles men* (1897–98) is a cycle of stories that tell of single episodes in the reign of Charles XII. More or less in almost all these works the high and solemn figure of the King stands out, unhappy and mysterious, who so well characterizes all the virtues and all the defects of his people. This cycle is a solemn monument erected not only to the memory of a King but to an entire people, the most militaristic among the peoples of Scandinavia. The King, conqueror at Narva and conquered at Poltava, is recalled with such grandeur of high-light and shadow that *The Charles men* has already become a classic of the Swedish nation.

Following these come *St. Göran and the dragon* (1900), *The pilgrimage of Saint Birgitta* (1901), *The forest murmurs* (1904), *The Swedes and their chieftains* (1908–10) and finally *New poems* (1916).

In 1916 the poet was awarded the Nobel Prize in literature.

Together with Heidenstam there entered into the lists against realism Oscar Levertin (1862–1906). *Songs and legends* (1891) and *King Solomon and Morolf* (1905) are important among his productions. His *Rococo stories* (1899) had a great success, as did also his literary essays *Poets and dreamers* (1898) and *Swedish figures* (1903), in which he passes in review the greatest historical and literary personages of his country.

But the greatest lyrist, the true creator of modern Swedish poetry, is Gustaf Fröding, who was born at Alster, Värmland, in 1860 and died at Stockholm in 1911.

In the poetry of Fröding, the vivid and dazzling artistic beauty of Snoilsky is united with fondness for country life, a lively sense of nature, such as one generally meets only in primitive poetry.

This is to be found in *Guitar and concertina* (1891) and in the *New poems* (1894), while in *Splashes and rags* (1896) the poet makes a pitiless and almost cruel examination of his own ego, an examination not inferior in sincerity to that which Strindberg offers us in his autobiography.

In his last years Fröding fell into a sort of visionary mysticism which associates him with Hölderlin and Novalis. In the collections of verse, *New and old* (1897) and *Spray of the Grail* (1898), he displays this subtle clairvoyance of his which permits him to wander freely in the boundless realm of fantasy.

Per Hallström (b. 1866) is known more as a writer of prose than as a poet. After going to America as an engineer, he returned with a little volume of poems, *Lyrics and fantasies* (1891), which engaged at once the favour of the public. America gave him also a taste for adventure and for the picaresque *genre*, which he shows in his stories. His ideas are in clear-cut contrast with those that prevailed at the time of naturalistic literature. He has in fact the old conception of matrimony and of the family, and on the basis of these convictions of his he has strenuously combated the supermen and the theories of free love in a comedy entitled *Erotikon* (1908).

The best-known book of Hallström is the collection of stories entitled *Thanatos* (1900), in which he maintains that if life is rich in content, death too is rich, beautiful, and may, if one observes attentively, make us understand that our existence, with its daily struggles and sufferings, has a profound meaning.

Hallström has furthermore written plays and comedies, *The Count of Antwerp* (1899) and others, taking his inspiration also from Italian subjects,—*Bianca Capello* (1900), *A Venetian comedy* (1901), etc.,—but these are lacking in directness, and when produced never receive the applause of the public.

Hallström is now perpetual secretary of the Swedish Academy, having succeeded the late Erik Axel Karlfeldt.

But the one who created the true Swedish prose, definitively withdrawing it from the influences of naturalism, was Selma Lagerlöf (b. 1858), the ex-schoolmistress, who unexpectedly revealed herself to be an able writer with *The saga of Gösta Berling* (1890–91). In this first novel she makes use of the analytic method of detail, as the preceding generation had already done, but secur-

ing from it an entirely different effect; she unites a
series of various episodes, joining them solely by
means of the unity of place, Värmland, the region
of dense forests and melancholy lakes. The attention of the reader is directed, through various
episodes, to the background of a single landscape.
The technique has a counterpart in art in those
paintings of the impressionist school that when
viewed nearby present only various unrelated spots
of color, while from a distance they give the effect of
a whole. All is vague, imprecise, nebulous; the very
language in this novel is a new language, full of inter-
jections and questions, enriched by neologisms which
at times prove audacious. It is a true return to romanticism with all its merits and its defects; it is
a true hymn to the romantic conception of existence.

Invisible links (1894) is the title of a collection
of stories, which confirmed and strengthened the
renown acquired by the authoress through her
novel. *The miracles of Antichrist* (1897) transports
us into the heart of Sicily. In this novel, full of
fierce love, assassins, revolutions, and betrayals,
one breathes a disordered romanticism through
which the Sicilians, as a French critic notes, are
so thoroughly Sicilian that they cease to be such,
an error into which writers of the North commonly
fall whenever they resolve to describe the peoples
of the South.

In 1902 Selma Lagerlöf gave the final touch to
her mighty national and religious epic which has
as its title *Jerusalem* and in which is told the sad

experiences of some Swedish emigrants in the Holy
Land. Some years afterward (1906–07) was published *The wonderful adventures of Nils* in which
at her ease and pleasure the fancy of the authoress
is given free reins. One meets again in this work the
profound sense of Swedish natural background of
which Lagerlöf provided an unforgettable example
in *The saga of Gösta Berling*.

In 1911 followed the novel *Liljecrona's home*
and in 1914 *The Emperor of Portugallia*. After
a brief interval of stories, *Monsters and men*
(1915–21), and after her violent novel against the
world war, *The outcast* (1918), Selma Lagerlöf
published her *Mårbacka* (1922) and *Ett barns mem-
oarer* (1930), both memories of her childhood, and
later two additional volumes of memories, *Dagbok*
(Diary, 1932) and *Höst* (Harvest, 1933), in which
shine all her fine and delicate art, all her noble and
serene womanliness.

The three last novels of the celebrated writer are
the trilogy, *The General's ring* (1925), *Charlotte
Löwensköld* (1925) and *Anna Svärd* (1928).

In 1909 Lagerlöf was awarded the Nobel Prize.

All the work of Lagerlöf concerns the love of
one's neighbour, love which involves also social and
religious elements. Under this aspect her work approaches that of Ada Negri and is closely related to
Karl Jonas Love Almquist.

Last of the great neo-romantic writers is Erik
Axel Karlfeldt (1864–1931). Born at Folkärna,
Dalecarlia, he was educated at the University of
Uppsala.

The titles of his poetic works are as follows: *Vildmarks- och kärleksvisor* (Ballads of the woodlands and of love, 1895), *Fridolins visor* (Ballads of Fridolin, 1898), *Fridolins lustgård och Dalmålningar på rim* (Fridolin's pleasure-garden and Dalecarlian paintings in rhyme, 1901), *Flora och Pomona* (1906), *Flora och Bellona* (1918), and *Hösthorn* (Autumn bugles, 1927).

Karlfeldt was elected a member of the Swedish Academy in 1904 and its Secretary in 1912. In 1920 he refused to accept the Nobel Prize. It was awarded him posthumously in 1932.

The art of Karlfeldt is broad and descriptive. His principal *genre* is the idyll of everyday life. In this field he is unique. The fundamental motives of his noble art are his love of nature, humanity and beauty in all its manifestations. The transporting and exalting power of his imagination, his astounding mastery of language and his poetic technique, his humour and pathos—all conspired to make him the foremost bard of his time, or at least, as some might prefer to put it: *primus inter pares*.

Peculiar to Karlfeldt is his love of Mother Earth. It was a standing psychic complex with him, a vital necessity, a religious cult which led to the glorification of the seasons, the flora and fauna, and the yearly festivals in a lyricism of such colour, rhythm, melody and harmony that it may justly be called *sui generis*.

A deep, religious undercurrent is felt in almost all of the poet's creations, but particularly, of course, in his later works. *Hösthorn* reveals it to us most convincingly, especially in the poem *Höst-psalm* (Hymn of autumn), where it appears in terms of transcendent beauty:

> *Allt korn av ädel sort*
> *skall glimma under slagan,*
> *då agnar hvirvla bort.**

These lines from *"Ur årets sagor"* (*Flora och Pomona*) might well be inscribed as a motto not only to *Hösthorn* but to all that Karlfeldt has written. His lyricism constitutes a collection of literary gems the lustre of which will increase in intensity as time passes.

Round these stars of greater magnitude move numerous smaller satellites, which, however, have brought a varied and abundant contribution to the literature of their country.

Pelle Molin (1864–96) earned a place in Swedish literature notably with his volume *Ådalens poesi* (The romance of Ådalen, 1897), a slender volume of interesting and well-written short stories.

Hjalmar Söderberg (b. 1869) is the impassioned describer of Stockholm, creator of various types taken from the life of the Swedish capital.

Albert Engström (b. 1869), artist and writer, is a humorist of great talent. He always accompanies his writings with amusing and very successful illustrations.

A confirmed sceptic is Bo Bergman (b. 1869), who by way of neo-romanticism has made himself

---

* All genuine, golden grain
beneath the flail shall glimmer
when the chaff is borne away.

proclaimer of a sort of neo-realism. His poems, *Selected lyrics* and *Eyes of life* (both 1922), are distinguished for a profoundly pessimistic intonation. His opposite is Anders Österling (b. 1884), who represents instead in Swedish literature a tendency toward aestheticism.

A Catholic author is Ernst Norlind (b. 1877), novelist and poet, while his colleague, Sven Lidman (b. 1882), is a follower of the doctrine of the "Friends of Pentecost." In the feminine camp the authoress Elin Wägner (b. 1882) continues to establish herself more and more.

An author who in these recent years has had a great vogue is Sigfrid Siwertz (b. 1882). His style is of a plasticity not inferior, according to some, to that of the greatest modern English prose-writers. His principal work remains for the present *Selambs* (Downstream, 1914–20), in which the history of a family is described from its origins until its decadence, a work considered as the best Swedish novel of the last fifteen years. Two very fine collections of stories are his *Old people* (1909) and *A handful of feathers* (1922).

Hjalmar Bergman (1883–1930) was a writer of wide resources. Bizarre, cynical and at times outright grotesque, he was author of numerous novels, stories and comedies, some of which have been translated into foreign languages. Among his best novels worthy of note are *The Markurells at Wadköping* (1919), which has also been dramatized, *Herr von Hancken* (1920), *The grandmother and Our Lord* (1921), *Madame Directress Ingeborg* (1924), and *The girl in the swallow-tail* (1925).

These novels full of spirit, vivaciousness and humour have made Bergman the most popular writer of modern Sweden.

Two writers of reputation are E. Gustaf Hellström (b. 1882), whose novel *Snörmakare Lekholm får en idé* (The lace-maker Lekholm gets an idea, 1927) is very popular in Sweden, and Henning Berger (1872–1924), author of various novels besides a successful translation of Omar Khayyám. Henning Berger recalls in his stories the life of the Swedes in America. *Over there* (1901), *Fata Morgana* (1911), *The heart on the wall* (1920), are novels palpitating with the nostalgia of a race for its distant land of origin.

Expressionistic tendencies are found in Pär Lagerkvist (b. 1891), author of symbolistic plays, *The last man* (1917), *The eternal smile* (1920), and *The way of the man who is happy* (1921), which have been great successes in the theatres of the North.

Ivan Oljelund (b. 1892), a converted ex-communist, has disclosed his spiritual torments in *New land* (1920) and in his story entitled *With a capital G* (1921).

Two authors who are young, but who are already well-known in their own country, are Harry Blomberg (b. 1893), and Ragnar Jändel (b. 1895 who with a profound sense of nature unites a s and serene joy of living.

Sweden has undergone a great loss with the untimely death of Dan Andersson (1888–1920), whose work reflects the tragic pessimism of the greatest Russian authors.

To these "seekers for God" one may add also
Carl August Bolander (b. 1888), who in his
novel, *Georg Wrede* (1917), reveals to us the new
atmosphere in which the Swedish literature of the
present has its being: a mysticism suspicious of the
old culture and anxious for new ideals.

We cannot bring to an end this brief excursion
into the field of Swedish letters without citing the
great explorer Sven Hedin (b. 1865), author of
travel books in which he tells of his adventurous
journeys particularly in the highlands of Asia, and
beside him one may mention the name of Frank
Heller, the pseudonym of Gunnar Serner (b. 1886),
a fantastic and fanciful traveller, who with his
witty extravagances has made all Europe laugh.

Despite its recognized present-day masters and a
number of promising younger voices, the contemporary literature of Sweden is, perhaps, largely in a
state of experimentation. After nearly half a century of unusual literary achievements which began
with Strindberg's *The red room* (1879) and closed
with Karlfeldt's *Hösthorn* (1927) a period of qui-
escence in Swedish letters is but natural. It must be
admitted that against the background of the 'eighties
and 'nineties with their literary giants, the present
standard-bearers of Swedish *belles-lettres* seem, with
some notable exceptions, to be insignificant. However, because of these exceptions, and because of an
abundance of youthful talent, the future,—though
it cannot of course be foretold with any degree of
certainty,—holds bright promise of new achievement.

SWEDISH-AMERICAN LITERATURE

by

ADOLPH B. BENSON, PH.D.*
Professor of German and Scandinavian
in
Yale University

THE first Swedes in America landed in Delaware
in 1638, so that the history of their literary
activity in this country is a long and interesting one.
But we need not dwell at any great length on the
productions of the early settlers, for most of them
were not literary, and their leaders were, naturally
enough, more concerned about the practical per-
manency of the colony and the saving of souls—
including those of the Indians—than about polite
letters. Their writings were for the most part
limited to official reports, personal diaries and correspondence, historical and geographical accounts
of the Swedish colony, and more particularly to
descriptions by the clergy of the parishes and pa-
rishioners. Most of the other material written by
Swedes in this country before about 1850 was
similar in character; in addition it was social, economic, scientific or ecclesiastical, anything but

---

* This article was originally to have been written by another student
of the subject, who in the eleventh hour was obliged for unavoidable
personal reasons to cancel his promise of coöperation. The present writer
therefore is a reluctant last-moment understudy or substitute, and the
results, will, he hopes, be judged accordingly. Under the circumstances,
he can at the most—to borrow a common phrase—increase the reader's
suspicion that there is such a thing as Swedish-American literature.

strictly literary, and most of the best-known lay authors at least returned later to their homeland and never became real Swedish-Americans in our present sense. We need but mention the engineer Per Lindeström (d. 1696) of the seventeenth century and the botanist Pehr Kalm (1716–79) of the eighteenth, whose travelogues on New Sweden and America respectively are now known internationally.

Then, too, the works of these men were finished and ultimately published first in Sweden,* as were the remarkable letters on America (1853–54) by Fredrika Bremer (cf. Swedish section) in the middle of the nineteenth century. The much-quoted writings by the early clergymen of New Sweden, such as Acrelius (1714–1800), Rudman (d. 1708), Campanius Holm (d. 1702) and others, belong in the field of history, especially in church history, rather than in *belles-lettres*. Nor do the early travelogues on America by minor Swedish citizens need to be considered here. Perhaps the nearest approach to anything literary by a Swede in America before 1800, let us say, were the letters in French written during the American Revolution (1780–82) by Count Axel von Fersen (1755–1810), the Swedish nobleman and friend of Marie Antoinette who in our struggle for independence served as

---

* Lindeström's *Geographia Americae* had been completed by 1691, but was not published until 1923 under the title of *Per Lindeström's resa till Nya Sverige 1653–56*. It appeared in Stockholm. An American translation by Amandus Johnson was published at Philadelphia in 1925.

Kalm's work appeared at Stockholm in three parts in 1753–61 under the title *En resa til Norra America*. An English translation of this appeared in Warrington in 1770–71. It was named *Travels into North America*. (Revised edition by Adolph B. Benson, New York, Wilson-Erickson, 1937. —Ed.)

colonel and first adjutant to General Rochambeau. These letters to his father, long since published (in an English translation in the *Magazine of American History,* April–July, 1879), are marked by a simplicity, directness and brutal frankness which stamps them as both literary and historical.

But the important fact here is that the several leaders of the Swedish colonists, most of them clerical, *did* begin to write *something,* somewhere, as soon as they had become well established, and this has remained the spirit and tendency among the Swedish immigrants down to the present time. Perhaps mention should be made, also, by way of further introduction, of the more or less useless seventeenth-century Swedish translation of Luther's Catechism into the Lenape Indian dialect (1696), which was published in Stockholm, at the King's expense, for distribution in this country. Incidentally, the first Swedish book printed in America was a translation of Count Zinzendorf's Moravian Catechism, which appeared sometime before 1750, the only work in Swedish to be published here before that date. At least the religious needs of the Swedes were to be satisfied.

Yet the Scandinavians have never been exclusively religious, and we have some early literary evidence that mundane thoughts entered into the minds of the Delaware colonists and their descendants. It is not without some significance that the first Swedish publication in America, and one of the very first items in any language to be printed in Wicaco (Philadelphia), was a group of eight Swedish songs,* compiled and edited by "Magister" Rudman, which appeared in 1701. In other words, despite the political absorption of the Swedes by the Dutch and English, something more than lacerated remnants of the Swedish language had remained, and we know from Kalm's *Travels into North America* that Swedish was kept up after a fashion in the Swedish churches and settlements, far into the eighteenth century. The Swedes mixed their English and Swedish together then just as many do now, a fact attested by the numerous examples cited by Kalm. Indeed, the language never died out entirely, as some recent students have surmised. Why should Count Zinzendorf (1700–60) have considered it necessary or expedient to publish a Swedish translation of his Catechism, if the language had disappeared?

Europe does not like to recognize any writing by American immigrants, and Sweden, on the whole, has that same attitude. For the most part, with one or two notable exceptions, she has maintained a superior, patronizing air toward the literary efforts of her sons and daughters in America, and those that she has recognized at all have ordinarily been subjected to a scathing, crushing criticism. Only lately has a more sympathetic turn of mind been noticeable. The writer feels that, after all, only an immigrant—or shall we say emigrant?—can really understand the literature of immigrants. Such a literature has to be judged from an entirely differ-

---

* The source seems to imply that the songs were not of a religious character, but the present writer has not seen them.

ent viewpoint than that of writers in a stable, thousand-year-old cultural community. Calmness and placidity yield to restlessness and a feeling of homelessness. The conditions of production, the motives for writing, the background, the experiences, sufferings and privations are all different. Psychologically and historically this literature, however, is important, for here we can literally observe the real birthpangs of the growing nation. It has been too much neglected.

To understand the Swedish-American literature, therefore, we must first of all have some knowledge of immigrant problems; we must preserve an open mind and a generous spirit, though some of the literary work will stand up well under the most severe scrutiny. The quantity of it is enormous. Almost two million Swedes have settled in America since the high tide of immigration started in the middle of the last century. Practically all could read and write; all brought some educational, religious, artistic or journalistic tendencies; and no group of them stayed very long in the same place without building a church or clubhouse and establishing a school, a college, a choral society, a newspaper or a magazine. Naturally, the amount of the printed output of such a people would be considerable, both in Swedish and English. The quality of the work was not all good; but neither was it all bad, even if the writers did not always belong to the so-called higher social classes. Most of the authors were educators, journalists and clergymen; but they came from all trades and professions, and from both sexes. A common theme was the yearning and vicissitudes of the immigrant himself, his troubles and tribulations on a new soil. The new-comer's "dog's life in America" was a favourite topic. America as a land of freedom was, of course, another. Religion and nature furnished the foundation for much poetry here as in Sweden, for the Scandinavians are either religious or nature-loving, or both, and sometimes so to the point of fanaticism. At all events, when they feel at all they feel deeply, and their interests and enthusiasms are intensive, a fact which is not always apparent externally.

The amount of Swedish verse written in this country is amazing. The Swedish lyrical mind and heart were certainly not lost in crossing the ocean. The present writer has a number of times served as one of the judges in the Swedish poetry contests conducted by the St. Erik Society of New York, and has been genuinely astonished at the variety of the themes, the frequent profundity of thought, and the technical workmanship.

Another activity popular with Swedish-American writers has been the creation of stories, sketches and plays that reproduce the mongrel dialect of Swedish and English, which can be excruciatingly comical.

In justice to Sweden, it should be noted here, too, that despite an initial reluctance for recognition, a few of the Swedish-American authors, especially poets, have been honoured in their native land by prizes, orders, medals or decorations.

So much for generalities and introduction. Now a few specific names and examples; and first a word about those who write primarily in English, most of whom are born in Sweden and are therefore immigrants. We shall never know the complete number of these, for the Swede is notorious for rapid Americanization and Anglicization of his name to the point of obliteration as a foreigner or hyphenated citizen. He is less nationalistic, either at home or abroad, than the Norwegian, for instance. However, we can mention Edwin Björkman (b. 1866), essayist, novelist, and translator of Strindberg, who has long been known to the American public for the high quality of his work; Warner Oland (b. 1880), well-known Hollywood star in Chinese characters, who has helped to translate some of Strindberg's plays; Velma Swanston Howard (b. 1868),* the excellent, recognized and beloved translator of Selma Lagerlöf and Strindberg; Hans Alin (b. 1893), a rather prolific and able author of plays, though an unsympathetic and censorious critic; and more recently Gösta Larsson (b. 1900), whose last novel, *Our daily bread* (1934), has been enthusiastically reviewed all over the country. Nor can the writer refrain from mentioning that the American poet, Carl Sandburg (b. 1878), is of Swedish extraction. Occupying a niche all by himself, is Dr. Frederick Peterson (b. 1859) of New York, perhaps the foremost Swedish writer of English verse, whose *Chinese lyrics* (1916) published under the pseudonym of "Pai Ta-Shun" (Pe-ter-son), revealed such a true Oriental spirit and colouring that even the best reviewers thought the author was a distinguished Chinaman.

A Swedish scholar and professor, Joseph E. A.

* (d. 1937.)

Alexis (b. 1885), of Nebraska, was in 1930 granted the *doctorat d'université* from the University of Paris for a thesis dealing with Swedish-American literature. It is an investigation of commendable order, though the reader would have liked to find more examples and interpretative criticism, both extensive and intensive, of the authors treated; but the work has a distinct value because of its bibliography, and the fact that a Parisian institution would acknowledge the subject at all should, indeed, count for something. Besides, the compilation looks and sounds strangely valuable and elegant in French, though it is certainly a curious novelty that this pioneer research, the title of which is *La littérature suédoise d'Amérique,* should have to appear in a Romance language. How many Frenchmen are really interested in it?—None of the above English-writing authors are included in Alexis's list.

Dr. Alexis in his bibliography enumerates seventy-seven Swedish-American writers whose works have been published as separate items since the year 1875. This does not include sundry minor contributions to newspapers and magazines, though undoubtedly many of the poems and stories later published separately in collections had originally appeared in the Swedish weeklies and monthlies of this country. Of course the list could not hope to be complete, and there is a good reason why it should not be. Of these seventy-seven, Alexis has chosen twenty-two for special attention, and so far as he knows, the present writer believes the selection on the whole to be a happy one. Alexis has in turn received his information from the library of the former Swedish Vice-Consul G. N. Swan of Sioux City, Iowa, and from the biographical and critical works by Ernst Skarstedt, especially *Våra pennfäktare* (Our writers, 1930), of which a new edition has appeared only recently. I mention this for the benefit of those who care to go into the matter more thoroughly. Incidentally, the first vehicles for the Swedish-American efforts were such newspapers as *Det Gamla och Nya Hemlandet, Svenska Amerikanaren, Svenska Tribunen-Nyheter, Svenska Kuriren, Svenska Amerikanska Posten, Nordstjärnan,* and *Vestkusten.*

Now a brief characterization of a few representative and outstanding Swedish-American writers.

First, chronologically, we must recall the name of August Hjalmar Edgren (1840–1903), scholar and teacher, whose pathetic alternate longing for Sweden and America sent him travelling between the two countries repeatedly, until, finally, Sweden won out. Edgren was an internationally famous philologist; he had a doctor's degree from Yale (1874), and is perhaps best known for his translations from the Sanskrit and for his renderings of Longfellow, Poe, Whittier, Lowell and Bryant. He did *Evangeline* into Swedish (1875), likewise fragments of *Hiawatha,* and a selection of poems by Tennyson. In his original poetry he shows himself to be a thinker as well as a master of form. He is classic, academic, yet simple and effective. He yearns for America; but once there he yearns still more for his fatherland. A professor in several institutions on both continents, he possessed a natural gift for languages and literature, an exquisite

aesthetic sense, and was a sincere and loyal interpreter of life. He scorned hypocrisy and super-
ficiality. Dignity of subject and harmony of words
and phrasing were two noteworthy poetic qualities
of this savant, and the present writer would add
a manly, penetrating beauty of feeling and soul.
Edgren was a restless, almost tragic figure, and
represents in many respects the inner, heartrending
split and dualism in the Swedish-American immigrant.

Perhaps the most gifted Swedish-American poet
to write in Swedish was another victim of this
dualism, namely, Magnus Elmblad (1848–88), a
vagabond genius and free lance. Constantly torn
between two worlds and tormented by an unconquerable weakness for alcohol, he finally succumbed
to the vice at the age of forty. He wrote equally
well, with lucidity and tenderness, in prose or verse.
He was noted for his profound sympathy for the
lower classes and the American Indians, whom he
considered badly cheated by the European settlers.
He wrote amusing *causeries* for the papers; made
translations from the German and English; and for
his poems drew on a large variety of subjects from
both Europe and America. His long poem *Allan
Roini* (1889), which treats of the struggle for independence by Herzegovina against the Turks, was
awarded a prize by the Swedish Academy. It glorified love of family, love of country, and love of
nature. *Azilla* (1878), another long poem, dealt
with an Indian maiden's sworn revenge on the
White Man. Elmblad loved to dwell on the peace-
fulness of the country as compared with the bustle

of the city, and his philosophy, despite frequent outbursts of pessimism, was one of practical resignation to the realities of life and enthusiasm for the ever-beckoning beauties of nature. He translated *The star-spangled banner* into Swedish. He passed away in poverty, in Sweden, and none who has read his vigorous verse can help regret the irregularity of his life and his early death.

A pioneer among the Swedish journalists of this country was John A. Enander (1842–1910), who served at various times as teacher, editor and general orator. He extolled American law and liberty, urging everybody to obey the former so that the latter might survive. He remained for many years a real factor, the grand old man, in the Swedish-American cultural life. He wrote poems also, on the Swedish language, on Sweden, and on the Chicago fire, for example, but his forte was in prose. His admonition to the Swedish immigrants to love their old country as they do their mother, and their new one as a bridegroom loves his bride, has become proverbial.

Our next choice is a clergyman, Ludvig Holmes (1858–1910). Though not profound or deeply philosophical, he versified easily, and his form was ever pure and readable. He chose a large variety of topics, including several humorous ones, like *Mulligans get* (Mulligan's goat). Three times honours came to him from his native land for excellence in poetry. Many themes were national, dealing with America or events in Swedish-American history. Naturally, his love for Sweden found expression in several items. Two volumes of poems came from his pen, most of them permeated with noble, elevated sentiments. The present writer will not soon forget the moments spent with Ludvig Holmes, when as a college student at Wesleyan he discussed all manner of topics with this genial and gifted personality. He was then pastor at Portland, Connecticut.

We have already referred to the writers who use the hybrid Swedish-American dialect in reproducing realistic humorous pictures of the influence of English upon the Swedish in America. The two most popular authors of this special *genre* are Aina Olson (b. 1866) and G. N. Malm (1869–1928). The latter, an artist of ability, a man gifted with an acute power of observation, a good-natured tolerance, and great skill in discovering a really comical situation, has immortalized himself in *Charli Johnson* (1909), a character who moves among the Swedish immigrants in Kansas and Nebraska. It is a faithful photograph of the manners and language of the people, with some gentle criticism of their mediocrities. He is never bitter. The book is a historical *Kulturbild*. *Härute* (Out here—in Kansas, 1919), a play in four acts, fiddles on the same popular string, depicting the immigrants during their period of assimilation.

The most original, interesting and eccentric of all Swedish-American writers was Ernst Skarstedt (1857–1929), whom we have already met. He was a poet, philosopher, historian, and critic, and erstwhile farmer, pioneer settler, journalist, musician and hermit. His father was a professor at the Uni-

versity of Lund, so that Ernst had the benefit of a
good education. But he hated the conventional life
of men, and after many attempts to live among
them, he finally retired, as he had done so often,
to the peaceful haunts of nature, where he ended
his fruitful and adventurous days. The present
writer knew him personally as a small, modest, exceedingly shabby-looking individual, with a brilliant mind. How he abhorred all pretension, hypocrisy and falseness! He possessed the ability to excite
admiration from friend and foe alike through his
fearless but non-personal criticism. All received the
same treatment. His rationalism had no place for
narrow dogmatism, but he was surprisingly fair to
all honest endeavours. "It is a lie," exclaims Skarstedt, "to say that God has ever forbidden us to
use our reason, the only light that can illumine the
path of life." His quest was to understand man and
nature. He is excellent in describing his own nomadic experiences or "dog's life" in America, as
he called it. The second edition of his work on
Swedish-American writers omits no really deserving name, it seems, and to this I refer for greater
completeness.

Ninian Waerner (1856–1905) was educated at
Uppsala and Berlin, studied art and music, and
emigrated to America, where he became a 'cellist
in an orchestra. Waerner is a poet, a real one,
humorous and melancholy, who occupies himself
mostly with sad, pathetic themes, the pain of separation or the non-realization of hopes. His sympathy for a suffering humanity is genuine, tender.
While he predominates in portraying sadness, with

great pathos, he can also describe scenes bizarre and fantastic. He, too, has published a series of amusing tales on his "dog days" in America.*

We have purposely limited this part of our discussion to a few noted men who have already passed on. It remains, by way of illustration, merely to mention some others, all of whom, except Carl Fredrik Peterson, are still living. Among the more important are: Vilhelm Berger (b. 1867) of the *Nordstjärnan* editorial staff, who has written a large number of stories and pamphlets dealing with Swedish-American conditions; Jakob Bonggren (b. 1852), the learned and venerable poet of *Svenska Amerikanaren*, whose philosophical tributes are split up between the home, Sweden and America; Oliver A. Linder (b. 1862), editor-in-chief of the same newspaper, poet, historian and humorist; C. A. Lönnquist (b. 1869), who is said to be a "sentimental poet, with profound sentiments and practical sense"; David Nyvall (b. 1863), educator, journalist, and poet; Carl Fredrik Peterson (1843–1901), a journalist who has depicted the struggles of the immigrant soul, both in verse and prose; G. N. Swan (b. 1856), the aforementioned prominent bibliophile and historian of Swedish-American writers; and Leonard Strömberg (b. 1871), clergyman, who is perhaps the most prolific of all Swedish-American authors. Alexis lists thirty-eight books by this pastor, most of them consisting of light, inoffensive, Christian and non-alcoholic novels—for Strömberg is a great

---

* In addition to the above authors, see also Henning Berger (p. 142), whose life and work in America entitle him to be named among the prominent Swedish-American writers.

temperance man—which have proved very popular in Sweden, where most of his works have been published.

It is obvious that the Swede in America has not accomplished much in the drama or the classical type of novel. But he has been true to his inherited tendency for lyric poetry, which is rich and stimulating. His prose literature deals, as does so much of his verse, primarily with the Swedish immigrant's physical and mental readjustment to his new American environment, with his gradual Americanization, acclimatization, and yearning for the Old World he left behind. Not that liberty has been a new idea to the Swedish immigrant, or that Americanization has been difficult; but the ties of kin, climate, nature, tradition and education cannot be torn asunder in a literate, sensitive and meditative soul without pain or anxiety. But it is seldom a pain of permanent despair or deep-seated pessimism; it is the passing pang that often accompanies a lingering, sensible optimism, tinged with humour and hope; it is the healthy resignation from which we have nothing to fear.

DANISH LITERATURE

DANISH LITERATURE

based on the treatise by
GIOVANNI BACH, Ph.D.
translated by
FREDERIKA BLANKNER, Litt.D.
Western Reserve University
and enlarged in collaboration
with contributors

EARLY PERIOD

THE earliest examples of Danish literature are the heroic legends. These were told and sung in the language of the Viking Period (c. 800–c. 1000 or c. 1100) but there are no records of them in that tongue. Gradually replaced as it was by Old Danish (c. 1100–c. 1550), only through the runic inscriptions can we glimpse the form and character of the language which was spoken prior to the eleventh or twelfth century.

But the contents of the legends have been brought to us through other channels. The Anglo-Saxon poem *Beowulf* still conveys some of the old stories to us and in the older periods of linguistic development the legends were related from one generation to another until they were recorded in Latin by the celebrated Danish chronicler, Saxo Grammaticus (c. 1150–c. 1220), in his *Gesta Danorum* (c. 1208). By the aid of other languages we thus have access to the ancient accounts of the feats of the hero Starkad, the shrewdness of Amled, and the great deeds of the legendary kings called the *Skjoldunger*.

During the early mediaeval times most of the writing was done by monks in the monasteries founded by the large monastic orders. They made annals and chronicles, nearly all in Latin. An English monk by the name of Aelnoth wrote about the year 1122 the *Historia ortus, vitae et passionis S. Canutis regis Daniae*, concerning the king who was killed in 1085 by the revolting peasantry and subsequently canonized by the church.

Almost a century later, the courtier Svend Aagesen (b. 1130) composed the *Compendiosa historia regum Daniae* (c. 1182), which almost prefigures the *Gesta Danorum* of Saxo Grammaticus.

Saxo Grammaticus, a priest by profession, entered the service of the Archbishop Absalon about 1180 and remained there until the death of the latter in 1201. Toward 1185, on the advice of this Archbishop, he began to write his history of the Danes—just referred to—from the time of Svend Estridsön (d. 1076), but later he added to this history that of earlier times, fusing both under the single title of *Gesta Danorum* or *Historia Danica*. The founts of his history are in part the old Scandinavian songs and traditions, in part information furnished him by the Archbishop Absalon.

The work is composed of sixteen books, of which the first nine contain traditions of the kings and the heroes down to about 950 A. D. Among these semi-legendary kings Hamlet is included. The other six comprise a period nearer to the author, who for that reason displays in them a greater certainty and veracity in the reporting of facts and presents a greater abundance of details, above all in the part which concerns King Valdemar and Archbishop Absalon.

The history is written in a Latin elegant and polished enough, similar in its sentence construction and in its vocabulary to that of Valerius Maximus and of Martianus Capella, which the learned Danish ecclesiastic took as model in the compilation of his chronicle.

There is very little to mention that is contemporary with the work of Saxo, with the exception of the small book *De profectione Danorum in Terram Sanctam* and some conventual chronicles of little account.

Successor of Absalon in the archbishopric of Lund was Anders Sunesön (1165–1228), who composed *Hexaëmeron,* a sort of theological encyclopaedia, in which he gathered all the fundamental questions of Catholic theology which he had studied at the Universities of Bologna, Oxford and Paris. He wrote also many ecclesiastical hymns which once were sung in the churches of the North.

LATE MEDIAEVAL LITERATURE

As previously stated, by about the beginning of the twelfth century, the language of the Viking Period had definitely developed into Old Danish, Old Icelandic, Old Norwegian, and Old Swedish. In the case of Old Danish this may be gathered from the collection of laws which date from about this time, and in the book of medicine of Henrik Harpestreng (twelfth century); but more important documents are offered us by the poetry, which was chiefly the work of monks and ecclesiastics, who through use of the mother tongue sought to diffuse among the faithful liturgical songs and prayers, translating them at times also from the Latin.

Contemporary with this poetry, born in the convent cells and intended to be sung in the churches, an anonymous popular poetry was taking form, which naturally made use of the language of the people. Influenced strongly by France and especially by England, the ballad was used in Denmark almost exclusively as an accompaniment for dancing. From the twelfth century dancing became very popular on the estates and in the castles of the royalty and the nobility. The dance took the form of a circle or a long waving line and was led by a *Forsanger* or leader who chanted the melody and the words of the numerous verses, while the dancing crowd joined in the chorus, which usually indicated the theme or idea of the song. The ballads were copied by the nobility in the sixteenth and seventeenth centuries and have come to us in many and varied forms, although no author ever appears to disturb the group character of their anonymity. The ballads may therefore be taken as a group expression of mediaeval attitudes toward the events and problems of life.

Although love and romance run through nearly all the ballads and form the principal theme of a considerable number of them, they may be divided into several main classes. The heroic ballads contain the story of legendary heroes like Holger the

Dane, Hagbard and Signe, Didrik (Theodoric from Verona), Aage and Else, etc. They are influenced both by foreign tradition and by the old heroic legends of Scandinavia. The songs of magic treat hereditary concepts of supernatural creatures and their power, as felt by a people recently converted to Christianity. These creatures inhabiting the waters and the woods thus symbolize the treacherous attraction exerted by these elements upon men and women. Here we meet the *Havmand* (merman) and the *Havfrue* (mermaid) and also the *Trold,* the monster of the deep, with his bewitching power. In the forests and on the meadows the *Elvermöer* (elf-maidens) enchant the young lover by their fatal spell. A magical power is attributed also to the runic characters.

The songs in which some of the legends are told are of great importance, because they bring into relief the new religious spirit diffused by Christianity. In them is found also the intermingling of Christian and pagan characters, but the latter often have nothing pagan about them except the name. Very beautiful is the legend entitled *The blind man and the Cross,* in which Christ, impersonated by the pagan god Balder, is stabbed by his blind brother Hödur, who when sprinkled with the blood regains his sight, only to realize his sacrilegious crime.

Other songs concern subjects from the Gospels such as *Mary Magdalene, The soul of the rich man,* etc.

But it is above all in the historical songs that the popular fancy participates, stirred by the unhappy or happy events of the great kings who followed

[165]

one another on the throne of Denmark. There are the songs of Valdemar I and of Valdemar II; there is the cycle of the songs of Marsk Stig, which tell us of the infidelity of the king Erik toward his groom Marsk Stig.

Beside the historical songs are those of chivalry, describing the court life of the time, in which the first lyrical impressions of the nascent Danish poetry are set like little gems.

THE REFORMATION

The Lutheran Reformation began to penetrate into Denmark under Frederik I in the first half of the sixteenth century, but only under the government of Christian III was the new religion everywhere recognized so that it became the religion of the State.

One may say that only with the Reformation, a typical expression of Germanism, is initiated the true cultural history of the Germanic countries, which up to that time had been orientated toward Latin culture; only with the Reformation do the great figures in the history of the northern lands begin to show themselves.

The first representative of the Lutheran ideas is Christiern Pedersen, the so-called "father of Danish literature," born about 1480. He studied in Paris and after returning home published a Latin-Danish dictionary of over 13,000 words.

While he was still in the bosom of the Catholic Church, Pedersen published pious works which later, when he had gone over to Protestantism, he heartily deplored. He translated and integrated the work of Saxo. Having become a Lutheran, he completed a translation of the Bible in 1543 and published many writings on the theological work of Luther. He passed some years of his life as a student at Malmö and died at Helsinge in 1554.

After the example of Pedersen, the monks who went over to Protestantism can no longer be counted. Another apostate is Hans Tausen (1494–1561), who dedicated himself with fervour and zeal to preaching the new religion, so inciting his hearers that at Viborg the citizens went to the point of demolishing twelve Catholic churches. Besides preaching he also translated the books of Moses and wrote a treatise on falsehood and truth.

The ex-Carmelite Frands Vormordsen (1491–1551) became the first Lutheran bishop of Lund and in that capacity published a little Protestant catechism.

The ex-monk Hans Spandemager (d. 1571) wrote the first Danish book of prayers.

Besides using works of piety for its propaganda Lutheranism made use, even greater use, of satire. A dialogue of the Swiss painter-poet Nicolaus Manuel was translated, a composition in which the sacrifice of the mass is derided. Other translations were made of the anti-Catholic works, and an original Danish book was written as well, *The story of the blacksmith Peter and of the peasant Adser* (c. 1533), which holds up to ridicule the miracles and the seven sacraments.

Despite invading Protestantism, Catholicism still

found some seasoned and militant champions, among whom Povl Helgesen (c. 1485–c. 1535) was the most important. Having as a young man entered a convent of Carmelites at Helsingör, he became, in 1518, an instructor in Sacred Scripture at the University of Copenhagen. At the beginning a sympathizer with the Lutheran doctrine, later he detached himself definitely from it, after Luther had burned the papal bull. He left nothing undone to save Catholicism in Denmark, but he did not succeed. His writings, almost all in Latin, were directed to that end, but in sign of derision they were pilloried in a small town of Denmark. Retired to Roskilde, the final stronghold of Catholicism, he passed there the last years of his life.

With the death of Helgesen, the final authoritative voice of the very small Catholic community was extinguished. The most outstanding personality of Protestantism was then Peder Palladius (Peter Plade, 1503–60), Bishop of Zealand and Professor of Theology at the University of Copenhagen. In his *Visitatsbog* (manuscript discovered in 1866, published in 1867) he describes the visits that he used to make in his diocese, and they give us at the same time an idea of Danish life in the sixteenth century. Palladius also wrote books on morality and in collaboration with a doctor he published even a little treatise in which he advises various methods of protecting oneself from the pest.

During this period the wave of the Renaissance, although weakened by its long journey, had already reached the countries of the North.

THE RENAISSANCE

Since with Protestantism the power of the clergy had fallen, that of the nobility became greater, and this naturally brought new interests into the cultural field, orientations toward present reality, toward life as it is lived, rather than toward things of the other world. Dogmatic theology continued to be studied, but along with it the natural and physical sciences were developed even more. Culture was being diffused; the influences of Italy, which like a beacon was pouring forth its radiating light over all Europe, were making themselves strongly felt. As in the other Scandinavian countries, efforts were being made likewise in Denmark to exhume the past; thus historiography and the scientific study of language arose. The songs and religious hymns were all translated into Danish, chiefly through the work of the poet Thomas Kingo (1634–1703).

Also of this period is the astronomer Tycho Brahe (1546–1601), to whom King Frederik II gave the island of Hveen in the Sound, so that he could establish an observatory there and carry on astronomical research.

The same king Frederik II was a true Maecenas of the arts and sciences, to which he contributed all of his great energy and his fine intelligence.

He favoured the exodus of Danish scholars to Holland, to Germany, and to Italy, so that they might complete their studies there and return to their own country with new experiences and new knowledge. One of these, Nicolaus Niels Steensen, came even to occupy the chair of anatomy at the University of

Padua and later became court physician to Ferdinand of Tuscany and a member of the *Accademia del cimento.*

Among the scientists besides Tycho Brahe, there are worthy of mention also Olaus Römer, discoverer of the finite velocity of light, and Thomas Bartholin, discoverer of the lymphatic vessels.

Distinguished in historiography were Anders Sörensen Vedel (1542–1616),—who, one may say, continued the work of Christiern Pedersen and published the Danish folk poems,—Niels Krag (1552–1602), Leonora Christina Ulfeldt (1621–1698) and Ole Worm (1588–1654), a true polyhistor, who did much for the awakening of antiquarian studies (runology) of the time.

Work in linguistic studies was done by Erik Pontoppidan (1568–1631), who wrote a Danish grammar; by Peder Syv (1631–1702), who published some *Considerations on the Cimbric language* (1663), a Danish grammar (1682), a collection of Danish proverbs (I–II, 1682–88), and the beginning of a Danish-Latin dictionary (1692).

The poetry of this period is still almost wholly religious and this is easily explained by the fact that an effort was being made by means of it to diffuse the new religion among the people, who are susceptible chiefly to the poetic form. Hans Christensen Sthen (1540–1610) and Anders Christensen Arrebo (1587–1637) are in the vanguard, but the great poet of the period is the previously mentioned Thomas Kingo. He already reveals his poetic genius in the *Spiritual chorus* (1673–81) and in the *Morning and evening songs* (1677–84), a collection of religious

songs, in which, however, there is a vision of nature
so fresh and intense as to make one think of the
greatest poets of the Occident.

Anders Bording (1619–77) may be considered as
the first Danish journalist. He in fact founded a
monthly magazine in verse, *The Danish Mercury*.

The first hints of the coming drama are noted in
Sthen, in Peder Jensen Hegelund (1542–1614) and
in the Biblical dramas of Hieronymus Justesen
Ranch (1539–1607), while Mogens Skeel (1650–
94), with comedies that show visible traces of imitation of Molière, is a forerunner of the great Holberg. Already scintillating in these, far-off and
fitful, are flashes of the Enlightenment.

LUDVIG HOLBERG

There are always great figures in the civil, literary and artistic history of a people who leave their
impression on an entire epoch. Such figures dominate undisputed through a long period of years
and leave behind them profound and ineffaceable
traces. One of these figures in the history of Danish
literature is Ludvig Holberg.

When he was born (1684), Denmark found itself, like the other Scandinavian countries, under
French influence. Politically and socially the consequences of the Thirty Years' War were still making themselves felt, a war from which Denmark had
emerged impoverished and damaged in every respect.

In politics absolutism was reigning, in literature
preciosity. The great vogue at that time in Denmark, as indeed in all Europe, was the novel of

Honoré d'Urfé, entitled *Astrea* (1610), a false and affected description of pastoral customs, a picture of the fancied felicity of the shepherds of Lignon; it was the reaction of a generation tired of wars, longing for a pacific and patriarchal conception of life. Sören Terkelsen translated a part of it into Danish, and inspired by the descriptions of idyllic love given in the novel, Johan Nist founded a pastoral order.

French became the common language, especially in society; German was adopted in the army; Danish remained for the people and the peasants. The old nobility had decayed and was displaced by one constituted in large part of adventurers who had immigrated during the wars. Ambition for position ruled everywhere, and poetry was reduced to a simple instrument of adulation, intended only to please the vanity and pride of the powerful.

Such was the condition of Denmark when Holberg opened his eyes on the world. We have already considered him in the section concerned with Norwegian literature, since he is a son of Norway, but the Danes claim him as their own, since his activity was in great part carried on in Denmark, where he lived from 1708 until his death in 1754, and since his work had a very great influence on all Danish literature.

The greatest importance of Holberg for Denmark consists in the fact that he created Danish prose, restoring to the language its former dignity. Furthermore, in his comedies he agitated problems and questions of high moral value, to which the Danish people had long been unaccustomed; once again he awakened a smile where sadness and desolation had reigned, laying bare the ills, the defects, the vices of the ruling classes. He purified the air of the arid theology and gloomy prejudices which were weighing on Denmark like a coat of mail. "Holberg," says Brandes, "represents illuminated absolutism in both Norway and Denmark."

The contemporaries of Holberg are of little importance. Hans Gram (1685–1748) and Jakob Langebek (1710–75) are both historians; Frederik Suhm (1728–98) wrote a *History of Denmark* (1782–1828) from the earliest times.

A history of the Danish church, *Annales ecclesiae Danicae* (1741–52), was written by Bishop Erik Pontoppidan (1698–1764). The Icelander Arni Magnússon (1663–1730) collected a great quantity of Icelandic manuscripts. Two continuators of Holberg's ideas are Frederik Christian Eilschov (1725–50), author of *Philosophical letters* (1748) and of *Philosophy for women* (1749), and Christian Falster (1690–1752), author of biting satires.

Distinguished in poetry was Hans Adolph Brorson (1694–1764), who wrote verses characterized by a sweet and gentle tenderness. They are religious poems, but as always happens in northern poets, the sense of nature, of landscape, is never lacking,—now soft and delicate as in Spring, now desolate as in Winter.

After the gloomy and graceless poetry of the period of the Reformation, one finds in these poems once more the gilded ray of the sun and the greening fields.

Rationalism penetrated into Denmark together with the French language and literature. The Encyclopaedists, Rousseau and then Klopstock and Schiller, were translated and placed within the reach of all. The German physician Struensee, a favourite of King Christian VII, sought at first to reorganize the State in accordance with the principles of reason, following the example of Frederick the Great. But his frivolity, the favouritism he showed the German language, and in addition his intimate relations with the queen gained the enmity of the people and he was arrested, condemned to death, and executed April 28th, 1772. After the brief dominion of Guldberg, author of works on natural theology, who limited or outright suppressed all the concessions made by Struensee, the period of the reforms was initiated with the work of the ministers Bernstorf, Reventlow and Colbjörnsen. In 1788 serfdom was definitely abolished and then in 1790 an almost complete freedom of the press was introduced, so that those seditious movements which had broken out in other countries were avoided in Denmark.

The study of theology was taken up again with renewed interest from the rationalist point of view. Christian Bastholm (1741–1819), court preacher, wrote a book on popular dogmatics and an ethics based on utilitarian deism.

A contemporary of Bastholm was Nicolai Edinger Balle (1744–1816), who published a catechism and fought with drawn sword the ideas of the Voltairean Otto Horrebow.

Jens Sneedorff (1724–64), Malthe Conrad Bruun (1775–1826) and P. A. Heiberg (1758–1841) are the principal political prose writers of the period. P. A. Heiberg published a work that at the time made a great stir, *The adventures of a banknote* (1793), in which he treats without reticence the most important questions that at that time inflamed public opinion in Denmark.

A temperament eminently caustic, he bitterly attacked the politics of Pitt and of the King of England, and for this he was condemned by the Danish government to a severe penalty. In 1798 he published a dictionary which makes one think of a similar one by Giovanni Papini. In this Heiberg explains in his own way words of current use, seizing every opportunity to find fault with the court, the aristocracy, the police. Some examples of these "linguistic studies" of Heiberg can give an idea of the style he adopted.

On the words "office or employment" he comments thus: "Like happiness, it is conceded by grace and not by merit."

On the word "king": "It is with the king in the state as with the cat in the house. 'It was the cat,' says the maid, if a key is broken or a piece of roast disappears. 'It is His Majesty's will,' says the Minister who wishes to revenge himself on some enemy of his. For the most part the cat and the king are equally innocent."

It is natural that such expressions should have gained the animosity of the ruling class, which thought to get rid of Heiberg by sending him into exile together with Bruun. Both took refuge in

Paris, where they died. In Denmark the freedom of the press had again been restricted and the democratic reforms previously conceded were in part withdrawn.

Knud Lyhne Rahbek (1760–1830) and Christen Henriksen Pram (1756–1821) kept themselves entirely out of politics. Both dedicated themselves to the theatre, for which they wrote comedies that at the time enjoyed some success. Rahbek was director of the Royal Theatre of Copenhagen, and editor of the magazine *The Danish Spectator*. In 1809 he composed a theoretic treatise on dramatic art which he published under the title of *Letters of an old actor to his son* (1782). When he married the authoress, Karen Margrethe Heger, a woman of elevated sentiments and of a very superior intelligence, his house, a little villa not far from Copenhagen, called Bakkehus (house of the hill), became a centre for the most distinguished personalities of the time. They were in great part the new men, the admirers of Goethe and of the first romanticists, among whom stood out figures like P. A. Heiberg, Baggesen, Grundtvig, the brothers Anders Sandöe Örsted (1778–1860) and Hans Christian Örsted (1777–1851), and above all the great poet Adam Gottlob Oehlenschläger, who married one of Heger's sisters.

STORM AND STRESS

The *Sturm und Drang* is a period of tempest and penetration, rising in Germany and through its very impetus and violence flooding all the countries of the North, where it found a region suited for its diffusion. The attention of the Scandinavian writers is turned from France to England and Germany and above all to Shakespeare, Goethe and Schiller.

As early as the second half of the eighteenth century a great figure arises in the field of Danish letters, Johannes Ewald, born November 18th, 1743, at Copenhagen.

Ever since his early youth Ewald had shown a character inclined to the fantastic and to adventure. His best beloved books were *Don Quixote* and *Robinson Crusoe,* which he sought to imitate when, at the age of twelve, he ran away from home with the intention of reaching the sea, taking a boat and disembarking on a desert island. He was a soldier in the service of the King of Prussia, then he went over to the Austrians, among whom he became first drummer-boy, then non-commissioned officer. In 1760 he returned to Copenhagen where he studied theology, and, under the influence of wine, to which he had submitted in order to lessen, as he believed, the pain caused him by gout, he discovered his poetic vein. In Denmark it is a trite, but correct saying that it was unhappy love that made Ewald a poet. He himself said that he considered his unhappy love for Arendse Hulegaard "the turning point in his life."

Already in 1766, on the occasion of the death of Frederik V, he wrote a beautiful funeral ode; a few years later a play of his appeared, *Adam and Eve.* In 1770 he wrote *Rolf Krage,* the first tragedy in Danish literature, in which one feels the imitation of Iffland and of Kotzebue. The same is true of *The death of Balder* (1774). However it may be, by means of these two plays the way was opened for the literary Renaissance of the old North.

In 1778 Ewald wrote *The fishermen*, a melodrama, in which he tried to reproduce life directly. These fishermen are still somewhat idealized, but so the taste of the time would have it. Rousseau was still dominant and with him his theory, according to which men in a state of nature are good, while culture has corrupted them and made them wicked. The popular song inserted in this play, *Kong Christian stod ved höjen Mast*, translated into English by Longfellow as "King Christian stood by the lofty mast," has become the Danish national hymn.

In 1780 the first volume of his complete works came out. He died in March, 1781.

Imitators of Ewald were Thomas Thaarup (1749–1821) and Ole Johan Samsöe (1759–96), while a nature entirely independent of them was Johan Herman Wessel (1742–85), a Norwegian emigrant, who wrote a parody tragedy, *Love without stockings* (1772), characterized by a disproportionateness between poverty of content and a loftiness of style in conformity with the most rigid French standards, making one think of the Italian comic-heroic poets of the sixteenth century.

This period numbers other writers, but writers of little value, in whom the imitation now of one, now of another great Danish or Norwegian author predominates. One among them, however, was elevated to European fame, Jens Baggesen (1764–1826).

The life of Baggesen was extraordinarily restless and disordered. A spirit independent and intolerant

of restraint, a true *Stürmer und Dränger,* he travelled the length and breadth of Europe, making the
acquaintance of the most outstanding personalities
of the period. At first he was a great admirer of the
French, above all of Voltaire, whom he sought to
imitate in his poetic work entitled *Comic tales*
(1785). Four years later,—to be exact in the spring
of 1789,—Baggesen left Denmark as a result of a
poem of his, *Holger the Dane* (1789), in which he
ridiculed his compatriots and expressed the wish to
become a German poet.

Removed to Hamburg, he made the acquaintance
of Klopstock; and from Hamburg, by way of
Frankfort, Worms, Mannheim, Heidelberg, Strassburg, he entered Switzerland, where at Zurich he
became an intimate friend of the Swiss poet Johan
Kaspar Lavater, one of the leaders of the movement of the *Sturm und Drang.* To this movement
Baggesen adhered fully and unconditionally, to such
a degree indeed that some time afterward, writing
to friends, he said: "Oh, if I could tear Voltaire out
of my consciousness I would give two years of my
life."

In March, 1790, he married Sophia von Haller
and shortly afterwards returned to Denmark, not
without first having made a visit at Jena to Schiller
and Reinhold. In the Danish capital he wrote
Labyrinthen (1792–93), a description of his journeys, a truly delightful work in which the spirit
of Holberg pulsates, but in which at the same time
one feels a veiled and diffused melancholy and occasionally also a deep and heart-breaking sadness.

From Copenhagen he returned again to Switzer-

land and from there to France, to Paris, in March,
1795, whence he wrote his friends that he thanked
God for having allowed him to be present at the
aftermath of the Revolution. "It is true that humanity is bleeding and the human heart bleeds at
the sight of carnage, but liberty, spirit of humanity,
lives and, rejoicing, the free soul ascends to heaven
among tears of blood."

Returned to his own country in the summer of
1796, he translated Homer into Danish hexameters;
but always restless, always yearning for distant
horizons, he returned to Germany, where his young
wife died. Two years later he married again, Fanny
Reybaz, daughter of the Swiss Minister to France.
In the autumn of 1800 he went to France, where
he planned to remain indefinitely, but he was seized
frequently by the desire to return to his own country and from there to go abroad again. In 1822,
once more in Paris, he lost his second wife and
a little son. Temporary imprisonment for debts
added to his misfortunes. During the last years of
his life he fought a losing fight with a severe illness.
In 1826, anxious to end his days in his native land,
he wished to return to Copenhagen, but October
3rd of the same year he died in Hamburg and was
buried at Kiel.

The work of Baggesen was as disordered as his
life: he tried his hand in many fields of literary
activity, but in none did he compose a true masterpiece, an immortal work worthy of enduring
through the centuries. His poems reveal, however,
a fervid imagination and an exquisite sensibility.
Denmark owes to him the creation of a poetical

style, elegant and pure, to which many poets of the youngest generation conformed. With his biting satire, he overturned many idols, freed Danish letters from French influence and smoothed the way for the great poets of the romantic movement, next typical expression after Protestantism of the Germanic spirit.

ROMANTICISM

The two mouthpieces of Danish romanticism were the Norwegian Henrik Steffens (1773–1845) and Schack Staffeldt (1769–1826).

While in Germany Steffens had read Schelling, Fichte and Schlegel; he had attended their lectures and had known also Goethe and Schiller, with whom he welcomed in the New Year of 1800.

With this accumulation of new experiences, new studies, and new impressions, he came back to Denmark in 1802.

Denmark at that time had just been through a severe ordeal. In the war between England and France, she had maintained the strictest neutrality, but under Frederik VI, this position was converted into an armed neutrality, which resulted in a conflict with England. A celebrated naval battle was waged in the Sound outside of Copenhagen, April 2nd, 1801, in which Denmark succeeded in maintaining her prestige and her dignity. It is said in this regard that the cannons thundering in that battle awakened the Danish muse. Certainly they contributed to the rebirth of a new national spirit, and new sentiments; of a new life and therefore of a new poetry. In this reinvigorated atmosphere saturated with vital and salutary elements, Steffens' voice echoed, extolling the new romantic creed.

Lively discussions were kindled, above all among the young generation which aspired to new ideals. And it was precisely among these ardent and militant youths that the great poet of the epoch arose: Adam Oehlenschläger.

Oehlenschläger was born November 14th, 1779, in Copenhagen. When he was one year old, his parents moved into the castle of Frederiksberg, of which his father was the overseer. He carried on his first studies in a school in Copenhagen, the director of which had offered to instruct him gratuitously in view of the family's scant resources. "The pathway of my youth," says the poet, "was not strewn with roses. I was dressed in the rags of the royal family, which had been sold at a low price by their wardrobe keeper."

He left school at the age of sixteen and became an actor, but for only two years. Then at once he gave himself over to indefatigable study to fill the gaps in his education.

Inspired in the summer of 1802 by Henrik Steffens, Oehlenschläger heralded the arrival of Danish romanticism with the poetic gem *Guldhornene* and followed it with a book of *Poems* (1803). In this collection the lyric drama *St. Hansaftenspil* not only speaks sarcastically of the pedantry of Rationalism, but bursts forth with a deluge of poetic ideas, expressed in a multitude of metrical forms.

Expanding and developing, Oehlenschläger continued in 1805 with his significant volume *Poetical writings,* a fine collection of lyrical and descriptive poems, which included his masterpiece, the epoch-making dramatic romance, *Aladdin, or the wonderful lamp,* which Brandes terms the corner-stone of Danish literature during the first half of the nineteenth century. In the latter poem the fortunate youth and his acquisition of the power of the lamp symbolize the romantic idea that the poet alone can penetrate into the spiritual realm of reality.

Having obtained a stipend from the Government, Oehlenschläger began later in the same summer to travel over Europe. His first halting place was Halle where he wrote his impressive tragedy *Hakon Jarl* (1807), based on the old historical writings of the North. At Weimar he visited Goethe whom he greatly admired, and elsewhere in Germany he made the acquaintance of other spiritual leaders of the day. He sojourned for a while in Berlin. At Jena he wrote works on historical and mythological investigation and inquiry. In Paris, in a little hotel in the *Rue des Bons Enfants,* amidst the tumultuous uproar of the French metropolis, he composed *Palnatoke* (1807), and *Axel and Valborg* (1808).

Later, on another of his trips to Paris, he was presented to the King, Louis Philippe, and dubbed the Corneille of Denmark. But it is not to Corneille, says a French critic, that one should compare him, but instead to Victor Hugo, since Oehlenschläger has accomplished in the Danish theatre the same revolution brought about by the author of *Hernani* on the French stage.

In Switzerland, as a guest of Mme. de Staël, he composed another tragedy, *Correggio* (1809), in which he dramatized the life of the great Italian painter. But his merit and originality consist in his having brought upon the stage and animated with his poetry, all those figures of warriors, pirates, skalds and Amazons, with which the Scandinavian myths and sagas are filled. "The reading of the plays of Oehlenschläger," Mme. de Staël has said, "arouses interest in two principal respects: first because the author has been able to adapt French regularity to diversity of situations, which pleases the Germans, and in the second place because he has represented in a way which is both true and poetic the story and the legends of the country inhabited at one time by the Scandinavians."

In his first tragedies, *Hakon Jarl* and *Palnatoke,* Oehlenschläger had not yet described the trials and torments of love; his exordium in this field, *Axel and Valborg,* was a master stroke. Some time afterward, he wrote *Hagbart and Signe* (1815). In both these plays he has represented amorous passion through the type characteristic of the northern nations. It is not the ardent love of Romeo and Juliet; but, as says Oehlenschläger himself, "the pallor of the moon in autumn lighting a forest of fir, does it not have a fascination of its own, in no respect inferior to the splendors of a summer night in the Italian countryside?"

The subject of the tragedy *Staerkodder* (1811) likewise is derived from a tradition of the North. The whole tragedy turns on the repentance of Staerkodder, who in his youth, excited by the perfidious advice of a priest of the god Thor, slew King Olaf.

The subject of *Robinson in England* (1819) is taken from a tradition according to which for some time it was believed that Daniel Defoe was not the author, but simply the editor of *Robinson Crusoe*.

The works of Oehlenschläger in the epic and lyric *genres* are not less numerous than his plays; the same freedom of spirit is found there, the same indifference as to form. The subjects likewise have been taken from Scandinavian history and mythology. *St. John's eve* (1803), *The little shepherd boy* (1818), *The gods of the North* (1819) and *The gospel of the year* (1823) are poems which even now are read with interest and delight.

Oehlenschläger's poetic vein was not quenched by age; at the age of seventy he was writing a tragedy on a national subject, *Kjartan and Gudrun* (1848), where one reads in the preface in verse: "The skald does not yet feel his blood congeal in his veins. He is still moved by the weeping of children, by the joys of adolescence; he delights in beauty; the oak grows green again for him each year." Oehlenschläger terminated his literary career with the publication of a poem entitled *Poetical art* (1848), in which are gathered the reflections of a man of both sentiment and intellect, and the heroic poem *Ragnar Lodbrok* (1849).

Oehlenschläger died in January, 1850, while his son, at his request, was reading him a passage of his tragedy *Socrates*, on the immortality of the soul. Thus he passed away tranquil and serene, as was his wish, a wish expressed in a lyric of his which was sung at his funeral:

"O forest, teach me to die as die the leaves, which wither silently. Spring returns again, the tree buds anew, and lifts its greening branches even into the blue of the sky.

"Bird of passage, teach me to fly toward far-off lands when the north wind blows, since when summer abandons our sky, in unknown climes an eternal springtime reigns.

"O airy butterfly, teach me to break these bonds which hold my spirit prisoner. Then I shall be no longer a creeping worm; I shall unfold freely in the air my dress of purple.

"O my Saviour, teach me to bear pain with saintly resignation, with peace of spirit. I would follow your standard! If Good Friday is full of sorrow, what more beautiful day than Easter?"

With such elevated and winged words one of the greatest Danish poets was carried to his last resting-place.

Oehlenschläger unfortunately registered too many foreign influences, especially German. For romanticism had need of a man of its own, and above all, need of reinstating the national spirit independently of foreign influences, at least immediate ones. And that new man was Bishop Nicolai Frederik Severin Grundtvig, the so-called "prophet of the North," born at Udby near Vordingborg, September 8th, 1783.

He studied theology passionately and was an ardent theological opponent of the rationalism then in vogue; he was also a famous historian, admirer of the Old Scandinavian literature, in which he sought to find the spirit and the tradition of his race; he was a poet, an orator, an educator and throughout his lifetime he coöperated in every way in the national rebirth of his country, weakened materially and morally by the reverses of fortune during the first quarter of the nineteenth century. Literature became an ideal refuge from the sad political and social reality. The glorious remembrances of the past served as consolation and instruction to the new generation.

With greater zeal and method than Oehlenschläger, Grundtvig explored the memories of the past and went to England to collect there the literary vestiges of the ancestors of his race. From these researches he drew the material for his work entitled *Nordens Mythologi* (1808), which made him famous throughout the North.

In a collection of lyrics in which he evokes the brilliant past of his nation, he shows less finesse but more vigour than Oehlenschläger. "His poems," a Danish critic has said, "are of granite beside those of Oehlenschläger's which are of marble; his harp has strings of steel." Both, however, have had followers; in fact from 1825 on a large number of poets derived their inspiration from the Scandinavian legends, and impressed on the people, together with love of the past, a sense of racial unity, and respect for the patrimony and cult of Danish glories.

The national reaction was accompanied by a religious reaction chiefly directed against the rationalism of the eighteenth century. There were two promoters of this movement: the court chaplain Jacob Peter Mynster, and Grundtvig, believer in his Lutheranism, but more of a liberal and polemic.

"Faith and liberty" is the motto which Grundtvig
and his followers assume and by which they are inspired in their propaganda. The school became the
fulcrum of the new education to be imparted to the
young, not so much the State school as the private
and independent institution. The school, according to Grundtvig, should have a basis at the same
time religious and national, should arouse, to cite his
own words, a spirit of Christian heroism; should,
with the study of the past, of the maternal language
and of the literary treasures of the race, nourish the
purest patriotic sentiment; should turn the hearts of
sons toward their fathers and the hearts of fathers
toward their sons, to help both to prepare, on the
basis of accumulated experiences of past generations, the future of the generations to come.

Personally, as an author, he contributed to the
realization of this ideal not only with the work above
cited, but in addition with the *Dramatic scenes of
the decline of the heroic epoch of the North* (1809-
11), and with *The struggle between Norns and gods*
(1808), in which he discloses in dramatic form the
ancient myths and the ancient legends, incorpo-
rated in the *Edda*.

Another masterly work of his is the *Compendium
of the world chronicle* (1812), in which he passes
in review all the most important events in the history
of the world, trying them on the touchstone of
Christianity. He translated the works of Saxo and
of Snorri Sturluson, coöperating in this way, together with Oehlenschläger, in the formation of a
Danish literary prose.

His religious faith, which took from him the

name of Grundtvigianism, does not originate in the Bible but in the teaching of the Apostles as the first testimony of true Christianity, of the word out of the mouth of the Lord, of the living word, as opposed to books which represent the dead letter.

In 1827 Grundtvig published in three volumes a collection of his sermons and in 1833 a *Compendium of the history of the Church*. From 1848 to 1851 he directed a weekly magazine, *Danskeren*, which carried periodically his articles and his compositions of historical, religious and social character.

Grundtvig died, almost a nonagenarian, September 2nd, 1872, amidst the lamentation of the entire Danish people, which by means of him had been able to find again the highroad of the spirit of its own race.

A great contribution to the work of Grundtvig was made by Bernhard Severin Ingemann (1789–1862), who has been called the Walter Scott of Denmark. His historical novels treating the period of the thirteenth and fourteenth centuries are still read with keen interest, since they give the Danish people the consciousness of its ancient greatness.

His poems, *Morning and evening songs* (1839), are, contrary to those of Grundtvig, sweet and sentimental, poems which every Danish child learns in school and never thereafter forgets. Besides a few unsuccessful plays, Ingemann wrote also some patriotic poems and the erotic cycle *The Shulamite and Solomon* (1839). He left in addition his autobiography,—in which he presents in lyric form his entire life,—directed toward the purpose of reviving in his people the racial and national spirit.

Johannes Carsten Hauch (1790–1872) and
Christian Hvid Bredahl (1784–1860), but especially the former, carry into Danish literature the
mystical current of German romanticism, the
hyper-sensibility of Tieck, Novalis, Jean Paul, the
philosophy of Schelling, and the theosophy of
Böhme.

Having lost a leg as a result of gangrene, Hauch
fell into the blackest melancholy, which led him
even to an attempt at suicide. Later, however, he
gave himself completely to poetry, and lived in
Rome where he was on friendly terms with Thor-
valdsen. He wrote the plays *Tiberius* (1828),
Bajazet (1828), and *Gregory VII* (1832), which,
rather than plays, are character studies; upon these
followed later *Svend Grathe* (1841), *The sisters of
Kinnekullen* (1849), *Honor lost and regained*
(1851), and *The youth of Tycho Brahe* (1852).

After 1834 Hauch began to write novels, especially historical novels. Among the most important
are *The alchemist* (1836), *A Polish family* (1837),
and *Robert Fulton* (1853).

He died in Rome and is buried there in the Protestant cemetery.

Christian Hvid Bredahl wrote plays, characterized by an enormous quantity of dialogues and
monologues, which make them give the impression
of dramatic scenes rather than of true plays.

All the writers mentioned up to the present time
had more or less adopted the philosophy of Fichte
or of Schlegel and they had become champions in
Denmark of the teachings of these philosophers.

DANISH LITERATURE

Johan Ludvig Heiberg (b. 1791) imported Hegelianism instead, to which he remained faithful throughout his life. But Heiberg was never a philosopher, he was only a popularizer, and his activity was carried on in the field of the theatre and above all in *vaudeville*. An admirer of Italian and Spanish literature, he wrote in 1813 the comedies for marionettes, *Don Juan* and *Walter the potter*, and in 1816 the romantic comedy *Well begun is half done*.

It was during his stay in Paris, a stay which lasted three years (1819–22), that Heiberg developed his taste for *vaudeville*. His first attempt in this type of theatrical literature was *King Solomon and Jörgen the hatter*, which was produced for the first time with great success in November, 1825.

Some time afterwards these were followed by *April fool* (1826), *The critic and the beast* (1826), *An adventure in the garden of Rosenborg* (1827). All these *vaudeville* sketches had the greatest success on the stage, to which the art of the actress Johanne Luise Heiberg, wife of the poet, impeccable as prima donna, contributed not a little.

Heiberg, to justify his art, which to some seemed superficial and light, wrote also a treatise on *vaudeville* and founded a magazine, *The Flying Post of Copenhagen*, in which Hans Christian Andersen, Andreas Nicolai de Saint-Aubain (pseudonym Carl Bernhard), and Carl Christian Bagger took the first steps of their literary careers.

As a thinker Heiberg revealed himself in the apocalyptic comedy *A soul after death* (1841) and in the poem entitled *Husband and wife* (1840).

When an old man he gave himself to the study of astronomy. He died at Bonderup, August 25th, 1860.

Like Oehlenschläger, so also Heiberg had his followers who continued his work, not always, however, with the same success.

Among these Henrik Hertz (1798–1870) is a distinguished author in whom one seems to hear the echo of the voice of Baggesen. He wrote also some comedies and dramas, in which he proved himself to be a romanticist full of power and sentiment. The mother of Heiberg, Mme. Thomasine Christine Gyllembourg (1773–1856), was a devoted and faithful admirer of her own son. She regularly wrote stories for her son's weekly magazine, stories which had enormous success, because the authoress, renouncing in them the old outworn world of the gods, of heroes and of cavaliers, had taken to treating directly the lower *bourgeois* environment of Copenhagen. Without any intention of irony or scorn, but with clear understanding of the life which was going on daily before her eyes, she wrote some little masterpieces in this form, such as *The family Polonius* (1827), *A story of every day* (1828), *Mésalliance* (1833), *The polar nights* (1834), *The extremes* (1835), and *One and all* (1840), brief stories which were avidly read by the Danish public, weary of the battles of the heroes and the cavalcades of the gods.

Another follower of the Heibergian current was Andreas Nicolai de Saint-Aubain (1798–1865), who also wrote stories of the *bourgeois* environment. With the shifting of gaze from heaven to earth, transition was imperceptibly made from romanticism to realism. Not only the people in the cities but also those in the country became the object of study and literary treatment. Thus Steen Steensen Blicher (1782–1848) described the wandering life of the gipsies on the heaths of Jutland. His masterpiece, *E Bindstouw* (1842), is a series of stories and poems, now humorous, now melancholy, but full of sentiment and pathos. The background is no longer composed either of scenes in Valhalla or of warriors' castles, but instead of natural landscapes, forests, meadows, dunes, the sea. A wholesome atmosphere, marine and resinous, penetrates all the Danish poetry of this second half of the nineteenth century.

Another writer tending to realism is Poul Martin Möller (1794–1838). *The adventure of a Danish student* (1823–24) is a masterpiece of humour, unfortunately incomplete.

Möller discussed his theories passionately in two treatises, *On irony* and *On affectation,* in which he breaks a lance in favour of verism.

But notwithstanding such deviations toward a realistic conception of life and therefore of art, romanticism still produced its poets, great poets, like Christian Winther, Emil Aarestrup, Ludvig Bödtcher, who have enriched Danish literature with true melody.

Christian Winther (1796–1876), "the most Danish of all Danish poets," published in 1828 a collection of lyrics including *Woodcuts*, little rustic and idyllic scenes in which the figure of the peasant is idealized. In 1835, after a trip to Italy, Winther published additional poems, wherein sweetness and delicacy alternate with a deep melancholy which especially in *Til Een* (To one) gives one the sense of world-sadness that attains its most noble and elevated expression in Leopardi, Heine and Byron. His most famous poem is *The flight of the deer* (1856).

Emil Aarestrup (1800–56) recalls Keats for mellowness of language. Carl Christian Bagger (1807–46) also wrote lyrics of exquisite workmanship, while in the poems of Ludvig Bödtcher (1793–1874) one meets a refined epicureanism, not free, however, from profound melancholy.

It was as a lyrist that Hans Christian Andersen (1805–75) also initiated his literary career.

The life of this very great author, a life which he called a fairy-tale, did not have a happy beginning. His parents were so poor that for a bed they made use of a bier that a short time before had borne the corpse of Count Trampe.

The first objects which struck the fancy of the little Andersen were the faded pictures hung on the walls of his hovel and a little box containing some earth in which purslane and sweet basil were planted, his mother's only garden, which, as he says poetically in his autobiography, "flourishes today in my story of the Snow Queen."

His ardent longing to hear fantastic unreal stories was encouraged by his father, who used to read him in the evenings the tales of the *Thousand and one nights* and the fables of La Fontaine.

Little Christian did not associate with the other children: all the time he was free from school he spent at home. In the evening, shortly after sunset, he would climb into his parents' great bed and try to sleep. "The flowered bed-curtains," he said, "closed me in on every side, dimming the light; I heard all that went on in the room, but at the same time I lost myself in my dreams and the real world no longer existed." Here already in embryo was the future singer of *The little mermaid* and *The little match-girl.*

Strange and interesting lad! At fourteen years of age he had still the innocence and credulity of a babe. He had heard it said by an old woman that the Chinese Empire was spread beneath the river of Odense, so that he did not believe it impossible that some bright moonlight night, while he was seated on a rock, the Prince of China, hearing him sing, could lure him to his kingdom and make him rich and powerful, at the same time consenting to let him return from time to time to Odense, where he wished to build a castle.

Quaint lad who at fourteen years of age was still sewing clothes for his marionettes and had a small thin voice of childish pitch.

Before he went to Copenhagen, a soothsayer prophesied for him that one day the city of Odense would be illuminated in his honour. He stayed in Copenhagen and the boy developed into a man; but deep in his heart there was always the child of former years, the solitary, dreaming, thoughtful lad before whose eyes, like images of a magic lantern, passed enchanted castles, sea-depths inhabited by blonde sirens, fairies who with their pallid gentle hands caressed his bloodless cheeks, deprived so early of a mother's caresses.

The first publication of the *Fairy-tales* was in 1835.

What always interests Andersen is that deep and silent life in beings which attracts us as mystery does. But in the innate human inclination to seek an explanation for all that occurs, he gives life and a voice to everything that comes under his eyes. And in this, above all, the imagination of Andersen consists, in endowing natural forces and inanimate objects with a soul. Now it is the wind that tells sorrowful tales, or a ray of the moon that speaks, or a dream transformed into a fairy who brings lovely stories to the little ones, placing under their closed eyelids the magic lantern of dreams.

What is most pleasing in Andersen is his sympathetic interest in little insignificant things, to which he gives a soul and a history. He remained ever a child with the qualities and defects of a child. An ingenuous and enthusiastic dreamer, he was on the other hand extremely sensitive to praise or blame, to such a degree that once he burst into tears because some little provincial newspaper had published a caricature of him. Suffering and the passing of years added to his character the note of melancholy, which at times in his tales is coloured by a light humour, this, however, never degenerating into bitterness or sarcasm. It is the same type of humour as is found in Dickens, but perhaps even more subdued. It is the humour that does not deride, but understands and sympathizes, the humour that knows how to say so many painful little truths without offending or irritating.

And this appears above all in his *The story of my*

life (1855), and also in his novels, *The improvisatore* (1835), *Only a fiddler* (1836), and in his plays.

The glory of Andersen, already great during the lifetime of the author, kept increasing and spread all over the world after his death. His fairy-tales, everlasting monument of the sensitiveness of his ingenuous dreaming spirit, represent a typical expression of the northern genius, in which shadow and light alternate and interweave in a thousand different ways, in which the inner life predominates and fancy delights in creating new worlds, new myths and legends.

Contemporary with Andersen was another great romanticist, Frederik Paludan-Müller (1809–76). *The dancer* (1833) and *Love and Psyche* (1834) are the two works of this author that precede his masterpiece *Adam Homo* (1841–8), a long narrative poem in three volumes. The author takes for the subject of his novel an ordinary man of his day and follows his progress in the light of the human ideal, a progress that, though externally symbolized by success in attaining the highest posts the State has to offer, spiritually signifies a continual decadence, an incessant compromise with his own conscience and dignity.

With this Adam, morally degenerate, Paludan-Müller contrasts, in other works of his, figures of high ethical value, such as the Indian ascetic in *Kalanus* (1854) and Benedict in *Benedict of Nursia* (1861).

Thus for the romanticism of Heiberg, of Bödtcher, of Winther, there was being substituted little by little an idealism pervaded with religious feeling, which already peeps through in the poem *Luftskipperen og Atheisten* (1853) and in the dramatic poem *Ahasverus* (1854) of Paludan-Müller. But the one who gave to this vague religiousness the concrete and definite form of a method, a doctrine, an idea, was Sören Kierkegaard (1813-55).

We have already spoken of this great philosopher at length in relation to Ibsen, in the section regarding Norway. Here it will be necessary to add that Kierkegaard fought with drawn sword the official Christianity of the State and all the petty forms of religion, to support instead an individual Christianity, heroic and consistent, like that of Brand's, a religion carried even to the point of paradox, absurdity or extreme consequences.

He wished to regenerate the faith and to revive integral Christianity. The last work of this great philosopher, *Öjeblikket* (The moment, 1855), is a bitter and violent pamphlet against the State Church and an admonition to his fellow-citizens to return to the pure founts of their religion.

This was his last testament. November 11th, 1855, Kierkegaard, worn, poverty-stricken, deluded, died in a hospital in Copenhagen.

The last romanticists were Meïr Goldschmidt (1819-87), Parmo Carl Ploug (1813-94), Jens Christian Hostrup (1818-92), the restorer of Danish comedy. These sounded in the literature of their country the last echoes of German romanticism. But at the same time the new political sympathies converging toward France, weariness of empty and evanescent romancings, and the need of thoroughly examining things and human events, favoured the advent of realism, then in vogue in French literature.

REALISM

Traces of realism are already to be found in Vilhelm Topsöe (1840–81). His novels, *Jason of the golden fleece* (1875) and *Scenes of new times* (1878), have a basis of that elegant scepticism which is characteristic of the novels of Flaubert.

But the great champion of realism was Georg Morris Cohen Brandes (1842–1927), the man who for more than thirty years was the Minos of Danish literature. His judgments were equivalent to the responses of the oracle; the older writers turned to him for applause and favour, the young for encouragement and advice. Many of the younger authors and poets used to come to read their works in his studio, and they considered themselves happy if they could return from it with a kind word, heartened, spurred to new works, new goals.

He descended into the literary arena as opponent of Rasmus Nielsen (1809–84), follower of Kierkegaard, who sustained the irreconcilability of religion and science. The two fields, according to Nielsen, should be completely independent, so that what one could accept from the viewpoint of faith one must refuse from the viewpoint of science. Against this stand Brandes reacted with his book *The dualism of our present philosophy* (1866).

In 1868 Brandes published a volume with essays on Hertz, Paludan-Müller, Aarestrup, Ibsen, and in 1870 a series of studies entitled *Critiques and*

[199]

portraits in which he undertook to consider also foreign writers.

But it was in 1870 when he sustained the examination on his doctor's thesis that Brandes established definitively the ideal mission to which he was to dedicate himself in Denmark, that is, to reconduct his generation, side-tracked by the dreams and caprices of romanticism, to the realities of life, to a practical sense of existence. To such an ideal he dedicated himself with greater zeal after a visit in the principal European capitals where he came in contact with the men most representative of realism: Taine, Zola, the brothers Goncourt. The enthusiasm which he aroused in his own country was equal only to that aroused many years before by Steffens, the apostle of romanticism.

The motto of Brandes was "freedom of inquiry and freedom of thought." Two very great writers of the North, Ibsen in Norway and Strindberg in Sweden, contributed their share toward demolishing the air castles constructed by romanticism. In England Mill and Darwin, in Germany Auerbach, Heyse and Keller, in Russia Turgenev, Dostoevski and Tolstoi offered to Europe works inspired by the crudest realism. The movement therefore was general, and Brandes was only the mouthpiece, the enthusiastic advocate who wished his country to conform to the current and taste then dominant throughout Europe. In opposition to the romantic tendency he sustained that a literature is shown to be alive by its ability and willingness to discuss problems. A work of art, then, was judged by him from its ideal value rather than from the aesthetic point of view. This conception of art thoroughly pervades Brandes' well-known *Main currents in nineteenth century literature* (1872–90), upon which followed, in order of their dates, *Danish poets* (1877), *Esaias Tegnér* (1878), *Men and works* (1883), *William Shakespeare* (I–III, 1895–96) and *Henrik Ibsen* (1898). Between his seventieth birthday and his death in 1927, Brandes wrote notable and comprehensive works on *Wolfgang Goethe* (I–II, 1914–15), *François de Voltaire* (I–II, 1916–17), *Cajus Julius Caesar* (1918), and *Michelangelo Buonarroti* (1921).

A lawyer with a case to plead,—so has Georg Brandes been defined; and this defect mars all his work, which is hardly more than a prolix debate, confused and indirect, in favour of a case extraneous to literature.

However, Georg Brandes should always be judged against the background of the intellectual aridity of the 'seventies. He found his country shackled by prejudices, shut off from the world, and his great importance lies in the fact that he led the currents of European intellectual life into Denmark. The difficulty that he encountered as well as the success he achieved in this is illustrated by the following characteristic incident. In 1870 Brandes was recommended for the Chair of Aesthetics at the University of Copenhagen, but because of his outspoken attacks on church traditions, and on other cherished traditions, he was not appointed. When he had attained fame, he was given the honorary title of professor (his Ph.D. degree made it possible for him to use the university auditorium for lectures), and in 1911,—forty years after the beginning of his lectures on *Emigrant literature,* the university which had rejected him as a teacher in 1870 honoured him with a great celebration. At that time it was remarked: "During these forty years it was not *Brandes* who changed his ideals."

The widespread attempt to underestimate the value of his work is, it appears, very largely due to the antagonism aroused by his consistent and aggressive atheism. If less attention is being paid to him now, it is most likely because he, in a sense, attained the goals he set himself, and accomplished his work, which was to awaken the people intellectually. He finished his task, and now the craving is for new gods.

Nevertheless, the teaching of Brandes bore some good fruits in art: the greater number of young writers, guided by foreign example and by the new literary taste formed in Europe, dedicated itself to writing novels directed toward the faithful reproduction of reality. The generation of 1870 may be characterized as "the generation of the experimental novel."

Through the work of Brandes, Danish narrative art regained consciousness of itself. The characteristic Danish tendency to psychology, to spiritual vivisection, the preference for impressionistic art, —to which the small canvas of the short story as well as the broad range of the novel is well adapted, —all assumed new vigour.

The Danish novel is not, however, a composition

which reaches the heights of the *epos,* as a novel of
Dickens or of Gogol, but it is a short story of large
proportions, a series of snap-shots of human life;
whence one may conclude,—as one of the critics
justly observes,—that the Danish were never truly
realists, but impressionists.

Sophus Schandorph (1836–1901), although ini-
tiating his literary career as a romanticist, revealed
realistic tendency in the collection entitled *From the
province* (1876), in which he describes the life of
the little Danish towns. *Five stories* (1879), *Folk
of slight importance* (1880), *Little stories* (1882),
The old pharmacy (1885), but above all the novel
entitled *Without balance* (1878), is the best that he
has produced in the field of realism.

With his death, Brandes lost a valiant supporter
for his cause, but other young and vigorous forces
filled the gaps that were being made, little by little,
in the circle of his followers.

April 7th, 1847, at Thisted, Jens Peter Jacobsen
was born. From his early youth he renounced the
possibility of a Christian vision of life and adopted
instead the theories of Darwin and the naturalistic
philosophy. In his *Niels Lyhne* one finds the following: "There is no God and man is his prophet."
He became even a resolute supporter of the evolu-
tionary doctrine and translated into Danish almost
all the works of the great English thinker.

His first attempts at poetry failed; only with
the story *Mogens* (1872) he began to attain a certain renown. In *Mogens* already one finds not only
a new vision of nature, but a new style, a style

plastic, meticulous, which with time came to seem even affected. This story earned him the lasting friendship of Brandes.

Both in *Niels Lyhne* (1880), the so-called Bible of atheism, and in the historical novel *Marie Grubbe* (1876), there is the same background of pessimism. Man is purely a creature of nature, with life maintained by his blood and senses; his life sad and his death painful. There is no dream, there is no hope that can save him from this cruel destiny. Such is the unhappy moral result to which the crusade against romanticism, proclaimed by Brandes, had arrived.

In *Niels Lyhne*, more important, perhaps, than the theme of atheism, is the exact and almost photographic description of the Danish soul, a Hamletic soul, in which, as a result of excessive indecision, impulses are almost never followed by action.

The protagonist wills, but when the moment for action comes, he gives up the struggle. This soft vacillating temperament, always in anxiety and distress, has been masterfully depicted by Jacobsen, who without fear of exaggeration, may be likened to the greatest Russian authors of the nineteenth century, whose spirit and disconsolate vision of life he has.

Besides being a great scrutinizer of souls, Jacobsen is also the greatest Danish prose-writer. He created a new Danish language; making use of the tonalities already offered him by Andersen, he developed a pictorial musical prose, which up to the present has remained unsurpassed.

Realism of the French style, indicated as a model

by Brandes, he adapted to the Danish temperament, and the result was that impressionism of which he remained the unquestioned leader. Not only this, but he never surrendered himself entirely to the hard and inexorable exigencies of realism; in the depths of his spirit, as in that of every man of the North, there always remained those lush and delightful romantic oases in which the soul concedes itself brief periods of repose, even while crossing the uncompromising and arid lands of naturalism. Very few have known, as has he, how to describe the sweetness of the full moon or the delicious fascination of the northern nights.

As he lived, so he died (April 30th, 1885), professing once again his atheistic belief.

Intimate friend and faithful admirer of Jacobsen was Edvard Brandes (1847–1931) brother of Georg. Edvard was an able and feared journalist and made use of the press to diffuse the doctrine of the so-called Brandesianism, that is, of radicalism in politics, of realism in literature and of atheism in religion. His work as an artist is much inferior to his work as a propagandist; but some of his plays inspired by Ibsen, such as *A visit* (1882), and a novel or so such as *A politician* (1889) and *Young blood* (1899), are not lacking in interest and literary merit. However, for the scenes that were too violent and characterized by the crudest realism, he was summoned to court.

In addition to ranking as an original author, Brandes was also the outstanding historian of the Danish theatre, acknowledged as a most able critic in a country where such criticism approaches the standard of art. He enjoyed, too, a certain measure of European fame as an Orientalist.

And, extending his activity outside the field of letters, Brandes served his country for years as a member of the upper house of Parliament, and crowned his public career by being Minister of Finance during the years of the World War,—a period that was indeed critical for a little neutral country adjoining one of the major belligerents.

Another declared realist was Erik Skram (1847–1923), author of the novels *Agnes Vittrup* (1879) and *Helen Vige* (1898) championing free love.

Karl Gjellerup (1857–1919) broke away from theological study, as described in *Germanernes Laerling* (Germanic disciple, 1882), and became a confirmed realist. Shortly afterwards he renounced his realism with the tragedy *Brynhild* (1884), in which he took for his subject an episode of the Nibelungs. Gjellerup was at heart a humanist and a classicist; hence, his withdrawal from the realistic and naturalistic school was the result of an inner development in the direction of what he considered a higher form of idealism. His break with Brandes, Gjellerup discusses frankly in his travel book *Vandreaaret* (The year of vagabondage, 1885). Deeply ethical by nature, he differed greatly with the Brandes group on the question of sex morality, a problem discussed by him with depth and seriousness of purpose in all his works, above all in the *Book of my love* (1889). Two of his novels are notable, *Minna* (1889), and *The mill* (1896).

His philosophical religious vision is revealed in its completeness in the cycle of stories entitled *The golden bough* (1917), which purposes to demonstrate the influence of Christ upon present-day humanity, and in his final works of Buddhist character.

In 1917, Gjellerup shared the Nobel Prize with H. Pontoppidan.

An unwholesome note of eroticism is found in the work of Herman Bang (1857–1912). In his first novels, *Stucco* (1887), *Tine* (1889), one hears the echo of the German-Danish war of 1864, of which Bang as a child had to suffer the consequences. Autobiographical instead are *Generations without hope* (1879), *By the roadside* (1886), *The white house* (1898), and *The grey house* (1901), in which the protagonist, differing from Niels Lyhne, who wills but cannot act, is outright incapable of willing.

As an impressionist, Bang is the greatest writer of Denmark, but in this impressionism of his one already feels a hint of decadence. "Weary," says a certain critic, "his sentences scintillate as among clouds, a style indicative of a dying culture."

A morbid sentimentalism is found above all in *Phaedra* (1883) and in *Mikaël* (1904). In the latter Bang bares the life of his own senses.

In *Without a country* (1906) the character of a gipsy, Joan, is depicted, who everywhere feels himself an alien; Joan is Bang himself, Bang who spiritually was a man without a country. And far from his fatherland he died, during a transatlantic visit.

The writer nearest to Bang, in taste and style, is Peter Nansen (1861–1918), though without

Bang's profundity and vigour of expression. Nansen
is the portrayer of elegant and sentimental Copenhagen, a subtle and impassioned *connoisseur* of the
feminine soul.

His novels, *Julia's diary* (1893), *Marie, a book
of love* (1894), *Peace of God* (1895), at the time
won an extraordinary success. They are three
simple novels, almost stylized, but pervaded by a
soft, delicate, sensual lyricism which makes the reading of them always attractive and pleasing.

We find a true realist in Henrik Pontoppidan,
born in 1857, a realist without fears and compromises, who in 1917 together with Gjellerup won the
Nobel Prize. He represents an antidote to the decadent literature of Bang and Nansen. With the enthusiasm of an apostle, Pontoppidan arrayed himself
against the lie of modern aestheticism, against false
social and political ideals. Already in his first book,
Clipped wings (1881), is foreseen the future
author of *Lykke-Peer*.

In the trilogy *Soil* (1891), *The promised land*
(1892) and *The last judgment* (1895), he gives
us an exhaustive picture of the religious and social
currents of the Denmark of his time. In the novels,
The old Adam (1894) and *The song of songs*
(1896), he holds up to ridicule the romantic af-
fectations of his generation.

Lykke-Peer (1897–98), the greatest work of
Pontoppidan, is the book of a man struggling with
life, but his is not one of those conflicts that ele-
vate men toward the highest spheres, it is not a
battle with a "giant Fate that exalts man while
crushing him," but, instead, it is a cynical and bit-

ter struggle. The hero of *Lykke-Peer* is, like the hero of *Adam Homo* by Paludan-Müller, the ordinary man eternally vacillating between the crass reality of life and the ideal which is never reached.

In *The kingdom of the dead* (1912–15, re-elaborated in 1917), a work published during the war period, Pontoppidan passes from the deepest desperation to faith in the return of man to the pure springs of life.

The realism of Pontoppidan is extraordinary in its minute particulars and in its almost cruel sincerity, which always accompanies the seeing of things as they are.

Pontoppidan's *The royal guest* (1908) undoubtedly is one of the most perfect short stories in Danish.

A specialist in emotional problems is found in Carl Ewald (1856–1908), son of the romanticist Herman Frederik Ewald. One feels in his novels the study of pedagogy which he made from his youth; his works, in fact, reveal an inclination to wish to impart ethical and social teachings. His novel, *My baby boy* (1899), is a masterpiece of its class, in which Ewald shows himself to be a profound psychologist and an able educator.

But the best things that he produced are the fairy-tales, the first of which appeared in 1882. These fairy-tales differ from those of Andersen, since they present a tendency markedly Darwinian and materialistic.

Ewald wrote also a very remarkable historical work, *Danish queens without crowns* (1906–08).

In respect to the aestheticism of his time, Karl

Larsen (1860–1931) represents the still virgin and original Danish element. In relation to the authors who were debating and agitating problems he is the pure artist who describes. His best book is *Doctor Ix* (1896), a sincere confession of the artist, who never reaches the point of being able to live life, since he is ever condemned straightway to transform into literature the fleeting instant.

A strange bizarre temperament is Gustav Wied (1858–1914). Wied as a writer is in a class by himself, but he has in common with the realists his aversion to every morbid sentimentality, to every romantic affectation. The essence of Wied's work is a bitter satire that often, however, succeeds in provoking laughter. In his heart is the gloomiest pessimism, the blackest desperation. Is he an impressionist? An individualist?

These questions would be difficult to answer, but certainly he is a controversialist by nature, the most vigorous perhaps that Denmark has had.

"Pray let us not make grand gestures, since all of us are men!" This is the motto which he affixed to his first book *Profiles* (1891), and it could be the motto of all his work.

The most important narrative books of Wied are: *Life's evil* (1899), *Knagsted* (1902), and *Pastor Sörensen & Co.* (1913), which three form a trilogy and contain numerous autobiographical elements; the two novels *The race of men* (1898) and *The fathers eat grapes* (1908); and the collection of tales entitled *The children of men* (1895), one of many by the author, sparkling in its lively humour. In

Wied's later years the drama became his favourite medium; significant among his plays are *The weaker sex* (1900) and *Dancing mice* (1905), especially the latter, where his mockery and great gift of caricature are vigorously expressed.

Other writers of this generation are Viggo Stuckenberg (1863–1905) who, together with Sophus Claussen and Johannes Jörgensen, founded the magazine *Taarnet* (The tower), which became the palaestra of the Danish individualists, Viggo Holm (1855–99), Niels Möller (b. 1859), Sophus Claussen (1865–1931), and Sophus Michaelis (1865–1932), all novelists and story writers, since in the program of Brandes, a program of uncompromising realism, there was no place for the lyric, forge of dreams and chimeras. Nevertheless, right in this period of time, the greatest poet of Denmark developed and one of the greatest of modern Europe, Holger Drachmann (1846–1908).

Having given his attention at first to painting, especially to the painting of marine scenes, and not finding encouragment and approbation at home, he emigrated to England and thence to France, where he took part in the war of 1870 and in the revolt of the Commune.

In 1872 he wrote his first book *With charcoal and chalk*, a collection of prose sketches which had some success. He wrote novels also and stories and plays, but only in the lyric did he find his true field of artistic expression. *Poems* (1872), *Muted melodies* (1875), *Songs by the sea* (1877), *Vines and roses* (1879), *Old and new gods* (1881), *New songs* (1892) constitute the best that Danish poetry can offer.

In 1883 Drachmann declared himself free from every attachment to Brandesianism and inaugurated a Danish movement of pure nationalistic tendency. He withdrew from the great leader of naturalism and realism, in the name of freedom of imagination and sentiment. "The last of the Danish romanticists" he has been characterized and such he was in temperament and in his art.

REACTION TO BRANDESIANISM

Brandes with his writings and his lectures had inoculated the mentality of his country with a poison composed of the most deleterious elements of European thought. Whatever was most subversive in romanticism and in literary naturalism, in positivism and in philosophical agnosticism in England, Germany and France, Brandes had given as pasture to the youth of the North: a monstrous individualism, a spirit of revolt which admitted no shackles, an unchaining of instincts. Such an attitude characterized Denmark of the period around 1880.

But already Gjellerup, as we have seen, had initiated revolution against this spirit of dissolution, a revolt which became open in Drachmann and culminated in the work of Johannes Jörgensen, who restored ethical and religious values which Brandes wanted intentionally to ignore or to combat outright as unwholesome and ruinous.

Contrary to many of his contemporaries, Jörgensen (b. at Svendborg, a village on the island of
Fünen, in 1866), passed from materialism to individualism. In 1896 after grave crises of conscience, he was converted to Catholicism, a conversion which had a decisive influence on Strindberg,
then vacillating between naturalism and mysticism.

One may follow the gradual slow conversion of
Jörgensen step by step through various books, from
the *Confession* (1894), in which he repudiates his
naturalistic and Darwinian theories, through a novel
of 1895, in which one already notes that the author
is finding himself at a decisive turning point of his
intellectual and moral life, and the *Book of travel*
(1895), telling of his journeys through Germany
and Italy, of his stay in the little mediaeval towns
of both countries, in Nürnberg, Rothenburg an der
Taube, Perugia, and Assisi. Already on the far-
off horizon is outlined the mystical figure of St.
Francis.

February 16th, 1896, Jörgensen solemnly renounced Protestantism and entered the Church of
Rome. Shortly afterwards, with the book *False life
and true life* (1896), he contrasted his past life, a
life of error and vice, with the new life inspired
by the practice of virtue.

His six-volume autobiography, *Mit Livs Legende*,
(Legend of my life, 1916–28) is of great importance
for the student of the *fin de siècle* spirit of modern
Danish literature.

Franciscan pilgrimages (1905) are the description of the delightful Umbrian plains, of the little
towns situated on the slope of the mountain, a

landscape which, indeed, became the favourite setting in which this author's imagination moved.

If the *Pilgrimages* are a delightful journal of travel, the *Life of St. Francis* (1902) is a marvellous canvas in which the saint is described with a fidelity and felicity of expression that make the book a masterpiece. It is evident that the author has examined all the ancient and modern sources; but rather than the critic it is the painter, the psychologist, that is revealed in him. The same may be said for the *Life of St. Catherine of Siena* (1915) and the *Life of Don Bosco* (1929).

In this spiritual renaissance Olaf Isted-Möller (1850–1913) and Edvard Egeberg (b. 1855) coöperated, as well as an accomplished group of authoresses who discuss in their novels problems of high spiritual value. Among these the foremost is Gyrithe Lemche (b. 1866).

But with the dethronement of Brandes, Danish literature lost its point of reference, its unity of directive, and split into innumerable tendencies, among which there was no one tendency that succeeded in having dominance over another.

One of the most outstanding personalities in the first thirty years of the twentieth century is Emil Rasmussen (b. 1873), an author who travelled much in Italy and drew from Italy the light and colour in which he developed all the characters of his novels. The landscape of the South, more than that of the North, is adapted to serve as scenario for his plays, in which passion bursts forth violent as a hurricane and men of powerful and direct instincts are as agitated as in a Dantesque whirlpool. In *Maffia*

(1906), *Chilly Eros* (1908), *What women want*
(1910), *The devil confessor* (1915), one finds an
atmosphere heavy and smoky, of morbid instincts,
of sick souls. *Way of the inferno* (1913) is a moving tale of Italian emigrants. His work *Polish
blood* opens a series of five novels (1918–26) in
which Rasmussen displays all the rich palette of his
dazzling colours.

Exactly the opposite of Rasmussen is Johannes
V. Jensen (b. 1873). If Rasmussen is a southern
temperament, an admirer of the instinctive and
impulsive man of the South, Jensen is the pure-
blooded Teuton, exalter of the energetic and hard-
working man of the sub-polar regions. For Jensen
the Teutonic is the superior race. The land of his
dreams, the land of adventures, is North America.

In *Himmerland stories* (1898–1910), he draws
with cunning and humour the type of the peasant of
Jutland, of the peasant bound to the soil, practical,
calculating, but also in certain moments dreaming
and poetic. In *Madame d'Ora* (1904) and *The
wheel* (1905), Jensen transports us to the vast
prairies of North America. In *The fall of the king*
(1900–01) he exalts the figure of Christian II, while
in the monumental series *The long journey* (1909–
22), including the following volumes in the order
of their sequence, *The lost land*, *The glacier*, *Norn
Guest*, *The Cimbrians*, *The ship*, and *Christopher
Columbus,* he describes graphically the development
of the Teutonic race from the Ice Age down to the
voyages of Columbus. This great racial epic is now
available in an English translation.

The union in his work of realism with imagination, an imagination truly grandiose and imposing, marks Jensen as the greatest living novelist of Denmark.

The Danish writer on social problems is Martin Andersen Nexö (b. 1869), in whom one finds a strong interest in Russian literature and above all in Dostoevski. *The Frank family* (1901), *Drizzle* (1902), *Pelle the conqueror* (1906–10), *Happiness* (1913), *Ditte, girl alive* and sequels (1917–21) are all novels in which the author treats figures of the proletariat, following them in their ideal ascent toward a better future.

Laurids Bruun (b. 1864) is a great stylist and a virtuoso of the Danish language. His production comprises about thirty-five volumes, of which the most important is the trilogy *Van Zanten* (1908–14), wherein he describes the beauty of the southern seas and the psychology of primitive men.

Knud Hjortö (1869–1933) and Harald Kidde (1878–1918) are two masters in the field of psychological analysis, while Otto Rung (b. 1874) takes pleasure in the description of strange and original temperaments.

The neo-mystic note is provided by the novel of Jens Anker Larsen (b. 1875), entitled *The philosopher's stone* (1923).

Founder of what became known as the Jutland movement was Johan Skjoldborg (b. 1861). Social in his attitude, Skjoldborg deals mostly with the hardships of life among the small farmers in the northwestern part of Jutland. His principal novels are *I Skyggen* (In the shade, 1893), *En Stridsmand*

(A fighter, 1896), *Kragehuset* (Crow house, 1899), *Gyldholm* (1902), and *Bjaerregaarden* (The Bjaerre farm, 1904).

Jeppe Aakjaer (1866–1930) together with Jacob Knudsen (1858–1917) and Jensen belong to this Jutland group; their preferred subject is the life led by the peasants in the peninsula of Jutland, once inhabited by the Cimbrians, progenitors of the modern Danes. *Folk in fustian* (1900), *People of Fjand* (1901), *Where peasants live* (1908), *Forces in ferment* (1916) are novels in which Aakjaer tells us with frank crudeness of the simple sane life of his land of origin. He tried his hand also in the lyric and the drama, but not with equal success.

Jacob Knudsen, a clergyman and a follower of Grundtvig, wrote powerful novels about social, cultural, moral, and religious problems. Conservative socially, he maintained that men's actions are determined by a character shaped by cultural inheritance. Religiously and morally radical, however, he championed man's independence from group dictation, but emphasized strongly the necessity of being rooted in a relationship to God. *Ferment* and *Clarification* (1902) picture this struggle with conflicting forces, and in *Fear* (1912) and *Courage* (1914) collectively named *Martin Luther*, he reveals through a biographical character analysis of the great reformer how his own basic fear was changed to courage through submission to God.

The animal world finds two great portrayers in Hans Kaarsberg (1854–1929) and Svend Fleuron (b. 1874).

In the art of the drama the first place is occupied by Helge Rode (b. 1870), whose plays often treat of the essence of life and death. His strongest plays are *Sons of kings* (1896), *On with the dance!* (1898), *Bartholin's day of joy* (1908), and *Count Bonde and his castle* (1912); these plays evidence the deepest pessimism, fed by a conviction of the absurdity of life.

Besides Gustav Wied, already cited, Denmark has lost a true dramatic talent in Hjalmar Bergström (1868–1914), whose plays *Mönter Street 39* (1904) and *Lynggaard & Co.* (1905) had in their day the greatest success. Bergström's best-known and most widely discussed play was *Karen Bornemann* (1907).

In the lyric, besides Drachmann who soars like an eagle above the others, worthy of note are Edvard Blaumüller (1851–1911), Viggo Stuckenberg, Sophus Claussen and Niels Möller, representatives of the individualistic current of the last decade of the nineteenth century.

Johannes Jörgensen brought into the lyric his mystical-religious note.

Thor Naeve Lange (1851–1915), Alfred Ipsen (1852–1922), Otto C. Fönss (b. 1858), Ludvig Holstein (b. 1864), Karin Michaëlis (b. 1872), Kai Hoffmann (b. 1874), Thöger Larsen (1875–1928), all indulged more or less in the individualistic current, while Valdemar Rördam (b. 1872) is the patriotic poet, author of hymns and songs very famous in Denmark, many of which have also been set to music.

DANISH LITERATURE

THE YOUNG GENERATION

After an exuberant period of expressionism during the twenties, a change toward a more sober attitude took place in the latter part of that decade. It can be seen in the poetry of Hans Hartvig Seedorff Pedersen (b. 1892), *I Dagningen* (At daybreak, 1927), and is concurrent with the general European disillusionment following as an aftermath of the world war and the golden age of prosperity.

After a brief lull a new generation of brilliant young authors again rises to the forefront, and during the first years of the present decade they have attained prominence in countries other than their own. They are a determined lot and are bravely facing a world staggering under the burdens inherited from war and social struggles. Realistic and sturdy in their attitude and style, they are, nevertheless, hopeful in their outlook. As yet it is too early to classify them in any way, but they give great promise.

Kaj Munk (b. 1898) has carved a name for himself as a dramatist with *En Idealist* (An idealist, 1928), *I Braendingen* (In the surf, 1929), *Cant* (Cant, 1931), *Ordet* (The word, 1932), and *De udvalgte* (The elite, 1933). Marcus Lauesen (b. 1907) created a sensation with *Og nu venter vi paa Skib* (Waiting for a ship, 1931), which his following books *En Mand og hans Fjende* (A man and his enemy, 1932) and *De meget skönne Dage* (The very beautiful days, 1933) have not attained. *Kaetteren fra Eisleben* (The heretic of Eisleben, 1934) is just off the press. Nis Petersen (b. 1897) became widely known by *Sandalmagernes Gade* (The street of the sandalmakers, 1931), a delightful and detailed story of second century Rome, and by his poetry. *Spildt Maelk* (Spilled milk), a novel of post-war Ireland, was just published (1934). Knuth Becker (b. 1893) impresses with his description of a bad boy, *Det daglige Bröd* (The daily bread, 1932) and *Verden venter* (The world is waiting, 1934). Jakob Paludan (b. 1896) whose novels,—for example *Markerne modnes* (The fields grow ripe, 1927) and *Fugle omkring Fyret* (Birds around the beacon, 1925),—have long shown promise, has risen to prominence with a description of a war-struck generation, *Torden i Syd* (Thunder in the south, 1932) and *Under Regnbuen* (Beneath the rainbow, 1933).

Under the leadership of these and others, Danish literature will merit watching during the immediate future.

DANISH-AMERICAN LITERATURE

by

GEORG STRANDVOLD

Associate Editor of Decorah-Posten

IT is a remarkable, and disheartening, fact that immigrants from Denmark have built, so far, no enduring landmark in the history of American literature; surprising, indeed, when it is remembered that the Danes are generally known because of their intellectual attainments. Somehow it seems as though the process of transplanting has stilled Danish song in the United States, and has eliminated it almost totally from the second and third generations of Danish-Americans. To the specialist in the history of migrations there is here plenty of food for thought.

Not that Danish-Americans have been inarticulate. On the contrary, they have written dozens of books, thousands of poems, but no single one is outstanding. Very few, if any, Danish-American literary works rank with the best produced in Denmark.

There is this further general observation to be made: the Danes in America have fostered no writer who has been able to devote all his time to literary pursuits; most of the authors must be classified as amateurs, many of them affiliated with the liberal section of the Danish Lutheran Church, practically none with the orthodox group within this organization.

In Danish-American *belles-lettres* one looks in vain for originality, imagery and daring; most books are mere narratives, dealing innocuously with some of the difficulties connected with the task of becoming acclimatized here—with yearning for the old home country, with admiration for the virility of the new.

Thus, judged from a strictly artistic viewpoint, Danish-American literature must, generally speaking, be considered rather mediocre. But if it is thought of as a mirror of pioneer and settlement life, this literature is important for the reason that it accurately reflects thoughts, dreams and everyday conditions among the Danes in this country; in a sense, most of these books are chapters of history rather than contributions to literature.

In the present brief survey only prose fiction and poetry will be discussed as it is felt that scientific, technical and religious works lie beyond the immediate scope of this attempt. It should be said, in passing, that Danish-Americans have produced numerous worth-while books in the scientific and technical field, most of them written in the English language.

A pioneer in Danish-American literature was Adam Dan (1848–1931), a minister in the liberal section of the Danish Lutheran Church of America. Coming to the United States in 1871 he wrote a number of pioneer stories, *Praerierosen* (The prairie rose, 1892), *Maleren* (The painter, 1901), *Vaarbud* (Coming of spring, 1902), etc. Notable among his collections of lyrics is his *Sommerlöv* (Summer leaves, 1903), and his song, *Saa langt, saa langt raekker Tanken frem* (So far away our thoughts do go), has rightfully been called "the national anthem of the Danish-Americans," for in its stanzas he gives beautiful and adequate expression to that longing for the home country which was an outstanding feature of early pioneer life.

Kristian Östergaard (1855–1931) is generally mentioned in the same breath with Adam Dan; both were ministers of the church, and both found their principal sources of inspiration in the life of the Danish immigrant farmers in the Middle West. Östergaard's *Anton Arden og Möllerens Johanne* (Anton Arden and Johanna, the miller's daughter, 1897) had the distinction of being the first Danish-American book to be published in Denmark, where it attained an unusual measure of popularity. *Nybyggere* (Pioneers, 1891), *Dalboerne* (The valley denizens, 1913), and *Et Köbmandshus* (The home of a merchant, 1909) also endeared Östergaard to his compatriots; he wrote a large number of songs, most of them expressing the immigrant's love for his new country and admiration for the majestic grandeur of American scenery.

Superior to Dan and Östergaard as a poet was Frederik Lange Grundtvig (1854–1903), a son of Nikolai Frederik Severin Grundtvig, famous Danish church reformer and founder of the folk high schools which have meant so much in the cultural life of Denmark. F. L. Grundtvig, too, was a minister, and with the exception of a few shorter works in the field of religious history he preferred

to express himself in rhymed verse. While he published no collection of his poems, they are scattered
throughout many song-books, one of which he
originally published himself. This *Sangbog for det
danske Folk i Amerika* (Song-book for the Danish people in America, 1889) is still being widely
used wherever Danes gather for their characteristic
community singing; the volume contains many
classics of Danish lyrical art, and most of Grundtvig's own songs are to be found here.

Among the older generation of writers Carl
Hansen (1860–1916) is the most accomplished artist. His short stories were widely read because he
was the first of the Danish-American group to
combine seriousness with an element of quietly
chuckling humour. Most of these stories are to be
found in his collections, *Praeriens Börn* (The children of the prairie, 1896), *Landsmaend* (Fellow-
countrymen, 1908), *Dansk Jul i Amerika* (Danish
Christmas in America, 1909), and *Nisqually*,
(1912). He wrote only one novel-length story,
Praerie-folk (People of the prairie, 1907).

Oluf Christian Molbech (b. 1860), a son of
Christian Knud Frederik Molbech, during his time
one of the outstanding prose writers and play-
wrights of Denmark, spent a good many years in
the United States and wrote as results of his observations here several novels, *Den gule By* (The yel-
low city, 1905), *Indianerliv* (Indian life, 1911),
Skovens Helte (Heroes of the forest, 1912) and
Over Havet (Across the sea, 1916). While he must
be classified as a Danish-American writer, he did
not deal especially with Danish-American subjects.

Emil Ferdinand Madsen (1861–1932) is known especially as the author of *Fra de stille Skove* (From the quiet woods, 1896)—a story of pioneer life among the Danes in America.

Jens Christian Bay (b. 1871), now chief librarian of the John Crerar Library in Chicago, made his literary *début* with a story, *Hvad Gud har sammenföjet* (What God hath joined together, 1898), and also has contributed a large number of short stories to the Danish-American Christmas annuals and other publications. He likewise compiled a valuable bibliography, *Denmark in English and American literature* (1915), and has written extensively in English as well as in German on subjects of particular interest to bibliophiles and botanists. It should be added that though Bay does not very frequently write poetry, when he does, he usually finds almost flawless forms of expression.

Almost forgotten, though still worth reading, are M. Sörensen's stories of immigrant life—*Traekfugle* (Migratory birds, 1903), *Udvandrerfolk* (Emigrants, 1904) and *Hinsides Atlanten* (Beyond the Atlantic, 1906), all written during the first decade of the present century.

Enok Mortensen (b. 1902), a Chicago minister, two years ago published a volume of ably written short stories, *Mit Folk* (My people, 1932), cast in a modern, realistic form, reminiscent of the style of Carl Hansen, and depicting Danish-American urban life. He is also the author of a play, *Livets Lykke* (Happiness of life, 1934) and a remarkably successful novel, *Saaledes blev jeg hjemlös* (Thus I became homeless, 1934), followed by a sequel (1936).

Also, it should be added that a great deal of valuable material has been buried in newspapers and periodicals during the last fifty or sixty years, much of it deserving rescue from the oblivion of bound files mouldering on library shelves. In fact, it may be said that the truest picture of immigrant life is to be found by a diligent search of the old newspapers.

While there are practically no dramatists among the Danes in America, there has been considerable activity in the lyrical field, in addition to what has already been indicated above.

John Volk (1843–1904) left behind him a literary monument, *Songs and poems in Danish and English* (1903), many of which were translations, others his own original poems. Ivar Kirkegaard (1869–1928), editor of a stately Danish-American monthly magazine, wrote prose and poetry with equal grace and fluency, and some of his best writings are preserved in a volume, *Halvkloden rundt* (Half-way around the earth, 1905), while his *Danske Dage* (Danish days, 1916), consists of lyrics only. Anton Kvist (b. 1878), must be considered the most significant poet among Danish-Americans of the present day, his *Fyr og Flamme* (Fire and flame, 1910) and *Danske Strenge* (Danish strings, 1916) containing much valuable poetry. Oscar Olafsson (b. 1883 *), an Icelander by birth, brought up and educated in Copenhagen and a resident of New York for more than a quarter of a century, in 1933 sent out a collection of exquisite verse, *Flora Danica,* subtly reminding the reader

* (d. 1937.)

of influence from Holger Drachmann, Heine and Byron. August L. Bang (b. 1887), probably the most diligent of all Danish-American song-birds, has for years been a steady contributor to the Danish-American press but has not yet found it possible to publish his writings between covers. Eckardt V. Eskesen (b. 1864), president of a large New York architectural terra cotta firm, published in Copenhagen a volume of poems, entitled *Mod Lyset* (Toward the lights, 1907), but has been silent since then.

Unique is C. L. Christensen (pseudonym Bror Enebo, b. 1878) whose slender volumes *Sagn* (Legends, 1922), *Fart* (Speed, 1931) and *Livets Röst* (Voice of life, 1931) contain some of the most exquisite lyrics written by Danes in America.

Though perhaps not wholly within the framework of a review of *belles-lettres*, there are several authors of books in other fields who should not be omitted from an account of Danish-American literary activity. Among them is Jacob A. Riis (1849–1914), a native of Denmark, who became widely known as the author of *How the other half lives* (1890), the autobiographical *The making of an American* (1901), *The battle with the slum* (1902), *Children of the tenements* (1902) and *The old town* (1909), which refers to his native city of Ribe, Denmark. Here, too, must be mentioned Carl Christian Jensen (b. 1888), whose *An American saga* (1927), an autobiography written in English, attracted much attention a few years ago, as well as Rev. T. M. Nielsen's (b. 1875) *How a Dane became an American* (1935).

Of interest is Morris Salmonsen's (1843–1913) *Brogede Minder* (Miscellaneous reminiscences, 1913), a charming volume of reminiscences of Chicago Danes. Rasmus Andersen (1848–1930), a New York minister for half a century, wrote extensively and mistily, chiefly religio-biographical books, but also ventured into the field of fiction with *Bispegaarden i Oklaho og Praestehuset i Utah* (The Oklahoma Bishop's home and the Utah parsonage, 1897), *Jörgen* (1906) and *Den foraeldrelöse Margrethe* (Margaret the orphan, 1907).

C. B. Christensen (b. 1858) published many years ago two very readable monographs, *Georg Brandes* (1896) and *Fra Amerikas Kultur* (A page of intellectual life in America; a biography of Nathaniel Hawthorne, 1898), which represent practically the only effort in the direction of literary history and criticism among Danish-Americans.

P. S. Vig (1854–1930) has published a large number of pamphlets as his contribution to Danish-American history. Thomas Peter Christensen (b. 1880), published in 1927 his *Dansk-amerikansk Historie* (Danish-American history), a useful reference book. Christian Rasmussen (1852–1926) began a comprehensive work, *Danske i Amerika* (Danes in America, vol. I, 1908, vol. II, 1927), which intended to present a complete history of his compatriots here; one and a half volumes were published at the time of his death in 1926, and no sequel is planned. Joost Dahlerup (b. 1874) also has done work in the historical field and, besides, has published a couple of volumes of fiction, notably *For Vind og Vove* (At the mercy of winds and waves, 1908).

A very considerable part of Danish-American writings, in prose as well as in metrical form, has been published in Danish-American weeklies, some of which are still in existence, notably *Den Danske Pioneer*, Omaha, Nebraska; *Nordlyset*, New York; *Dansk Tidende*, Chicago; *Dannevirke*, Cedar Falls, Iowa; *Bien*, San Francisco; *Luthersk Ugeblad*, Blair, Nebraska; *Det Danske Ugeblad*, Minneapolis and Tyler, Minnesota; and a few others.*

Norden, Racine, Wisconsin, 1903–1916, represents the only ambitious attempt at an illustrated monthly Danish-American magazine.

During 1936 the second generation of Danish-American writers began to show activity, and in English Sophus Keith Winther (b. 1895) published his *Take all to Nebraska*, and Niels Peter Gravengaard (b. 1865) his *Christmas again!*, both full-length American novels dealing with Danish pioneer life, chiefly in Nebraska. Both authors are sons of Danish immigrants.

One circumstance which is of importance in connection with Danish-American literature is the fact that nearly everyone who has written has done so *con amore;* with exceedingly few exceptions Danish-American authors have had to publish their

---

* The history of these papers, and of many more which have vanished, is told in a separate chapter in *Norsk-Amerikanernes Festskrift*, edited by Johannes B. Wist, Decorah, Iowa, 1914; in *Den danskfödte Amerikaner*, edited by Max Henius and privately printed, Chicago, 1912, pp. 95–102; and in Thomas P. Christensen, *Dansk-amerikansk Historie*, Cedar Falls, Iowa, 1927, pp. 135–157.

books at their own expense since no publishing house has been established among them; a few have succeeded in having reputable houses in Denmark take over their books, but there is not one of all these writers who has ever earned riches as a result of his literary activities. The work has always been one of love, love for their people.

While this survey cannot pretend to be complete, it does, its writer feels, comprise a majority of the names and books of any significance in Danish-American literary annals.

ICELANDIC LITERATURE

ICELANDIC LITERATURE

by

RICHARD BECK, Ph.D.

Professor and Head of the Department of
Scandinavian Languages and Literatures
in the
University of North Dakota

EDDIC AND SKALDIC POETRY

DOWN through the centuries literary interest has characterized the Icelandic nation to a remarkable degree. The liberty-loving Norwegians who principally colonized Iceland (874–930) brought with them not only rich and varied traditions, but a love of poetry as well. In fact, not a few gifted poets were among these settlers. Moreover, in ancient Iceland the poetic genius of the North soon found ample native material in addition to the great store from abroad; and in this isolated island of the North Atlantic the epic tradition of the Scandinavian countries, and of the Germanic race, was destined to blossom forth in its full vigour and beauty. The story of how Iceland became the treasure-house of ancient Germanic and Scandinavian lore is as fascinating as it is unusual, but unfortunately beyond the scope of this survey.*

The main stream of early Icelandic literature divides itself into three branches: the Eddic poems, the skaldic or court poetry, and the sagas.

The Eddic poems are preserved in a unique and priceless thirteenth century manuscript collection, the *Elder* or *Poetic Edda,* which came into the possession of the Icelandic bishop, Brynjólfur Sveinsson in 1643, and is now in the Royal Library at Copenhagen under the title *Codex regius.* This collection consists of a large number of poems dealing with the early mythology, moral teachings, and heroic legends; within these types the poems differ, however, in style and spirit; the metres are alliterative, simple but dignified, as befits the generally elevated themes. Neither the author nor the compiler of these poems is known to us. Their date of composition ranges from 800 to 1100, broadly speaking, although on this point scholars continue to differ considerably. These poems were not, on the other hand, put into writing until after 1100, most of them probably between 1150 and 1250. Here is not the place to consider the much debated question of the home of the Eddic poems. One thing is certain, they have been preserved in Iceland and there only. Although traditional in nature, and although they have come down to us more or less mutilated, the best of them, at least, have

* For this see: Sir William A. Craigie, *The Icelandic sagas,* Cambridge Manuals, 1913; Knut Liestöl, *The origin of the Icelandic family sagas,* Oslo, 1930; Bertha S. Phillpotts, *Edda and saga,* New York and London, 1931; and Halvdan Koht, *The Old Norse sagas,* New York, 1931. Several of these books contain good bibliographies on the subject, including lists of English translations of the sagas and the Eddas.

clearly been fashioned and polished by a master hand.

The *Poetic Edda* opens dramatically and most appropriately with *Völuspá* (The sibyl's vision), which has been called *A Scandinavian Genesis*. It is even more than that as it deals not only with beginnings but also with the ultimate destiny of man and this world. In this sonorous and mighty lay we listen to an inspired prophetess addressing her revelations to the assembled gods and to humanity at large. Her words are mystical and terse, dealt out with a sparing hand, but impressive and profound, and therefore difficult of interpretation, a task made doubly hard as the poem has reached us deplorably mutilated. Withal, its grandeur and sweep are always in evidence, and it is clearly the work of a poet endowed with rare mastery of form and equally rare imaginative power.

On a level with *The sibyl's vision* in interest and significance is the group of poems entitled *Hávamál* (The sayings of the High One), which has been referred to as *A Scandinavian Book of Proverbs*. It is largely a collection of wise precepts tersely expressed. Here we find the most direct and the most complete presentation of the old Scandinavian philosophy of life. These poems contain rules of social conduct, as true and useful in our own day as they were a thousand years ago, but in an even greater degree they express moral principles applicable to any situation in life, ethical teachings always the same. The experience, through centuries, of the northern nations is here summed up concisely and graphically.

Remarkable alike for its racy humour and narrative excellence, is the *Thrymskvida* (Lay of Thrym), which tells of how Thor regained his stolen hammer. The characterization of Thor himself is particularly masterful. Among the heroic poems of the *Poetic Edda* a whole cycle preserves an older Northern version of the German *Nibelungenlied*, the very theme which Wagner immortalized in his *Ring of the Nibelungs*. These poems are rich in vivid descriptions and frequently also in penetrating psychological interpretation; in them the epic ideal of the race finds a vigorous, and at times a magnificent expression.

From the tenth to the thirteenth century there flourished in Iceland the skaldic or court poetry, which differs fundamentally from the Eddic poems. All of the latter are anonymous, whereas the names, and in many cases the lives, of the skalds, or court poets, are known to us. The Eddic poems preserve mythology, ethical views, and heroic lore; the skaldic poetry almost exclusively sings the praises of kings and chieftains. Finally the metrical form of the Eddic poems is simple, though elevated; that of skaldic poetry highly complicated. These Icelandic minstrels not only developed intricate, sonorous verse-forms; they added an even more characteristic feature:—the use of a poetic diction all their own, abounding in metaphorical and descriptive expressions (*kennings*), frequently far-fetched and fantastic. As a result much of the skaldic poetry suffers from recurrent phraseology and sameness of themes, and from a lack of personal feeling. Generally speaking, therefore, these poems have much greater historical and cultural than literary value. Nor is that a cause for surprise; they were frankly professional productions not infrequently written purely for personal advantage; and the old Scandinavian chieftains, like their Germanic kinsmen elsewhere, most desirous of a noble renown, naturally cherished and honoured the poet, who could, more surely than anyone else, guarantee lasting fame to the great deeds of his master.

The oldest existing skaldic poems are ascribed to the Norwegian, Bragi the Old, who is said to have lived during the earlier part of the ninth century. He was followed by a number of Norwegian poets associated with the court of King Harald the Fairhaired (860–933), who held his poets in high esteem. The leading Norwegian court poet of the tenth century was Eyvindr Finnsson, who wrote a famous memorial poem in honour of his beloved king, Haakon the Good, *Hákonarmál*. Written in Eddic metre, an admirable vehicle for its theme, the poem pictures excellently the vigorous king and breathes genuine admiration for him.

Beginning with the middle of the tenth century and on to the end of its hey-day the Icelanders monopolized the art of skaldic poetry and brought it to its highest excellence. The first of these Icelandic poets known to us by name, as well as the greatest of them all, was Egill Skallagrímsson (900–983). A man of no ordinary mould, rugged alike in features and character, he is the very embodiment of the Viking spirit. Along with his indomitable will, which defied even the gods themselves, he possessed, however, a deep sensitiveness. He was a master of metrical form and excelled in graphic descriptions. The full measure of his poetic genius is seen in his *Sonatorrek* (Sons' lament), a memorial poem mourning the loss of his two sons. Born out of inexpressible sorrow and utter despair, the poem quivers with deep, though subdued, emotion, revealing at the same time the noble manliness of the author. In a strikingly original manner the poet pours out his heart in this forceful and remarkable dirge, one of the greatest poems in Icelandic literature.

Kormákr Ögmundarson (c. 935–c. 970) is preeminently the love poet among the Icelandic skalds; his verses, alive with warm, sincere emotion, record his unhappy love for Steingerdr, his Laura; they reveal him as a poet of genuine lyric gifts. Unfortunately, many of his delicate songs have come down to us sadly mutilated. Hallfredr Óttarsson (970–1007), the first of the Icelandic court poets to deal with Christian themes, eulogized his master, King Olaf Tryggvason, in a memorable, highly personal poem. Sighvatr Thórdarson (995–1045) was the court poet as well as a cherished friend of King Olaf Haraldsson (Saint Olaf), whom he mourned in a notable poem and in several exquisite shorter songs. His poem, *Bersöglisvísur,* written as a reprimand to King Magnus, son of Saint Olaf, is remarkable for its sane frankness and so impressed the young king that he mended his ways. Sighvatr's poetry is spontaneous, simple in language, and refined. Another Icelandic poet of the eleventh century was Arnórr Jarlaskáld, noted especially for his poem in honour of King Magnus the Good; eloquence and sonorousness are his principal qualities. After 1100 the skaldic poetry began to decline, although it continued to be written down to the fourteenth century.

The art of the skaldic poetry is admirably interpreted in the *Prose* or *Younger Edda* by Snorri Sturluson, the great Icelandic historian (1178–1241). In this *ars poetica* of his he discusses in detail the poetic diction together with the metrical principles of skaldic verse, illustrating his discourse with numerous examples from the works of earlier poets or of his own composition. Although apparently not a poet of great native ability, Snorri has obviously been a resourceful master of metrical form. This significant handbook of his begins with an illuminating and refreshing exposition of Old Norse mythology, primarily based on the Eddic poems, knowledge of which is indeed necessary for a full understanding of the numerous skaldic allusions.

ORAL AND WRITTEN SAGAS

Equally as notable a contribution to world literature as the Eddic poems and the skaldic poetry are the *Icelandic sagas;* and they are even more unique since they are entirely in a class by themselves, a thoroughly Icelandic production, without a literary counterpart.

Sir William A. Craigie's definition of the saga-literature is both concise and accurate; "The general title of *Icelandic sagas* is used to denote a very extensive body of prose literature written in Iceland, and in the language of that country, at various dates between the middle of the twelfth century and the beginning of the fifteenth; the end of the period, however, is less clearly marked than the beginning. The common feature of the works classed under this name, which vary greatly in length, value, and interest, is that they have the outward form of historical and biographical narratives; but the matter is often purely fictitious, and in many cases fact and fiction are inseparably blended."

The written sagas were the outgrowth of a long oral tradition, and this is clearly reflected in their structure and style. Story-telling was an unusually popular form of entertainment in ancient Iceland, and the story-tellers, or "saga-men" as they were called, acquired rare mastery of their difficult art. We know, however, the names of but very few of the authors proper of the sagas or of those who committed them to parchment. Doubtless the writers felt that they were merely recording for posterity traditional material which was, so to speak, public property; therefore, they did not, except in few instances (as in the *Historical sagas*), attach their name to the story. Clearly, they were not much concerned about their own literary fame.

Of the Icelandic sagas the large group commonly referred to as *Íslendingasögur* (Sagas of Icelanders), some thirty-five in number, has the widest appeal. Although dating, in their written form, from the twelfth and thirteenth centuries, they are popular reading even today. These stories generally tell of people who lived in Iceland, and frequently deal with individual families; hence the title often used, *The Icelandic family sagas.* They are also similar in that their authorship is shrouded in mystery. They differ, on the other hand, not only in "length, value, and interest," as already suggested, but also in faithfulness to historical fact. There is also considerable variety in their subject-matter, although they centre nearly always around tragic issues and end on a tragic note; the tragedy is, however, relieved by touches of humour and romance. Nevertheless, only one of the *Sagas of Icelanders* is a comedy, *Bandamanna saga* (The story of the confederates), full of rollicking fun, a clever and vigorous satire on the political leaders of the day. Let no one think, however, that because they are tragic in theme, the *Sagas of Icelanders* make dull reading; like all true tragedies, told with literary artistry, they stir the reader and ennoble him.

The historicity of these sagas is still a subject of debate. They have been weighed in the balance of the most searching criticism. The result is excellently summarized in the following words by one who can speak with authority: "Yet, after the purgatory of critical examination, the sum of facts retained by the sagas is still so large that they alone permit us to write the history of centuries" (Koht). On the other hand there is full agreement about the significance of the sagas as an expression of the life and the culture of the age which produced them. They cast a flood of light not only upon the civilization of Iceland of old, but no less upon the whole realm of ancient Scandinavian and Germanic culture.

The *Sagas of Icelanders* are, however, much more than cultural-historical documents of first importance. As works of literature they rank with the most excellent of narratives. Their style is forceful, clear, and concise. There is strict economy of phrase; and the story is generally told in a simple and straightforward manner. The sagas are characterized by still another great literary quality; they are free from comment on the writer's part, from all intrusion of his own person. He has the *rôle* of an impartial observer, zealously keeping himself in the background. Very rarely does he condemn or extol the conduct of his men and women; as a result the story is not burdened with direct moralizing. The saga-writer knows his art and his audience; he leaves something to the imagination. The sagas are rich in eloquent silences and suggestive omissions, and this is not the least remarkable of their literary excellences.

Usually the sagas are told with great technical skill; there are quick turns of dialogue and often a brilliant evolution of plot. The best of the *Sagas of Icelanders* are unified and logical in construction, each event following the other as decreed by the law of cause and effect. "We see, step by step, incident after incident, how the strands of tragedy are being woven, or how great events may spring from small causes" (Phillpotts). Here is, indeed, the realism of life itself.

Without resorting to minute psychological analysis, the saga-writers excel in character-delineation. Their men and women are revealed through their own actions and utterances, and through public opinion. This is after all the way we learn to know people in real life; and the saga-writers use this simple method artistically and effectively. They succeed in drawing full-length portraits not only of the important persons, but of the minor characters as well. Professor Koht does not exaggerate when he writes: "Indeed, the Icelandic sagas present a whole gallery of individualized and interesting characters which stand out before us so clearly and palpably that we seem to know them personally."

Through the magic of their literary art the saga-writers succeeded in investing their story with the appearance of reality and in making their characters flesh-and-blood creatures. Because of this artistry and vitality the sagas are still "a living literature." These early writers of Iceland accomplished even more; they anticipated, indeed, in a degree developed, one of the most modern of literary forms—the novel.

Of the Icelandic sagas *Njáls saga* (The story of Burnt Njal) is the most elaborate and the most famous; here the art of the saga reaches its highest development. Sir George W. Dasent, whose translation of this saga into English has itself become a classic (in *Everyman's library*), says: "This tragic story bears away the palm for truthfulness and beauty." Penetrating character-portrayal, narrative excellence, and tragic intensity here go hand in hand. Of the other longer sagas the *Egils saga*,

Laxdaela saga, and *Grettis saga,* are especially worthy of attention. Among the shorter sagas *Hrafnkels saga Freysgoda, Gísla saga Súrssonar,* and *Gunnlaugs saga* are of particular interest. In fact, all of the sagas make interesting reading, despite their difference in literary merit and historical accuracy.

Akin in spirit and style to the *Sagas of Icelanders,* carrying on the heroic tradition of the North, are the *Historical sagas,* which were written in large numbers in Iceland during the twelfth and thirteenth centuries; this was the great period of recording in writing the varied and vast oral literature, poetry and prose, described above. The pioneer writers in this field were Saemundur Sigfússon (1056–1133) and Ari Thorgilsson (1067–1148), both of whom have been surnamed "The Learned"; the latter has also been called "the father of Icelandic history," and not without justification. His *Íslendingabók* (Book of Icelanders), which admirably summarizes the early history of Iceland, was the first historical work written in Icelandic. It has justly been styled "a model of historical method," and constituted a sound foundation for later Icelandic historical writing. In a class by itself is the *Landnámabók* (Book of settlements), which describes the colonization of Iceland by districts, lists the names of the settlers, and traces their family. This is a record without a parallel elsewhere. Iceland of the troubled thirteenth century is depicted in the *Sturlunga saga,* an extensive compilation, a large part of which was written by the historian

Sturla Thórdarson (1214–84), an impartial interpreter but not a brilliant stylist.

The Icelandic historians did not, however, con-
fine themselves to their own country; they wrote
sagas dealing with Denmark, the Faroese Islands,
the Orkneys, and Greenland (including an account
of the Icelandic discovery of America). Neither
was the old mother country, Norway, neglected. A
large group of sagas tells of the lives and achievements of the kings of Norway. By far the most
important is the *Heimskringla* (The globe) by
Snorri Sturluson, the greatest of Icelandic historians, referred to above. Beginning with prehistoric times this remarkable work relates the story
of the kings of Norway down to the year 1177.
Scientific accuracy, sound critical judgment, and
mastery of style characterize the *Heimskringla* and
mark Snorri not only as one of the greatest of
historians but no less as an unusual literary artist.

The early history of the Icelandic church is told
in a number of *Eccleciastical sagas*, many of which
are the lives of individual bishops. These works are
highly informative, but differ greatly in historical
importance and literary interest.

Finally there is a large body of *Mythical* or *Romantic sagas* dealing with more or less legendary
heroes of prehistoric times; here the fancy and the
fantasy of the unknown authors have a free play,
and the supernatural is much in evidence. Not infrequently, however, these sagas are artistically and
effectively told, as a rule in a fluent, idiomatic
language. Among the most important and interest-

ing are the *Völsunga saga,* which preserves an early
version of the Nibelung legend, and the *Fridthjofs
saga,* an exquisite story of romantic love. The Swedish poet Tegnér based his far-famed narrative
poem of the same name on this saga.

As elsewhere in the Northern countries the ancient laws were the first material to be recorded in
writing in Iceland. Several law collections, written
during this period, are still in existence; the most
significant is the *Grágás,* which contains the laws
from the period of the Icelandic republic (930–
1264), a veritable gold mine of information relative to the life and the culture of early Iceland and
thereby also of ancient Scandinavia.

During this period, so rich in the writing down
of literary material which had originated or taken
shape in Iceland, a number of stories, sacred and
secular, were also translated into Icelandic from
foreign sources. The handwriting is already on the
wall. Internal events and currents of thought
from abroad were joining forces in thwarting the
creative genius of the Icelanders.

DECLINE OF CLASSICAL LITERATURE—NEW TYPES
OF POETRY

With the loss of political independence (1264)
and the gradual disappearance of the Althing (the
Icelandic parliament) as the centre of national life,
Icelandic literature declined. The period from
1300 to 1540 produced little of literary significance in prose. Older sagas were diligently copied
and compiled, romances and other fictitious tales
flourished, and annals were written in large num-

bers. The skaldic poetry was a thing of the past, its place being taken by the rich production of poems on religious subjects, written in Eddic metres or the sonorous verse forms of the skalds. The most noteworthy among the earlier poems of this type is the *Sólarljód* (Sun song), from around 1200, which has been called *An Icelandic Divine Comedy*. Didactic in spirit it is primarily a vision poem, characterized by deep feeling and lively imagination, containing passages of sheer beauty. The most remarkable literary production of the fourteenth century was the sacred poem *Lilja* (The lily), consisting of no less than a hundred stanzas. It was written by the monk Eysteinn Ásgrímsson (d. 1361), the leading poet of the day, and is an eloquent and masterfully constructed interpretation of mediaeval Christology. It long remained popular and found many imitators; a new edition of it has just been published in Iceland. Poetry of this kind continued to flourish far into the sixteenth century, appearing in new metrical forms which harmonized better with the religious themes than the old skaldic metres.

The names of several poets from the latter part of this period have come down to us. By far the most important of these, alike for his sacred and secular poetry, was the great patriot Jón Arason (1484–1550), the last Catholic bishop of Iceland. He also deserves a place in the literary history of his country for having brought there (about 1530) the first printing press.

After 1300 there arose in Iceland the *rímur*, a narrative type of poetry, in reality a series of ballads, which remained extremely popular down to the nineteenth century. The basic metre is the alliterated, four-line stanza, doubtless foreign in origin; the rhyme-schemes, however, vary greatly and the metaphorical and descriptive expressions of skaldic verse appear here in great abundance. The themes are especially drawn from the mythical sagas, romances, and other fiction tales of the earlier days. Frequently the *rímur*-poetry is sadly lacking in beauty and artistic excellence; but it has considerable cultural and linguistic significance. It made the people at large realize what tremendous wealth the Icelandic language possesses and kept alive their sense of poetic form. Conventional ballads, originally from foreign sources, also circulated in large numbers in Iceland from 1400–1600. Particularly beautiful is *Tristrams kvaedi* (The Tristram poem), melodious, gripping in theme, with a haunting refrain.

FROM THE REFORMATION TO THE ENLIGHTENMENT

During the second quarter of the sixteenth century echoes of the Lutheran Reformation began to reach Iceland. The introduction of this significant religious and cultural movement did not, however, come about as the result of public sentiment; the Reformation was imposed upon the Icelandic people by royal decrees and military force; hence it was not, any more than in Norway, followed by a cultural and literary awakening as had been the case in many lands. Nevertheless, it brought with it fundamental changes in the cultural life which soon expressed themselves in the literature of the period. Stories of the saints naturally disappear, and the old religious poetry is replaced by Lutheran hymns. Edifying and explanatory works in prose, intended to spread and interpret the Lutheran teachings, appeared in large numbers. Most significant, not least linguistically, are Oddur Gottskálksson's translation into Icelandic of the New Testament (1540) and Bishop Gudbrandur Thorláksson's translation of the Bible (1584). Bishop Thorláksson, a man of great learning and initiative, and of varied interests, also published a new hymnal (1589), in the noteworthy introduction to which he pleads for the insistence on poetic excellence in hymn-writing, indeed a much needed admonition in that day.

From now on until far into the eighteenth century, the only printing press in Iceland was under the direction of the bishops of Hólar in the North, and its activity was almost entirely limited to the publication of religious works. Secular literature continued, nevertheless, to flourish, circulating freely in manuscripts. The hymn-writers and secular poets are legion; especially numerous are the authors of the popular *rímur*. A new type of ballads (*vikivakar*) first appears early in the sixteenth century and remains in favour down to the nineteenth; from a literary point of view the refrains of these songs are generally the most interesting, often highly lyrical and genuinely beautiful. The leading poet of the sixteenth century was the pastor Einar Sigurdsson (1539–1626), whose best poems combine deep feeling and fluent language.

The sixteenth and the seventeenth centuries were characterized by a renewed interest in historical and antiquarian studies. Many annals and biographies were written, more important, to be sure, as historical sources than as literary productions. Of the annalists Jón Egilsson (1548-1634) and Björn Jónsson (1574-1655) deserve special mention, while the most noted historians and antiquarians were Arngrímur Jónsson (1568-1648), Thormódur Torfason, or "Torfaeus" (1636-1719), and Árni Magnússon (1663-1730), the founder of the famed "Arna-Magnaean" collection of Icelandic manuscripts in Copenhagen. With these historical and antiquarian investigations and writings was laid the foundation for the fruitful later study of Old Icelandic antiquities and the road was paved for an awakening of Northern literature.

Two poets from the seventeenth century have a permanent place in Icelandic literature: the hymnologist Hallgrímur Pétursson (1614-74), who towers high above his contemporary writers of sacred songs, and Stefán Ólafsson (1620-88), also a clergyman, who was a very popular lyric poet, writing both on religious and secular subjects, but at his best in his satirical and humorous pieces. With his hymns on the Passion of Christ, *Passíusálmar*, Pétursson takes his place among the great Lutheran hymn-writers of other lands. Profound and sincere religious feeling here expresses itself in simple, though eloquent, language. Generation after generation of Icelanders have sung these hymns and committed them to memory, and their influence on the religious and moral life in Iceland is far beyond estimation. This becomes clear when attention is called to the fact that no less than forty-eight editions of them have been printed to date (1666–1929). Pétursson's memorable funeral hymn, *Alt eins og blómstrid eina* (Even as a little flower), is to this day generally sung at Icelandic funerals. He also wrote secular poetry of great merit, often characterized by rare metrical skill.

Of the prose-writers of this century two stand out: Jón Magnússon (1610–96), a clergyman, whose *Píslarsaga* (Story of torments), a vivid account of his long warfare with alleged witch-craft, is a cultural-historical document of first importance; and Bishop Jón Vídalín (1666–1720), justly renowned for his fiery and forceful eloquence. His volume of sermons, *Jónsbók* (1718–20), equally remarkable for inspiration, oratory and keen observation, remained popular reading in Icelandic homes down to the latter part of the nineteenth century, and has profoundly influenced Icelandic thought.

ENLIGHTENMENT AND AWAKENING

The years 1750 to 1835 were in Iceland a period marking the beginning of a national awakening and progress. Industrial and trade reforms were initiated, which gradually lifted the people out of the depths of poverty and hopelessness, the result of centuries of oppression, famines, and adverse physical environment,—reforms which later brought in their train complete financial freedom and paved the way for political independence. In these and other attempted improvements is seen the practical interest of the Enlightenment movement, which now had reached Iceland and expressed itself vigorously in the literature of the day, side by side with a pronounced national and antiquarian tendency. Other forces contributed to a greater vitality and variety of the literary production. The church no longer monopolized the printing of books; a new printing press, devoted to the publication of secular literature, was established in 1773. Of great importance was also the organization of various literary societies, which existed for a shorter or longer period and issued a number of useful publications. Most significant of these is the Icelandic Literary Society (*Hid íslenska bókmentafélag*), which was founded in 1816, and is still active, having contributed greatly to the cultural life of the Icelandic people. Nor must the work of the Royal Society of Northern Antiquities of Copenhagen, which was founded in 1825, be left out of the reckoning; with its editions of a number of the Old Icelandic prose works, which were eagerly read in Iceland, it aroused and made more wide-spread the interest in the saga-literature and strengthened the national spirit.

The most important writer during the earlier part of the period was Eggert Ólafsson (1726–68), a gifted poet as well as a distinguished scientist; he had been deeply influenced by the Enlightenment and wrote edifying and inspirational poems in its spirit. His greatest literary production is his *Búnad-*

arbálkur, a series of poems eloquent in their praise of country life. Ólafsson may, however, principally be looked upon as the leader in a nationalistic movement. He sought to awaken the dormant national feeling of his countrymen and strove to create richer Icelandic prosperity and culture on the heritages of the past. The preservation and the purification of his mother tongue were especially dear to his heart. His poetry vibrates with deep love for his native land and genuine admiration for its history and ancient literature. As a result his patriotic poems are generally the most successful, and not a few of them strike a new note. He is the co-author of a monumental natural-historical work *Reise igiennem Island* (Journey through Iceland, 1772), which ranks as "the first authoritative and comprehensive description of Iceland and its inhabitants" (Hermannsson). Although Ólafsson died in the prime of life he exerted a lasting influence on the cultural life of his country.

The leading poet of the latter part of the eighteenth century was Jón Thorláksson (1744–1819) who spent most of his days in very straitened circumstances as a rural clergyman in northern Iceland. An unusually interesting personality, he was a man of a brilliant mind and a poet of great gifts; his extensive original production ranges from bitter, sometimes malicious, satires to elevated hymns breathing deep religious feeling. Excellent as many of his original poems are, particularly in their rare mastery of form, they are far overshadowed by his numerous verse translations. Through these he enriched the literature of his country in a degree surpassed by very few, if any, of his compatriots past and present. Besides a number of minor ones, his translations include three great masterpieces: Pope's *Essay on man,* Milton's *Paradise lost,* and Klopstock's *Messias;* of which the two last named are especially successful. Fluently rendered into the elevated verse-form of many of the Eddic poems, these translations cleared the road for the poets of the following century.

Sigurdur Pétursson (1759–1827) is to be remembered as the pioneer Icelandic dramatist, but his comedies are of small literary merit. Benedikt Gröndal (the elder, 1762–1825) was highly regarded as a poet in his day. His translation of Pope's *Temple of fame* is fluent and accurate.

An outstanding figure during the latter part of the period was Magnús Stephensen (1762–1833), a versatile writer, but lacking in genuine poetical ability. The truest and foremost advocate of the Enlightenment, he may be considered the representative of a tendency largely anti-national. A sincere patriot in his way, he sought, in harmony with his views, to build Icelandic culture on the foreign models of his age. He desired to educate his people in full accordance with the spirit of eighteenth century Enlightenment. National characteristics, traditions, and language he valued little. He was a man of the widest interests and the most extensive activities, occupying the highest judiciary office in the land, and moulding public opinion through his numerous publications. Because of these far-reaching contacts, despite his limitations, he accomplished much and has left an indelible impression upon the history of the era.

Among the prose-writers of the day the pastor Jón Steingrímsson (1728–91) holds a place of prominence because of his autobiography; this is a work equally charming in its simplicity and sincerity of style. It presents a truthful and vivid picture not only of the author himself and his experiences, but of his age as well.

THE LAST HUNDRED YEARS—PROGRESS AND LITERARY ACTIVITY

The nineteenth century is of special importance in the history of Icelandic literature generally, and even more so in the history of Icelandic poetry. This period was one of further national awakening, politically and intellectually, and of marked progress in every sphere of life. A new, independent Iceland was emerging, receiving its constitutional freedom in 1874 and its political sovereignty in 1918.

Naturally, the literature was affected by the new currents of thought which swept the country. It is even customary to speak of a Renaissance in Icelandic letters during this era. At any rate, no one will deny that the national awakening produced a richer literature than Iceland had possessed for centuries. Both the renewed interest in ancient Icelandic writings and vitalizing foreign influences played here a part. Lyric poetry flourished especially.

The great philologist Sveinbjörn Egilsson (1791–1852), author of the *Lexicon poeticum* (1860), a monumental dictionary of the language of skal-

dic poetry, was the teacher of many of the romantic poets of this period and in a sense their forerunner. He was a poet of considerable ability; but
holds a prominent place in the history of Icelandic
letters because of his prose translations of the
Homeric poems. Remarkable alike for beauty and
purity of language, they profoundly influenced
later Icelandic poets.

The writer who introduced romanticism into
Icelandic poetry was Bjarni Thorarensen (1786–
1841), a virile and individualistic poet, and one
of the greatest Iceland has produced. As a student
at the University of Copenhagen he had come under
the influence of the Danish poet Oehlenschläger,
who was the leader of the romantic movement in
Denmark. Nevertheless, Thorarensen owed still
more to ancient Icelandic poetry, in particular the
Eddic poems. He not only frequently uses the old
verse forms, but he succeeds exceptionally well in
reproducing the spirit of the old poems. He is more
concerned with the contents than with the form of
his poetry. Vigour, depth of thought and rich imagery characterize his best poems. He wrote much
occasional poetry, and his obituary pieces are both
powerful and original. His patriotic poems and his
love poems also are outstanding.

With the name of Thorarensen is coupled that of
Jónas Hallgrímsson (1807–45), although the two
are in many ways a contrast. The latter was one
of four progressive, young Icelandic students in
Copenhagen, who founded the annual *Fjölnir*
(1835–46), dedicated to the purpose of arousing
their countrymen, and no less of improving the

literary taste and of purging their native tongue of foreign importations and imitations. Their crusade had far-reaching consequences. Significant and gifted as were his co-workers, Hallgrímsson is the one who primarily concerns us. He excelled in exquisite lyric form, being the master of simple and flowing style. His diction is unusually pure and he was a powerful force in the movement for the purification of the Icelandic language. He was a romanticist, deeply influenced by Heine, but there is much classical restraint in his poems. He, too, like Thorarensen, owed not a little to old Icelandic poetry. By profession he was a natural scientist, and he had a keen eye for the peculiar beauty of Iceland, throughout which he had travelled extensively. He wrote descriptive poems of unusual charm; he transmutes everything into sheer beauty, the dross into gold. Love of his native land, its scenic grandeur, and its history permeates his poetry. He is still one of his nation's most popular poets; and he has had great influence on succeeding writers. With his short stories he became the pioneer in modern Icelandic story-writing.

Other important poets of the first half of the nineteenth century were Sigurdur Breidfjörd (1798–1846) and Jón Thóroddsen; the latter will be discussed with the novelists, where he primarily belongs. Breidfjörd carried on with great success the tradition of the *rímur*-poetry. He also wrote shorter poems and epigrams. Many of the latter are veritable gems, fraught with deep feeling, tersely and excellently expressed, or containing striking pictures. He has influenced later Icelandic

writers. Hjálmar Jónsson (known as Bólu-Hjálmar, 1796–1875) belongs with these writers, although he outlived them by a quarter of a century.
He was endowed with great poetic genius, which
the most adverse of circumstances tended but to
strengthen. His life-long struggle with poverty, and
the lack of understanding on the part of his contemporaries, embittered him, however. His poems, therefore, often take the form of laments and scathing
denunciation of his age. They are, none the less, rich
in striking originality and rugged force. Jónsson can
be supremely eloquent, and his darts never miss the
mark.

During the latter part of the nineteenth century,
a number of gifted poets carried on, more or less,
the traditions of Thorarensen and Hallgrímsson.
The influence of romanticism is seen in the works
of these poets combined with strong national feeling. Not infrequently do they find inspiration and
subject-matter in the sagas and the history of their
country. Grímur Thomsen (1820–96) was at his
best in historical and narrative poems. He depicts
powerfully unique historical characters. His descriptions of external nature are vivid; his style is
vigorous and clear-cut. Although a widely travelled
man and a cosmopolitan, he is profoundly Icelandic. His study of Lord Byron (*Om Lord Byron*,
1845) was a pioneer work of its kind in the Scandinavian countries. Benedikt Gröndal (the younger,
1826-1907) was the most thorough-going romanticist among the Icelandic poets. His poems are uneven; the most successful ones reveal bold imagination and whimsicality. His style is lofty, at times

excessively elaborate. Much more interesting and significant are his two mock-romances, notably *Heljarslóðarorusta* (The battle of the field of death, 1861), a burlesque on the battle of Solferino, which stands alone in the humorous literature of Iceland. Gisli Brynjólfsson (1827–88), an admirer and imitator of Byron, wrote especially political poems, love songs, and occasional pieces. He was a great lover of freedom and wrote beautiful poems on that subject. He is, however, frequently lacking in originality.

Steingrímur Thorsteinsson (1831–1913), who was extremely productive as a writer, both in prose and poetry, won much popularity with his graceful lyrics. His best productions are his patriotic poems descriptive of scenery, his love songs, and satirical epigrams. He translated masterfully into his native tongue a number of significant works, including the *Arabian nights,* Shakespeare's *King Lear,* and Andersen's *Fairy-tales,* not to forget a sizable volume of the choicest lyric and narrative poems from many languages.

Matthías Jochumsson (1835–1920), a clergyman in various parts of Iceland, was both a versatile and a prolific writer, a lyric poet, a journalist, and a dramatist. He is generally looked upon as the greatest Icelandic poet of the second half of the century. He was unusually many-sided and wrote on a great variety of themes. His poems on subjects from Icelandic history are particularly noteworthy, as are his elegiac and memorial poems. His religious poems and hymns, reaching at times the highest peaks of inspiration, breathe deep faith and

strong idealism. Jochumsson's literary taste sometimes fails him; but at his best he combines startling
imagery with profound thought; his style is forceful and eloquent. His inspired hymn Ó, *Gud vors
lands* (Our country's God), written for the mil-
lennial celebration of the settlement of Iceland in
1874, has deservedly become the Icelandic national
anthem. In literary significance Jochumsson's
dramas rank far below his poetry. *Útilegumennirnir*
(The outlaws), written in 1861, has, however, remained a popular stage play down to the present
day. Like Thorsteinsson, Jochumsson rendered the
literature of his country inestimable service with
his excellent translations of major and minor
foreign masterpieces, included among which are
Shakespeare's *Hamlet, Macbeth, Othello, Romeo
and Juliet*: Byron's *Manfred*; Ibsen's *Brand*; and
Tegnér's *Frithiof's saga*.

Kristján Jónsson (1842–69) was a poet of great
promise, but died before reaching maturity. His
poems are melancholy and pessimistic. At times his
workmanship is faulty, but he wrote several pieces
of high quality both in thought and form. Jón
Ólafsson (1850–1916), a journalist and a political
leader, wrote glowing patriotic poems and exhortations to his countrymen. Love of his country and
love of freedom are the strongest notes in his
poetry. His translations of Björnstjerne Björnson's
Norwegian peasant stories, including the widely
known *Synnöve Solbakken*, are admirably done.
His brother, Páll Ólafsson (1827–1905), belongs
in this group of poets, although he carries on a dif-

ferent tradition. Like Bólu-Hjálmar he was a peasant, and he "represents in perfection the best qualities of the unschooled Icelandic poet" (Craigie). His verses are very spontaneous, frequently humorous or satirical in character. He also wrote convivial songs and charming love poems. He is a master of the Icelandic quatrain (*ferskeytla*). His poems still retain their popularity.

The most productive, and in many ways the leading Icelandic hymnologist of the century was Bishop Valdimar Briem (1848–1930). He has written many deeply felt and beautiful hymns, which grace the pages of the Icelandic hymn book, but his most notable work is the two-volume collection *Biblíuljód* (Bible songs, 1896–97), well characterized as "metrical pictures of biblical events." In a work of such magnitude, naturally, all the poems are not of equal merit, but many of them are remarkable for their exceptional musical quality, graphic nature descriptions, and soaring flight of the imagination.

Different kind of distinction was achieved by Jón Árnason (1819–88), who has a special place in the history of Icelandic letters because of his extensive collection of Icelandic folk- and fairy-tales (1862–64), compiled and in many cases retold by him. This folk-literature, the accumulated wealth of centuries, is an invaluable source of information concerning the cultural life of the Icelandic nation. In these tales we can, as it were, hear the very heartbeats of the common people; their joys and sorrows, their dreams and aspirations, together with their ideals and ethical views, find a vigorous expression in stories forceful and graceful in style, of rare life-likeness.

In 1882 four Icelandic students in Copenhagen founded the periodical *Verdandi*, of which, however, only one volume was published. These young authors had come under the influence of Georg Brandes, and through their new organ made themselves the champions of realism in literature. Two of the group, Gestur Pálsson and Einar H. Kvaran, are primarily significant as novelists. A third one, Hannes Hafstein (1861–1922), the first Icelander to hold the office of minister for his native land, was a very gifted lyric poet. Vigour, freshness, and youthful ardour are his outstanding qualities. His descriptive poems are both vivid and powerful. His spirited exhortations, patriotic poems, and love songs are of lasting merit. Thorsteinn Erlingsson (1858–1914), though not a member of the *Verdandi*-group, was a self-acknowledged follower of Brandes and his realism. Erlingsson was a radical both in religion and politics; he fiercely denounced religious bigotry and social injustice. In many of his poems he expresses his views fervently and eloquently. He has the tenderest sympathy for all living things, for the weak and the suffering. He also wrote exquisite patriotic lyrics and nature poems. He was a master craftsman, and his perfection of form has won general admiration. One of his favourite verse-forms was the quatrain, which he used with rare success. Through his social and political opinions, and no less because of his lyric art, he has had tremendous influence. His major work is the narrative poem *Eidurinn* (The oath, 1913), a series of songs on a tragic love theme, combining lyric beauty with social satire; unfortunately, only the first part of this work was completed.

Brief as our survey of nineteenth century Icelandic poetry has been, it reveals, nevertheless, that Iceland produced during that period an unusually large group of gifted lyric poets. And poets continue to flourish in Iceland; every year adds new names to the already long list. Only the most prominent of present-day Icelandic lyric poets can, however, be mentioned. Among the older ones, whose works partly belong to the nineteenth century but in a much larger degree to the first quarter of the twentieth, the following deserve to be named: Jón Thorkelsson (1859–1924), Bjarni Jónsson (1863–1926), Sigurjón Fridjónsson (b. 1867), Thorsteinn Gíslason (b. 1867), Gudmundur Magnússon (1873–1918), Sigfús Blöndal (b. 1874), Gudmundur Gudmundsson (1874–1919), and Sigurdur Sigurdsson (b. 1879). All these have written poetry of a high order or distinguished themselves as translators, and in not a few cases both holds good, but any adequate account of their work is out of the question because of our limited space.

Special attention must, however, be called to Einar Benediktsson (b. 1864), who is commonly recognized as the greatest Icelandic poet now living. A lawyer by profession he has held public offices in Iceland and also interested himself in politics and journalism. He has been called an Icelandic Browning, and not without reason. His poems contain profound philosophical thought expressed in lofty style. He grapples with the deepest problems of human existence. He has also written impressive descriptive and nature poems. He has travelled extensively and has spent much of his life outside of Iceland; nevertheless, he has lost none of his Icelandic characteristics. His love for Iceland and his faith in the future and the mission of his nation are written large everywhere in his poems. He is original in style as well as in the treatment of his themes, but he is not always easy to understand. Benediktsson has also to his credit several excellent translations including a remarkable version of Ibsen's *Peer Gynt.*

Of the younger present-day Icelandic poets the following are the most prominent: Stefán Sigurdsson (1884–1933), Jakob Thorarensen (b. 1886), Jakob Jóhannesson Smári (b. 1889), Davíd Stefánsson (b. 1895), Jón Magnússon (b. 1896), Jóhannes Jónasson (pseudonym Jóhannes úr Kötlum, b. 1899) and Tómas Gudmundsson (b. 1901). All seem destined to occupy a lasting place in the literature of their country. The women are also making a noteworthy contribution to modern Icelandic poetry. In the forefront among these are Ólöf Sigurdardóttir (1857–1933), the sisters Herdís and Ólína Andrésdóttir (twins, b. 1858), Theodóra Thóroddsen (b. 1863), and Unnur Benediktsdóttir (b. 1881). The last named, who writes under the pen-name of "Hulda," has written several collections of lyric poems, besides volumes of short stories, sketches, and fairy-tales. Her latest book, just published, is a cycle of songs, constituting what may be termed a spiritual autobiography, written with tender feeling and delicate lyric charm.

Present-day Icelandic poets cannot readily be classified according to "schools" of poetry. Many tendencies, old and new, meet in their works. Realism plays an important part, but neo-romanticism is also very evident, as well as a strong national note,—a new interest in folk-poetry and folk-lore. This literature is, however, too near to us for any final estimate.

Considered as a whole the last hundred years have been a remarkable period in the history of Icelandic poetry. And it continues to flourish notwithstanding the increasing interest in novels, short stories, and dramas, as will be seen below. Moreover, present-day Icelandic poetry is richer both in variety of themes and in variety of verse-forms than ever before. In this respect there has been a marked gain. Stephan G. Stephansson and Einar Benediktsson, to name but the two greatest, have here set a worthy example: "each of these has, in different ways, shown that the traditional form of Icelandic poetry is capable of being made the vehicle of profound and sustained thought to an extent not hitherto attempted or realized" (Craigie). And the younger Icelandic poets may well follow the leadership of these men. They should strive to open up new horizons, to enrich Icelandic literature with new themes without sacrificing the precision of form so characteristically Icelandic.

The creative activity of the Icelandic writers of this period, during the last sixty years especially, has been directed into other channels besides the broad stream of Icelandic poetry. Novelists and writers of short stories increase with every year, and Icelandic dramatists have won recognition at home and abroad.

Jón Thóroddsen (1819–68), already referred to, became the pioneer novelist of modern Iceland with his novels *Piltur og stúlka* (Lad and lass, 1850) and *Madur og kona* (Man and wife, 1871). He found models or, better, inspiration, in some of the works of Sir Walter Scott; for Thóroddsen was far from being a slavish imitator of anyone. His novels, although romantic in spirit, present vivid and truthful pictures of Icelandic rural life. He succeeds admirably in characterization; here is a whole group of sharply individualized, flesh-and-blood creatures. His spontaneous humour adds brightness and colour to the story; his style, clearly influenced by the Icelandic sagas, is concise and vigorous. Thóroddsen also wrote lyric poems, but these lack depth and originality. Nevertheless, he wrote smooth and graceful verses, enlivened by his fine humour. Several of his poems are still very popular.

Gestur Pálsson (1852–91) was, as previously indicated, a full-blooded realist, one might even say a naturalist. He was a journalist by profession and an able essayist; he is, however, especially remembered for his short stories of Icelandic rural and town life. His bitter pessimism here expresses itself in cutting satire, exposing relentlessly the faults of human kind and the hollowness of time-honored social practices. Despite that fact, Pálsson's human sympathy can readily be detected; he portrays his characters with keen understanding and frequently with striking realism. In his stories there is traceable a definite influence from the works of Alexander Kielland, the Norwegian novelist.

Einar H. Kvaran (b. 1859) is without doubt one of the most significant writers of present-day Iceland; of the older generation he is surely the most productive and most versatile man of letters, and he enjoys great popularity. Editor of several papers and periodicals, a charming essayist, and the champion of many important causes, he has been, for over half a century, a vital force in the literature and the intellectual life of his nation. He is also a gifted lyric poet and a dramatist of note, but his greatest contribution is in the field of fiction. His hand is never surer, his touch nowhere more delicate than in his short stories, not a few of which are masterpieces of finished art. His novels, of which he has written several, deal generally with life in Reykjavik, the capital of Iceland, during the first two decades of the present century. They are graphic and truthful pictures of society, but still more profound psychological studies. Kvaran began as a realist, and his literary method remains that of the realist. His philosophy of life, as it appears in his mature works, is on the other hand the very antithesis of the materialism and scepticism commonly associated with realism in literature. He places the emphasis on spiritual values. In his later novels particularly, as well as in some of his shorter stories, his interest in spiritualism is a dominant note. These later works of his have, as a matter of fact, been severely criticized for savouring too much of spiritualistic propaganda. Nor can it well be denied that his special views are here sometimes so much in evidence that the art of the novelist suffers. Kvaran's novels—especially *Ofurefli* (The unconquerable, 1908), *Gull* (Gold, 1911), and *Sálin vaknar* (The soul awakens, 1916)—are characterized by many great literary qualities:—skill in story-telling, sympathetic and often masterful character delineation, fluent and mellow style, at times good-naturedly humorous, but not particularly virile or striking. Perhaps its greatest quality is its sincerity; as a rule Kvaran succeeds in giving to his narrative the impression of living reality. A broad understanding, rich humanity, and a fundamental belief in the inherent goodness of man are generally characteristic of his works of fiction as of his dramas; in literary artistry the latter are, however, inferior to his best stories.

Gudmundur Fridjónsson (b. 1869), largely a self-educated man, a farmer in northern Iceland, has, despite adverse circumstances, won for himself a prominent place among present-day Icelandic writers. He is one of the leading lyric poets of the day, and has besides written a great number of essays and newspaper articles, several volumes of short stories, and one novel. Having lived all his life close to the soil, he interprets Icelandic rural life with minute knowledge and penetrating understanding. His short stories are rich in local color and in full-length portraits of the rugged and solid farm-folk of Iceland. Fridjónsson is the arch enemy of the superficialities of the city culture and the mechanization of modern life. His style is robust and original but at times not free from artificiality.

Gudmundur Magnússon (1873–1918), who

wrote mostly under the pen-name Jón Trausti, was an extremely productive writer, an essayist, a lyric poet, and a dramatist, but will longest be remembered as a novelist and a writer of short stories, attaining high rank in both these branches of literature. Intimately acquainted with rural and town life alike, he interpreted both effectively; the former in the novel *Halla* (1906) and in the series *Heidarbýlid* (The heath-farm, 1908–11); the latter notably in *Borgir* (1909). His historical novels are also noteworthy. Himself a fisherman in his earlier years, he has written excellent short stories of the life of the fishermen, splendid in characterization and breathing the atmosphere of the sea. But his literary art, particularly in his longer works, is far from flawless, and his style lacks polish; on the other hand, his narrative is vivid and fluent; he also succeeds in creating a number of strong, unforgettable characters. His descriptions and interpretations of the life of his day are a significant contribution to the cultural history of Iceland.

Jónas Jónasson (1856–1918), a clergyman, wrote historical fiction, but is more successful in his realistic, satirical short stories; he is, however, more important still as a folklorist. Jón Stefánsson (pseudonym Thorgils Gjallandi, 1851–1915), a farmer, wrote realistic stories of rural life, but achieved much greater distinction with his well-told and sympathetic stories of animals.

Icelandic fiction of the post-war period is characterized by conflicting tendencies, a commingling of the old and the new. As in the case of the lyric poetry of the period, this literature is too near to us for an objective evaluation. Of the large number of novelists that have appeared on the scene only the most prominent ones will be briefly considered. Kristín Sigfúsdóttir (b. 1876), who has written a successful stage play, *Tengdamamma* (Mother-in-law, 1923), has ably interpreted Icelandic rural life in her novels *Gestir* (Guests, 1925) and *Gömul saga* (An old story, 1927–28), especially in the first part of the latter; she has also written good short stories on similar themes. Fridrik Ásmundsson Brekkan (b. 1888) has likewise written short stories of merit. His principal work, however, is the significant historical novel *Saga af Brodur Ylfing* (The story of Brother Ylfing), which was originally published in Danish in 1924 and was well received in the Scandinavian countries; a revised translation by the author was published in Iceland in 1929. Here stirring events and impressive personalities are convincingly portrayed; the clash between the old and the new, between Paganism and Christianity is presented with deep understanding. Gudmundur Gíslason Hagalín (b. 1898) is the author of several volumes of short stories of everyday life, especially of the life of the Icelandic fishermen; splendidly told tales, revealing and sympathetic. His latest novel *Kristrún í Hamravík* (Kristrun at Hamravik, 1933), which has just come off the press, is hailed as a great stylistic achievement and an important cultural document. Halldór Kiljan Laxness (b. 1902) has already much varied literary production to his credit, including volumes of short stories on different subjects. His principal books as yet are the highly autobiographical, chaotic novel,

Vefarinn mikli frá Kasmír (The great weaver from Kashmir, 1927), and the more firmly knit two-volume serial of contemporary life, *Thú vínvidur hreini* (Thou, pure vine, 1931) and *Fuglinn í fjörunni* (The bird on the beach, 1932). Written in colorful and eloquent, although uneven style, these works are obviously the product of an author endowed with keen observation, strong power of characterization, and unusual narrative talent; but they are marred by excesses and lack of taste. Withal Laxness is unquestionably the most gifted of the younger Icelandic novelists, at least of those writing in their native tongue, and he appears certain to make a signal contribution to Icelandic fiction, especially when (as may be expected) he rids himself of the tendency to exaggeration which has detracted from the general excellence of his works to date. His great mastery of language, coupled with his psychological penetration, admirably seen in his portrayal of the soul-life of children and young people, will then appear to still greater advantage.

Many of the leading writers of short stories of the period, being at the same time the most prominent novelists, have already been mentioned. Others who have written short stories of special merit, although far apart in selection of subject-matter and literary excellence, are: Thorsteinn Erlingsson (1858–1914), Theodóra Thóroddsen, Sigurjón Fridjónsson (b. 1867), Einar Thorkelsson (b. 1867), Theodór Fridriksson (b. 1870), Sigurdur Nordal (b. 1886), Jakob Thorarensen (b. 1886), Davíd Thorvaldsson (1901–32), and Axel Thorsteinsson (b. 1895); and still others could be added to the list.

Several of the novelists considered have been essayists as well; and it is pleasant to record that this form of literature is finding increased favor in Iceland. Especially gifted essayists in addition to the ones already referred to are: Gudmundur Finnbogason (b. 1873), Sigurdur Gudmundsson (b. 1878), Sigurdur Nordal (b. 1886), and Thorbergur Thórdarson (b. 1889).

Several Icelandic authors of our day have chosen to write in foreign languages, doubtless mainly because of a desire to reach a larger circle of readers than their countrymen of some one hundred thousand. This was true of Jónas Gudlaugsson (1887–1916), who wrote three volumes of excellent lyric poetry and an equal number of widely read stories in Danish; others have followed the same course. In the forefront of Icelandic writers now living, who have thus sought a larger public through the medium of a foreign tongue, stands the novelist Gunnar Gunnarsson (b. 1889). Enormously productive, he is one of the most widely read writers in Scandinavia, and known far beyond the boundaries of the northern countries; what is more significant still, his standing as a literary artist is commensurate with his popularity, for no unbiased critic will deny him a high rank among the leading Scandinavian novelists of today. One of his most important works is the series *Borgslaegtens Historie* (The story of the Borg family, 1912–14), available in an abridged English translation under the title *Guest the one-eyed*. This is a gripping story, in particular the third volume containing the account of Guest, the mysterious wanderer, who does penance for his former sins until death releases him. A powerful theme—the regeneration of a soul steeped in crime—is here well handled. Simple but strong characterization goes here hand in hand with a graphic description of the Icelandic scene. Two of Gunnarsson's most important and most popular novels are *Edbrödre* (The sworn brothers, 1918) and *Salige ere de enfoldige* (Seven days' darkness, 1920), which have both been translated into English. The first one is a fine historical novel, noted for its effective characterization and its vivid portrayal of Old Norse culture; the other, a profound psychological study, is a very original and a highly provocative book. The strongly autobiographical five-volume series *Kirken paa Bjerget* (The church on the mountain, 1923–8) is probably, however, the author's greatest work. Gunnarsson is noted for his insight; he excels in revealing the innermost soul-life of his characters; he also possesses great technical skill, which is apparent not only in his novels but no less in his short stories; he has also tried his hand at the drama, with but moderate success.

Kristmann Gudmundsson (b. 1902) writes in Norwegian; and since his arrival in Norway ten years ago he has written, in the language of that country, a volume of short stories and seven novels, aside from a great number of sketches, stories, and articles in various papers and periodicals. He has already won for himself a high place among the younger writers of Norway. Nor is his literary recognition confined to Norway or the other northern countries; his books have been translated into many languages and have been much read. *Brudekjolen* (The bridal gown, 1927), his first novel and the only one as yet translated into English, instantly won him recognition. Against a background of scenic grandeur, the author pictures vividly the everyday life of rural Iceland, and even more the emotional life of people of strong feelings over whom traditions hold a mighty sway. Gudmundsson writes with sympathy and psychological penetration in a vigorous and varied style. His later novels, especially *Livets morgen* (The morning of life, 1929), *Den blaa kyst* (The blue coast, 1931), and *Det hellige fjell* (The holy mountain, 1932), show a marked development of his literary genius. He depicts the unfolding emotional life of young lovers particularly beautifully and delicately. Many of his short stories are also examples of high narrative art.

With his charming juvenile stories, which have reached a tremendous circulation in numerous languages, Jon Svensson (b. 1857) has gained much renown. He early left Iceland and has for years had his residence in Holland, where he is a priest of the Jesuit Order. His stories, based on his experience as a youth in Iceland and elsewhere, are written in German.

Three writers stand out in present-day Icelandic drama. Indridi Einarsson (b. 1851), an economist by training, for years state auditor and later Chief of the Bureau of Statistics for Iceland, is the oldest of these; and Icelandic dramatic art owes more to him than any other individual. The National Theatre of Iceland, now being erected at Reykjavik, is largely the result of his untiring efforts and the realization of his fondest dreams. Already while a student in college he wrote his first drama, *Nýársnóttin* (New Year's night, 1872), a romantic, lyrical play which has enjoyed great popularity. Several years after came the realistic drama *Skipid sekkur* (The ship is sinking, 1902), dealing with contemporary life; but his later plays draw their themes from history and folk-lore; of these *Sverd og bagall* (Sword and crozier, 1899) has appeared in an English translation (*Poet Lore*, Vol. XXIV, 1912). These dramas, although uneven in structure and excessively rhetorical, are frequently impressive and generally well adapted for the stage. Einarsson collaborated in an Icelandic translation of Ibsen's *Vikings of Helgeland*, and has also translated a number of Shakespeare's historical dramas and comedies (still in manuscript); then it is not surprising that his later works show influence from these giants of the drama.

The greatest Icelandic dramatist to date is Jóhann Sigurjónsson (1880–1919), the son of a farmer in northern Iceland. After spending three years in the College of Iceland, he studied veterinary science for several years in Copenhagen; whereupon he devoted his time to literary work, always his main interest: he made his home in Denmark and wrote both in Icelandic and Danish. His first play, *Dr. Rung* (1905), the tragedy of a young Copenhagen scientist, is primarily a psychological study, rich in lyric qualities, but weak dramatically. All the poet's later dramas are Icelandic in theme and setting, and he gains immeasurably by being on familiar ground. *Bóndinn á Hrauni* (The Hraun farm, 1908) is, in the revised Danish version of 1912, "a pleasant dramatic idyll of contemporary country life in Iceland"; the author's grip on his material is still uncertain, but the dialogue is effective and there are notable lyric passages.

With his *Bjaerg-Ejvind og hans Hustru* (Eyvind of the hills, 1911) Sigurjónsson reached his full dramatic power, and nowhere is his literary art greater. This stern and impassioned tragedy of the outlaw and the woman who sacrifices all to share his lot is equally notable for magnificent poetry, penetrating characterization, and stark reality. The last act, with the outlaw and his wife face to face with starvation, as the storm rages about their lonely hut in the mountain wastelands, is a masterpiece of psychological insight and dramatic art. Sigurjónsson's next drama, *Galdra-Loftur* (1915), is like *Eyvind of the hills* based on an Icelandic folk-tale, centering around an Icelandic Faust. Hence the supernatural is here a prominent element; but the drama is first and last the tragic love story of Steinunn, the heroine, and Loftur, the student of black magic, who seduces her. The clash between their temperaments and their conceptions of love becomes the central issue of the drama. Impressive as this tragedy is, it is not as firmly knit structurally as *Eyvind of the hills*, but there are some intensely dramatic scenes, passages of pure beauty, as well as splendid and delicate characterization. *Lögneren* (The liar, 1917), Sigurjónsson's last drama, is written on a theme from *Njáls saga* (The story of Burnt Njal), generally acclaimed as the greatest of the Icelandic sagas. The dramatist has in many respects succeeded in creating an impressive drama out of the old saga material; nevertheless, there is no gainsaying that his work is overshadowed by the great classic which inspired it and furnished its theme.

Considered as a whole Sigurjónsson's best works are characterized by dramatic intensity, profound understanding of the human heart, and not least by a richness of pure, exalted poetry. His *Eyvind of the hills* which has been staged in many countries and translated into a number of languages, is, together with *The Hraun farm*, available in an English translation.

Gudmundur Kamban (b. 1888) has made a name for himself as a dramatist, novelist, writer of short stories, and an essayist. As he has studied dramatic art diligently and been engaged in directing theatrical performances both in Denmark and Iceland, he has an intimate familiarity with the stage. His works have appeared both in Icelandic and Danish. He achieved a great theatrical success throughout the Scandinavian countries, especially in Copenhagen, with his *Hadda Padda* (1914). This and his next drama, *Kongeglimen* (The royal wrestling, 1915), which depict modern Icelandic life, are romantic in spirit, written on a love theme, and recall the works of Jóhann Sigurjónsson. The scene of Kamban's later dramas is laid outside of Iceland; three of these, *Marmor* (Marble, 1918), *Vi Mordere* (We murderers, 1920), and *Örkenens Stjerner* (The stars of the desert, 1925), were inspired, or at least colored, by the author's sojourn in

America (1915–17). These plays are realistic and very critical of modern society. *Vi Mordere*, a penetrating study of marriage, combines keen pscychological analysis and individualized characters with excellent dramatic technique. Justly estimated as Kamban's best drama, this play was a great success on the stage both in Copenhagen and Oslo. More genial and tempered, although akin in theme, is *De arabiske Telte* (The tents of the Arabs, 1921). The author's latest drama, *Sendiherrann frá Júpiter* (The ambassador from Jupiter, 1927), is a dramatic romance, scathing in its indictment of western culture, but too abstract for success on the stage.

Kamban's novel *Ragnar Finnsson* (1922) is a challenging and a well-constructed story, notable also for the convincing and keen character portrayal. Much more significant an achievement, however, is his historical novel, *Skálholt* (1930–32), a dramatic recreation of seventeenth-century Iceland. Although by no means a flawless production, this is a work conceived on a large scale, presenting a number of unusual, vividly portrayed persons against a colorful background. A genuine Icelander, Kamban is also a full-blooded cosmopolitan. He is a reformer much concerned about the moral and social problems of the day; he does not excel in creative power, but his mastery of dramatic form is remarkable. Of his works *Hadda Padda* alone has been translated into English.

CONCLUSION

This rapid survey of Icelandic literature down through the centuries clearly brings to light that

from the "Saga Age" to the present literary production has never ceased in Iceland. At times the
fire has burnt low, but there have always been living embers on the hearth. Every century produced
some writers of note. The ancient literature never
entirely lost its hold on the people; the voices of the
masters were never silenced altogether. In fact,
there is a marked continuity in Icelandic literature
from its beginning to our day. Moreover, as the
preceding pages indicate, the present literary production of Iceland is unusually large in proportion
to its population of but a little over one hundred
thousand. Needless to say, it is not all of high
quality. Several of the Icelandic writers of the
last fifty years have, however, in common with
many of their predecessors, added to the literature
of their country works of genuine and lasting merit,
deserving of attention beyond the shores of Iceland.
There is to be sure a good deal of uncertain groping,
experimenting, on the part of the younger Icelandic
authors; but not a few of them promise well for the
future.

Historical and philological studies are pursued
diligently in the modern land of the sagas, and increasing attention is given to investigations in the
natural and physical sciences; the stimulating influence of the recently established University of Iceland (1911) can already be seen. In the realm of
sculpture, painting, and music notable progress is
being made. Einar Jónsson (b. 1874), the sculptor,
has won wide fame for his strikingly original,
beautiful and thought-provoking works. Icelandic
painters are rapidly gaining recognition at home

and abroad, as are Icelandic composers and singers. The visitor to Iceland is impressed with the varied activity and the spirit of growth in the cultural life of the small nation inhabiting that historic island of the North.

ICELANDIC-AMERICAN LITERATURE

by

RICHARD BECK, Ph.D.

*Professor and Head of the Department of
Scandinavian Languages and Literatures
in the
University of North Dakota*

No account of Icelandic literature of the last hundred years would be complete without a mention of the contribution made by the Icelanders in America. In spite of adverse circumstances they have vigorously maintained the literary tradition of the home-land; and this literary production of theirs is all the more remarkable when one bears in mind that they are only some thirty thousand in number,* and that they have resided on this continent for only a sixty-year period. Nor must the significant fact be overlooked that they have cultivated their literary interest in the time they could spare from earning their living at various occupations, or from discharging exacting public duties. They have been prompted by love of literature and not by mercenary motives.

In Stephan G. Stephansson (1853–1927) the

---

* For material in English on the Icelanders in America, see: B. B. Jónsson, "Following Lief Ericson," in *The American-Scandinavian Review*, March–April, 1915; and Thorstina Jackson, "The Icelandic communities in America," *Publications of the Norwegian-American Historical Association*, III, 1928.

Icelandic-Americans possessed a truly great poet, unquestionably one of the greatest that Iceland has produced. At the age of twenty he migrated with his parents to America, where he was three times a pioneer. He was a farmer all his life, an entirely self-educated man. He was, however, an unusually widely read individual, and, despite the hard toil of pioneer farm-life, a prolific writer. His poems have been published in five large volumes. His production is therefore nothing short of amazing, and he wrote on a variety of subjects. His nature poems are rich in picturesque detail and deep thought. Nor are his many poems on themes from the sagas and other northern lore less forceful or less poetic. A fearless spokesman of the oppressed, he frequently found inspiration in current events. His love of Iceland and things Icelandic is one of the strongest notes in his poetry, although his interests were world-wide. His originality is one of his chief glories. His workmanship is on the whole admirable; and his language is rich, pure, and beautiful. But he is at times obscure.

Other Icelandic-American poets of merit are: Jón Runólfsson (1855–1930), Kristinn Stefánsson (1856–1916), Thorbjörn Bjarnarson (pseudonym Thorskabítur, 1859–1933), Kristján N. Júlíus (b. 1860), Jóhann Magnús Bjarnason (b. 1866), Sigurdur J. Jóhannesson (b. 1868), Magnús Markússon (b. 1868), Guttormur J. Guttormsson (b. 1878), Thorsteinn Th. Thorsteinsson (b. 1879), and Einar P. Jónsson (b. 1881). These writers, all of whom have used the Icelandic language as their medium of expression, differ, of course, in their choice and treatment of themes, and in their artistry. They represent various tendencies; and they do not, by any means, all deserve the same place as poets. They have, however, in their different ways written many fine poems. And here have only been enumerated the most worthy of those Icelandic-Americans who have published their poems in book-form. There are several others, who, in a fuller account, would have been deserving of mention. Of these Mrs. Jakobína Johnson (b. 1883) must be singled out because of the unusually high quality of her work. Runólfsson, Jóhannesson, and Jónsson have also ably translated English and American poetry into Icelandic, as has Jónas A. Sigurdsson (1865–1933), a poet in his own right.

Clearly, the Icelanders have not lost their appreciation of poetry or their ability to write verse when they migrated to new shores. Guttormur J. Guttormsson, one of the most virile and original of the group of poets mentioned, the only one born on this continent, is also the author of a volume of one-act dramas, profound in thought and generally strikingly distinctive in theme and dramatic method.*

Although a few Icelandic-Americans have tried

---

* Richard Beck, the author of this section on Icelandic literature, is, himself, among the Icelandic poets in America. Born (1897) and reared in Iceland, with the A.B. degree from the State College of Iceland, he holds the degrees of Master of Arts and Doctor of Philosophy from Cornell University and since 1929 has been Professor and Head of the Department of Scandinavian Languages and Literatures in the University of North Dakota. Parallel with his scholarly publications, he has carried on the composition of his original poems in Icelandic, of which he has published a collection, *Ljóðmál* (Songs, Winnipeg, 1929). He is a frequent contributor of original poems to Icelandic, Icelandic-American, Norwegian-American, and American publications.—ED.

their hand at writing poetry in English, Laura Goodman Salverson (born in Winnipeg, of Icelandic parentage, 1890) is the first, and so far the only one, to have published a volume of original poems in that language—*Wayside gleams* (Toronto, 1925), containing poems of considerable literary value. Christopher Johnston (d. 1927), an Icelander by birth, contributed a number of delicately wrought lyrics to Canadian and American papers.

Several Icelandic-Americans, including Johnston, have on the other hand devoted themselves to the translation of Icelandic poetry into English, with varying success. Among these Mrs. Jakobína Johnson excels particularly, having to her credit a large number of excellent translations. Gudmundur J. Gíslason (1877–1934), Runólfur Félsted (1879–1921), Vilhjálmur Stefánsson (b. 1879), Skúli Johnson (b. 1888), and Páll Bjarnason (b. 1882) have also made a name for themselves as translators of Icelandic poetry; and still others could be mentioned. Mrs. Johnson has in addition translated several significant Icelandic dramas into English (still in manuscript).

The creative literary interest of the Icelanders in America has to date primarily found expression in lyric poetry. The prose writers are much fewer in number than the lyric poets, although some Icelandic-American authors have, as might be expected, cultivated both the literary forms in question.

Of Icelandic-American authors of fiction, writing in Icelandic, Jóhann Magnús Bjarnason, already listed among the lyric poets, has been by far the most productive and is in some ways the most gifted. His works have been much read by his countrymen on both sides of the Atlantic. He has written several interesting, often highly romantic novels, abounding in vividly described and peculiar characters. Better constructed, generally speaking, and hence more effective artistically are many of his short stories, of which he has published a large number. He is also the author of numerous beautiful fairy-tales; here as elsewhere the strength of his narrative art lies in its simplicity and sincerity. Besides their literary value, Bjarnason's prose works have considerable cultural-historical significance, as they are graphic pictures of Icelandic pioneer life in America.

Besides Bjarnason the following Icelanders in America have written noteworthy short stories: Gunnsteinn Eyjólfsson (1866–1910), Thorsteinn Th. Thorsteinsson, Jóhannes P. Pálsson (b. 1881) and Gudrún H. Finnsdóttir (b. 1884). Aside from Guttormur J. Guttormsson (see above) Pálsson is the only Icelandic-American dramatist of consequence, the author of several thought-provoking one-act plays.

Several of the lyric poets and prose writers already referred to have also written, in the Icelandic language, articles and essays of literary merit. This is equally true of a number of the Icelandic clergymen in America, notably Jón Bjarnason (1845–1914), Fridrik J. Bergmann (1858–1918), Björn B. Jónsson (b. 1870), Rögnvaldur Pétursson (b. 1877), and Guttormur Guttormsson (b. 1880). Bjarnason's

Icelandic translation of Lewis Wallace's *Ben Hur* (1911–12) is a notable achievement.

Writing in English, Laura Goodman Salverson has gained literary recognition for a number of well-written short stories which have appeared in various Canadian publications. She is also the author of three full-length novels, of which *The viking heart* (1923), though uneven in excellence, was very favourably received. This is a story of Icelandic pioneer life in Canada, told with not a little understanding and sympathy.

Bogi Bjarnason (b. 1888), a journalist by profession, has written able short stories and sketches. In Baldur Jónson (1887–1917), who left a small volume of charming and highly individualistic essays, *Leaves and letters* (Wynyard, Saskatchewan, 1918), Icelandic-American and Canadian literature lost a writer of uncommon promise. John G. Holme (1877–1922), a very gifted journalist, for a period city editor of the *New York Evening Post*, was also an essayist of no mean ability.

Vilhjálmur Stefánsson, the son of Icelandic pioneers in Manitoba, who has already been mentioned as translator of Icelandic poetry, has won wide fame as a brilliant writer no less than as an intrepid and resourceful explorer. His many books and numerous articles on his experiences and explorations in the Arctic, and on other subjects, reveal the master of varied and vigorous style as well as the keen observer.

In proportion to their small population the Icelanders in America have, during their sojourn of sixty years on this continent, published a surprisingly large number of papers and periodicals, although only a few are now in existence. These have, in varying degree, maintained and stimulated literary interest among their readers.

It should be noted that many of the writers mentioned reside or resided in Canada; hence in a more restricted sense their production may be termed Icelandic-Canadian.

As in the case of Norwegian-American literature, and the same doubtless holds true of other foreign literatures in this country, it is to be regretted that only a small part of the best things which have been produced by Icelandic-American writers is accessible to the English-speaking reader.

FINNISH LITERATURE

FINNISH LITERATURE

by

RICHARD BECK, Ph.D.

*Professor and Head of the Department of
Scandinavian Languages and Literatures
in the
University of North Dakota*

THE TWO NATIONAL LANGUAGES

ALTHOUGH belonging racially to the Finno-
Ugrian group, the Finns are generally included
among the Scandinavian nations because of their
close political and cultural connection with Sweden
for centuries (1154–1809). During this period
Swedish became the official language and continued
as such under Russian rule (1809–1917). Nevertheless, the Finnish tongue was by no means forgotten; it was not only preserved by the native
Finnish population, but on frequent occasions it
was permitted and used in the courts of the land.
It was not, however, until 1841 that Finnish was
taught generally in the lower schools. In 1902 it
was established on an equal level with Swedish as
an official language. The National Movement in
Finland, which gathered strength after 1809, although its beginnings can be traced much farther
back, came to a climax in the declaration of Finnish
independence in 1917. With the growing national

consciousness of the Finns, the demand for the pre-
dominance of the Finnish language has increased
apace; the two languages, Finnish and Swedish, are
as yet, however, "the national languages of the Republic," the former being spoken by a vastly larger
number of the population.

As a result of the two languages existing side by
side in Finland for centuries, one finds there two
literatures, Finnish and Swedish. Withal, the works
of the writers of Finland, whether in Finnish or
Swedish, are generally characteristic productions of
the soil and the environment.

LITERATURE IN FINNISH *

During the Middle Ages a rich and varied folk-
poetry, in the Finnish language, flourished in Finland, but no written literature in Finnish has come
down from that period. The Reformation, to combat Catholicism whose language was Latin, succeeded in bringing about a rebirth in Finland of
the national language for literary purposes. Bishop
Mikael Agricola (c. 1508–57), the pioneer in the
field, contributed notably to this movement by
translating the New Testament, which was published in 1548, and by publishing an *A-B-C book*
(1542), *The catechism* (1543), *The book of
prayers* (1544), and *The book of hymns* (1551),
all in the Finnish language. The work of Agricola

---

* Strictly speaking, of course, Finnish literature in Finnish is not a
Scandinavian literature, since Finnish is not a Scandinavian language. However works written by Finns in Finnish as well as in Swedish are here included
for the sake of completeness and because, as previously stated, Finland though
not racially and nationally one of the Scandinavian countries is generally
mentioned among them for historical, cultural and geographical reasons.
—Ed.

was continued and developed by other writers of the sixteenth century. Bishop Ericus Erici (c. 1545–1625) materially strengthened the progress of the movement with the publication (in 1621 and 1625) of a large collection of sermons in Finnish, a work which was widely used and highly valued for a period of nearly two centuries. A Finnish translation of the whole Bible appeared in 1642. During the seventeenth and the eighteenth centuries, on the other hand, poetry in the Finnish language consisted in occasional and religious poems of no literary significance.

In the second half of the eighteenth century the figure that stands out is that of Henrik Gabriel Porthan (1739–1804), who, though not writing in Finnish, held high the flame of his nationalistic faith until with the treaty of Tilsit (1809) Finland passed under a new master. Porthan prepared the groundwork upon which later the Finnish Literature Society was founded through the work of three great writers: Lönnrot, Runeberg, Snellman. With his pioneer studies in Finnish folk-poetry Porthan aroused interest in this remarkable and extensive oral literature, an interest which grew strong after 1809 and bore fruit in the works of many of the Finnish romantic poets, who not only paid much attention to the folk-literature of their country, but also wished to create written literature in the Finnish language.

The first notable collection of Finnish folk-poems was published (1822–31) by Zachris Topelius (the elder, 1781–1831), the father of the famed poet. His work was carried on with great energy by Elias Lönnrot (1802–84), who was untiring in collecting a vast number of Finnish folk-songs, which still lived on the lips of the people in the country-districts, and who accomplished the still greater task of weaving these songs together into the impressive epic *Kalevala* (1835), justly called "the national epos of Finland," ranking with the world's greatest works of its kind. The English-speaking reader will get an idea of its stylistic effectiveness, its haunting sonorousness, by turning to the excellent English translations by Crawford and Kirby, or to Longfellow's *Hiawatha*, which, at least in verse form, is definitely imitative of the Finnish classic. Needless to say, the publication of the *Kalevala* gave a fresh impetus to the awakened interest in the Finnish language and to the development of literature in that tongue. Lönnrot also collected and edited (1840) significant lyric folk poems (*Kanteletar*). He was also the first secretary and during a long period the most zealous worker of the Finnish Literature Society which was founded in Helsingfors in 1831 and has with its numerous publications contributed greatly to the revival of interest in the Finnish language and Finnish traditions. Since 1841 it has published the valuable annual *Suomi*.

No great poets, writing in Finnish, appeared, however, during the first half of the nineteenth century; the three most worthy of attention are: Jakob Judén (original Finnish name Juteini, 1781–1855), Abraham Poppius (1793–1866), and Samuel Gustaf Bergh (pseudonym Kallio, 1803–53). Besides these there were a number of unschooled poets, "folk-poets" one might call them, who wrote on contemporary themes in the old ballad style. Foremost of these was Paavo Korhonen (1775–1840) whose poems were published by the Finnish Literature Society in 1848.

For a period the progress of literature in Finnish was retarded by the censure ordinance of 1850 which restricted the publication in that language to books on religious and economic subjects. In 1863 this decree was annulled and Finnish gradually gained the same position in public life as Swedish, a change which was likewise accompanied by greater political freedom generally. Since then Finnish literature has flourished vigorously, original productions as well as numerous translations. Periodicals and papers also grew rapidly in number.

August Ahlquist (pseudonym A. Oksanen, 1826–89) and Julius Krohn (pseudonym Suonio, 1835–88), who wrote in the spirit of the great national poets Runeberg and Topelius and emphasized artistry of form and purity of language, became the forerunners of the great poets of the next generation. Ahlquist was especially active in the interest of the purification of the Finnish language.

Important as these writers were, the first truly great figure in modern Finnish literature is A. Stenvall (pseudonym Aleksis Kivi, 1834–72), the son of a village tailor. A writer of original genius, potent imagination, and marvellous style, he is the author of the first important drama in the Finnish language, an excellent comedy of peasant life, *The parish cobblers* (1864). His greatest work is, nevertheless, the novel *Seitsemän veljestä* (Seven brothers, 1870), in which one does not know whether to admire more the vigorous realism or the delightfully harmonious style. This classic of Finnish peasant life, where the real and the allegorical mingle effectively, appeared in an English translation in 1929. "It is symbolic of the struggles of man to subdue the intractable forces of nature, both in the world around him and in his own breast. Kivi selects the moment when the wild nomadic life of half civilized man is being transformed into the more disciplined life of a civilized community. Man has to break in wild nature with a plough and force the desert to produce crops for his use, and he has to break his own self-willed soul, as one breaks in a wild horse" (Arthur Reade). Hence, *Seven brothers* is a work possessing a strong universal appeal. Kivi also wrote highly personal lyric poetry of distinguished quality. He contributed immeasurably to the development of Finnish prose style.

Finnish literary men of note, contemporary with Kivi, or nearly so, were the dramatist Kaarlo Bergbom (1843–1906), remembered especially as the founder and first director of the Finnish national theatre, the lyric poets J. H. Erkko (1849–1906), Paavo Cajander (1846–1913), Arvi Genetz (pseudonym Jännes, 1848–1915), and Kaarlo Kramsu (1855–95). Erkko, noted for his patriotic poems, is also a dramatist who has written on themes from the *Kalevala*. Cajander has rendered several of Shakespeare's dramas excellently into Finnish. Jännes is the author of a masterful Finnish translation of Runeberg's famous poem *The elk-hunters*.

The naturalistic tendency of the eighties found two important representatives in Minna Canth (1844–97) and Juhani Brofeldt (pseudonym, Juhani Aho, 1861–1921). Canth, an unusually gifted authoress, wrote novels, but was primarily a dramatist who dealt forcefully and frankly with the social problems of her time, an untiring spokesman of her sisters in bondage and the labouring class. Her works savour at times too much of propaganda, but more often, because of their sincerity and truthfulness, rise to the level of genuine literature.

Aho was the son of a rural clergyman and simplicity of life was ever characteristic of him. He began his writing with very realistic stories of Finnish peasant life, turning later to descriptions of the life of the wealthier classes. A sojourn in Paris (1889), where he made a thorough study of the literary methods of leading French writers, influenced his writing profoundly and beneficially, making it more direct and concentrated. This is clearly seen in his important series of short stories and sketches *Chips* (1891–1921), greatly varied in subject-matter, many of which are masterpieces of literary art, containing superb pages worthy of the greatest literature of the world. Among Aho's novels the gripping story *Outlawed* (1890) reveals his narrative power at its height. With tragic intensity and concentration he depicts here the struggle against the social environment of an individual seeking self-realization. Aho's cultural-historical novel *Panu* (1897) interprets penetratingly the conflict between paganism and Christianity in mediaeval Finland. As a distinguished Finnish

literary critic has observed, Aho's greatness consists in his psychological portrayal and his lyric
moods. Culturally and historically his works are
also of first importance as they reveal truthfully
the temper and the conflicting tendencies of Finnish life in later years. A brilliant stylist, Aho may,
together with Kivi, be looked upon as the father of
modern Finnish prose.

Other writers of note belonging to the eighties
are Hjalmar Nortamo (pseudonym Nordling, b.
1860), a humorist; the novelist Arvid Järnefelt
(1861–1932), a profound psychologist, who, influenced by Tolstoi, dealt largely with social questions; Teuvo Pakkala (1862–1925), who in dramas
and stories described masterfully the life of the
proletariat in the small towns, but is still better
known for his excellent children's books; Santeri
Ivalo (original Finnish name Ingman, b. 1866),
author of historical novels; and the lyric poet, Kasi-
mir Leino (1866–1919).

A group of special interest are a number of realistic writers of Finnish peasant life who were themselves peasants. The first and most important of
these was Pietari Päivärinta (1827–1913), who
late in life, while he was confined to bed with a
broken leg, wrote his highly autobiographical and
vivid novel of peasant life, *Elämäni* (My life,
1877), which was followed by other, though less
successful, works of similar nature. Several authors
carried on this tradition, including the gifted Santeri Alkio (b. 1862) and Heikki Kauppinen (pseudonym Kauppis-Heikki, 1862–1920).

Various literary tendencies, such as realism and

[298]

neo-romanticism, are represented in the works of the numerous Finnish writers who have appeared since the turn of the century.

A worthy successor of Kivi and Aho was Vihtori Peltonen (pseudonym Johannes Linnankoski, 1869–1913) who won wide fame with his novel *The song of the blood-red flower* (1905), which has been translated into many languages. Nevertheless, in *The fugitives* (1908) a novel of peasant life, the author reaches greater heights artistically. Linnankoski was a poet of genuine feeling and imagination, a writer of brilliant style.

Of a considerable number of women prose-writers four especially deserve attention. Maila Mikkola (pseudonym Maila Talvio, b. 1871) has written several realistic novels about both the life of the peasants and the upper classes. A strain of optimism, however, runs through her works and the characterization is often highly romantic. Hilja Haahti (b. 1874) began her career as a writer of lyric poems, but her chief productions have been in prose. All her writings are characterized by a religious and patriotic spirit. The *Israelin tyttäret* (1903) is her most finished work artistically. Her style is flowing and she has gained wide favor especially for her writings for the youth. Aino Kallas (b. 1878) has published a number of well-written short stories descriptive of life in Estonia and eastern Finland. Maria Jotuni (b. 1880) has written effective stories and dramas characterized by pronounced realism, one might well say naturalism, and robust humour.

Akin in spirit and literary treatment are the

novels of Joel Lehtonen (b. 1881), a poet of great gifts. Other contemporary prose-writers of note are Ilmari Kianto (b. 1874) who has written stories of rural life; Volter Kilpi (b. 1874), whose delicately wrought stories are highly symbolic, and Kyösti Wilkuna (1879–1922), author of several historical novels.

Of the younger prose-writers Frans Emil Sillanpää (b. 1888) is the most important, having to his credit novels as well as several collections of short stories. He excels in psychological insight and in nature descriptions, and succeeds admirably in picturing the everyday life of the peasant. All these qualities are marked characteristics of his beautiful though tragic novel *Silja* (1931), which was published in an English translation in 1933. The heroine, the peasant girl Silja, is a figure which lingers long in the reader's memory.

Among the leading novelists of the youngest group is Mika Valtari (b. 1908).

Foremost among the recent poets writing in Finnish stands Eino Leino (1878–1926), an amazingly productive author, who wrote novels, short stories, and literary studies, besides several collections of verse. He did noteworthy work in all these branches of literature, but his many-sided genius found its fullest and finest expression in his lyric poetry, which covers an unusually wide range of themes. Among other significant literary productions he has translated Goethe's *Iphigenia* and Dante's *Divine Comedy* into Finnish. Leino had a large share in the new development of the language and form of Finnish poetry.

Besides Leino, modern Finland possesses several other lyric poets of established reputation. Otto Manninen (b. 1872) has written poetry of a high order, which combines deep personal feeling and masterful form. By his numerous and important translations, including the *Iliad* and the *Odyssey*, and Molière's comedies, he has rendered Finnish literature inestimable service. Kyösti Larsson (pseudonym Larin-Kyösti, b. 1873) is another gifted and prolific poet who has won great popularity. V. A. Koskenniemi (b. 1885), first a professor of literature and later rector of the University of Turku, has written poetry notable for its intellectual quality and finished form and is considered Finland's best living poet. A mention may be made of Juhani Siljo (1888–1918), whose promising literary career was cut short in the World War, and of the poetess Hilja Madetoja (pseudonym L. Onerva, b. 1882), who is one of Finland's most versatile and prolific woman writers of today, having written successful novels and dramas aside from collections of poetry; but her genius burns brightest in her lyrics.

Among the many Finnish poets who have produced distinguished works during the last few years the following are outstanding: Erkki Kivijärvi (b. 1882; *Heinäkuu*, 1920); Heikki Välisalmi (b. 1886; *Talven maassa*, 1922); Hugo Jalkanen (b. 1888; *Kuutamo-oodi*, 1914); Einari Vuorela (b. 1889; *Kullanhuuhtoja*, 1932); Lauri Pohjanpää (b. 1889; *Poems*, 1910–35); Viljo Kojo (b. 1891; *Talvikuva*, 1919); Aaro Helakoski (b. 1893; *Poems*, 1920–35); Katri Vala (b. 1901; *Paluu*,

1924); Yrjö Jylhä (b. 1903, *Runon pursi,* 1934); and Uuno Kailas (1901–33) whose tender, brooding and melancholy, yet beautifully wrought, poems assure him a permanent niche in the gallery of Finnish poets.

LITERATURE IN SWEDISH

The beginnings of Swedish literature in Finland are associated with the monastery at Nådendal where the monk Jöns Budde (d. about 1500), the leading writer in Finland during the Middle Ages, translated and revised several religious books between 1484 and 1491. His works are particularly significant from a linguistic point of view.

The pioneer poet in Finland, writing in Swedish, was, on the other hand, Sigfrid Aronus Forsius (c. 1550–1624), clergyman and astronomer, who wrote poetry as well as almanacs and scientific works. The founding of the Academy at Åbo (1640) and the establishment there of the first printing press in Finland (1642) greatly encouraged the development of Swedish literature in Finland. Olof Vexionius (1656–90) was the first Finn to publish a collection of original poems. A poet of much greater gifts was Torsten Rudén (1661–1729) whose love poetry and occasional poems were in great favour at the time. Jakob Chronander (d. 1694) was the pioneer dramatist, his student comedies possessing considerable merit. Mystery and morality plays also were written.

Finland's first significant poet was, however, Jakob Frese (1690–1729), at best in his deeply felt personal lyrics, who like his country's leading poet of the next generation, Gustav Philip Creutz (cf. Swedish section), resided in Sweden. Creutz' foremost work, the pastoral poem *Atis and Camilla* (1761) is a charming story of youthful love clothed in language of rare beauty.

As already referred to in the discussion of Finnish literature in the Finnish language, the central figure in the cultural life of Finland during the latter half of the eighteenth century was the historian Henrik Gabriel Porthan, who not only did pioneer work in his chosen field, but exerted as well a profound influence on literature. He was one of the founders of the cultural and literary society "Aurora" at Åbo, and the first editor-in-chief of its publication, Finland's first literary magazine. He was also the pioneer in scientific study and treatment of Finnish folk-poetry. Through his varied and far-reaching cultural and literary activities he aroused the Finnish national feeling, which was of fundamental importance for the progress of his country after 1809.

A number of Finnish poets, younger contemporaries of Porthan's, were influenced by him, including the gifted satirist and critic J. H. Kellgren (cf. Swedish section), and the still more important Frans Michael Franzén (cf. Swedish section), whose earlier poems, from the last decade of the eighteenth century, are the high-water mark of pre-romantic Swedish poetry. His poem in memory of Gustav Philip Creutz combines in a rare degree originality and imaginative quality, and won for its author the coveted prize of the Swedish Academy. Mikael Choraeus (1774–

1806), a versatile writer, was in turn an admirer and imitator of Franzén, although far below his master in ability and artistry.

During the first quarter of the nineteenth century Swedish poetry in Finland was, generally speaking, of an inferior quality, highly imitative. Worthiest of inclusion are the three poets J. G. Linsén (1785–1848), A. I. Arwidsson (1791–1858), and A. G. Sjöström (1794–1846); much more important than the poetry of these writers was, however, the contribution made by them toward a further strengthening of the Finnish national feeling, and here they were building on the solid foundation laid by their predecessors, particularly Porthan.

After these "lean years" came the "golden age" of Swedish literature in Finland (1830–63). Helsingfors, where the University had been located following the fire at Åbo in 1827, now became the literary centre. Finland's great masters of Swedish verse and prose, Runeberg and Topelius (cf. Swedish section), blazed forth on the literary horizon, producing one masterful work after another, Runeberg finding for his lyric and narrative genius a classic expression in a number of poems, including the incomparable cycle *Fänrik Ståls sägner* (The songs of Ensign Stål, 1848 and 1860). He also gave to Finland its beautiful national anthem *Vårt land* (Our land), which breathes lofty idealism and patriotism of the noblest kind. Topelius embodied his romantic spirit and love of the ideal in mellow and musical lyrics, and in his great historical prose work, *Fältskärns berättelser* (Tales of an army surgeon, 1851–66), not to forget his masterful books for children.

Other poets of the period are J. J. Nervander (1805–48), who early forsook poetry for science; Rafael Hertzberg (1805–96), who earned for himself great popularity with his poems and stories as well as with his able translations of Old Finnish folk-literature; Fredrik Cygnaeus (1807–81), a many-sided and gifted lyric poet, but primarily remembered as Finland's first great literary critic, and Lars Stenbäck (1811–70), whose poetry is aflame with intense feeling.

Women writers of that day who, besides labouring diligently for the emancipation of women, made a name for themselves in literature, are Fredrika Runeberg (1807–79), wife of the poet, who wrote short stories and historical novels; Vilhelmina Nordström (1815–1902) and Adelaide Ehrnrooth (1826–1905).

Johan Vilhelm Snellman (1806–81) is remembered as his country's first notable publicist, a champion of Finnish national feeling and Finnish language.

Of writers appearing about the middle of the nineteenth century two in particular deserve to be remembered: Emil von Quanten (1827–1903), author of the widely known and popular song *Suomis sång,* and Josef Julius Wecksell (1838–1907), a truly gifted poet, whose tragedy *Daniel Hjort* (1862) is a work of lasting importance in Swedish-Finnish dramatic literature.

The foremost literary representative of the eighties was Karl August Tavaststjerna (1860–

98), author of distinguished prose and poetry. His story *Childhood friends* (1886) is the first realistic novel written in Swedish in Finland. With his drama *Affairs* (1890) he similarly introduced literary realism to the Swedish stage of his country. His novel *Hard times* (1891) is, nevertheless, his most successful and most mature prose work, equally remarkable for excellent characterization and great narrative skill.

A thoroughgoing naturalist and a very productive writer was J. Ahrenberg (1847–1914), whose best stories portray eastern Finland. To the last decade of the century also belong the dramatist Gustaf von Numers (1848–1916), the lyric poets V. K. E. Wichmann (b. 1856) and Jonatan Reuter (b. 1859), the novelist Helena Westermarck (b. 1857), the poet and story-writer A. Slotte (1861–1927), and the writer of short stories Konni Zilliacus (1855–1924). Werner Söderhjelm (1859–1931) was the most important literary critic of Finland during the last decade of the nineteenth century and the first years of the twentieth.

A worthy successor of Topelius and Tavaststjerna was Mikael Lybeck (1864–1925), whose numerous works in verse and prose, poems, dramas, and novels, reveal deep seriousness and whose literary form is marked by classic restraint. Realism and symbolism both are in evidence in his works, and he is capable of penetrating psychological interpretation.

About the turn of the century a number of gifted writers appeared on the scene, many of whose works are coloured by the political and social conflicts of the day. Hjalmar Procopé (1868–1927) has written several volumes of poems, whose chief characteristics are simplicity, sincerity, mastery of form, and pronounced intellectual quality. Impressive and forceful patriotic poems and charming descriptions abound in his production. Arvid Mörne (b. 1876) has taken an active part in the political and social struggle, but owes his place in the modern Swedish literature of Finland especially to his vivid and deeply felt poems dealing with the life and the scenery of the Swedish-speaking coast-districts of Finland; he is also a novelist and dramatist of note. Bertel Gripenberg (b. 1878) won already with his first volume of poems in 1903 a high place among modern Swedish-Finnish poets, a position which his later work has more than justified. He is the master of an unusually rhythmical and sonorous verse, the sonnet being one of his favourite forms. His earlier poems written in the spirit of the enjoyment of the passing hour are characterized by erotic passion. His later poems breathe, on the contrary, a deep feeling for the stern beauty of the interior of Finland and a worship of heroic deeds. Many of Gripenberg's poems deal directly with the social and political conflicts of the time, praising the fight waged by the few against the many. He has translated into Swedish Oscar Wilde's *The ballad of Reading Gaol* and Edgar Lee Master's *Spoon River anthology*.

Nino Runeberg (pseudonym Alceste, b. 1874) has written a drama of merit, but his chief literary contribution is his lyric poetry, often possessing charming folk-song quality. Jacob Tegengren (b.

1875) is noted for his nature and religious poetry. Richard Malmberg (pseudonym Gustav Alm, b. 1877) has written well-told, highly ironic novels of modern life and excellent short stories. Emil Zilliacus (b. 1878) has to his credit poetry notable for its clear, classic form, while Joel Rundt (b. 1879) excels in nature-descriptions. Josefina Bengts (1875–1925), Hugo Ekholm (pseudonym Hugo Ekhammer (b. 1880) and Henrik Hildén (b. 1884) have written truthful and effective stories about the life of the common people in various parts of Finland.

Gustaf Mattson (1873–1914), a leading publicist and editor, is the author of travel books remarkable for their artistry of style, keen observation and rich humour. John William Nylander (b. 1869) has written colourful and realistic sea stories, and Eirik Hornborg (b. 1879) an educator, author, and influential political figure, has written novels also dealing with the life of seafaring men and historical subjects.

Yrjö Hirn (b. 1870), a brilliant aesthetician, literary historian, and essayist, has written a number of noteworthy works in those fields and is a personality of great significance in the cultural life of present-day Finland. Other literary critics of consequence are Emil Hasselblatt (b. 1874), Gunnar Castrén (b. 1878), Olaf Homén (b. 1879), Torsten Söderhjelm (1879–1907), and John Landquist (b. 1881).

Since the beginning of the twentieth century a large number of able and in some cases unusually gifted writers have augmented the already large group of Swedish-Finnish authors. Ture Janson (b. 1886) is primarily a novelist and writer of short stories, charming in their perfection of style and fine irony. Sigrid Backman (b. 1886) has aroused attention with her novels which combine realistic descriptions and romantic character-portrayal.

By far the most outstanding of these younger Finnish prose-writers, and without any doubt one of the greatest writers of Swedish prose in Finland, is Runar Schildt (1888–1925). His short stories and dramas are notable for their excellence of style, psychological penetration, and deep human sympathy. The weak and forgotten have in him a most sympathetic spokesman. Along with Lybeck, Schildt is the leading dramatist in modern Swedish-Finnish literature.

In the group of younger lyric poets Jarl Hemmer (b. 1893) holds the place of honour. He is a richly endowed poet, whose love of beauty and enthusiasm express themselves in melodious and vigorous poems. He has also proved himself a talented prose-writer.

Other contemporary lyric poets are Greta Langenskjöld (b. 1889), Erik Grotenfeld (1891–1919), and Ragnar Ekelund (b. 1892). Modernism and expressionism have their representatives in Edith Södergran (1892–1923), and Elmer Diktonius (b. 1896); a similar tendency is found in the short stories and essays of Hagar Olsson (b. 1893).

Clearly much literary activity is going on in

Finland in both the Swedish and the Finnish languages, an activity notable both for its richness and variety, with the Finnish element rapidly gaining ground.

FINNISH-AMERICAN LITERATURE

by

GEORGE SJÖBLOM
Formerly Editor of Valvoja *and*
New Yorkin Uutiset

COMING from a country which, in the opinion
of many observers of note,* is among the most
advanced and progressive in Europe today, it is
quite natural that Finns in America should have
built up a literature of their own. In this endeavour
they have had some things in their favour, while certain other considerations are against them. Among
the favourable circumstances is the fact that there
has been no obstacle of illiteracy to be overcome,
Finns being among the most literate people in the
world; and the fact that the Finns in America have
brought with them one of the outstanding habits
of their homeland: reading.

On the other hand, the very uniqueness of the
Finnish language tends to limit the literary output,
as the publishers must face the fact that their po-
tential book-buying public cannot be found outside the group of some three hundred and fifty
thousand Finnish-Americans. For while the literature of Finland is partly in Swedish and partly in

* For example, see: Cecil Gray in his monograph *Sibelius*, Oxford Univer-
sity Press, 1931; T. W. Atchley, *Finland*, London, 1931; Eugene van Cleef,
Finland, the republic farthest north, Columbus, Ohio, 1929; Agnes Rothery,
Finland, the new nation, New York, 1936.

Finnish, that of the Finnish-Americans is practically all in Finnish, except for a few works in English. The publishers, therefore, are not willing to take such risks as can be assumed by American or even by Scandinavian publishing houses, with their wider fields. And even with all their prudence our publishers * have found that the production of books is an unprofitable business, that it is, in fact, possible only as a sideline to newspaper publishing. Another negative feature is that the readers of Finnish usually follow the flourishing literature of Finland itself, the variety and quality of which is such that only the most intrepid of the Finnish-American *littérateurs* can consider attempting to keep abreast of it.

There have been, however, upward of fifty authors among the Finns in America since the beginning of the "modern immigration" of Finns in the 1870's. (There are no records of writers among the early Finnish colonists who helped to wrest the Delaware valley from the wilderness in the seventeenth century.) In the limited space at our disposal, it is obviously impossible to try to encompass the output of these fifty or more writers with adequate factual and critical observations. We must content ourselves with mentioning their names and giving a general idea of the nature of their work.

In the field of fiction the following names are outstanding: Akseli Rauanheimo (1871–1932),

* The principal publishers of the books mentioned in this section, as well as of other books by Finnish-American authors, are the Finnish Lutheran Book Concern, Hancock, Mich.; Carl H. Salminen, Duluth, Minn.; the Finnish Newspaper Company, 4418 8th Avenue, Brooklyn, N. Y.; and the Raivaaja Publishing Company, Fitchburg, Mass.

Johannes Virtanen (b. about 1895), Kalle Potti (1871–1935), Sara Röyhy (b. 1852– ?), E. A. Hedman (b. 1866), John Lauttamus (b. 1870), John Parkkila (b. 1885), William Risto (b. about 1885), John E. Rantamäki (editor of *Amerikan Suometar*, Hancock, Mich., b. 1889), Hillevi Koski (b. 1890), Helmi Kangas,* Matti Herneshuhta, Eva Vitkala and Antti Aho.

Perhaps many of the stories by these authors would scarcely stand the test of expert criticism. Most of them are noticeably subjective and analytical; the authors seldom write purely for the sake of entertainment. The majority of the stories are somewhat fictionized memoirs or chronicles about the life in the Finnish communities, both known and remote: yarns about miners, lumber-jacks, farmers, and mill-workers, who must struggle anew for their existence in a strange land; their peculiar problems, their hopes and frustrations, their indomitable courage or long-suffering patience and their quotas of successes and failures (Risto, Hedman, Lauttamus, Potti). A few of the writers (notably Röyhy, Vitkala, Kangas and Koski) have more or less completely forsaken all realism and permitted their fancies to soar unrestrainedly into romance and adventure.

The historical novel was successfully attempted by Akseli Rauanheimo, a remarkably versatile newspaperman who was appointed Consul General of Finland in Montreal, Canada, some time after Fin-

* The majority of biographical dates appearing in this section have not been previously published and have therefore called for special investigation. It is regretted that in a few cases dates have had to be omitted because unobtainable.—ED.

land had become an independent country. *Uuteen maailmaan* (1921), among his many books, is a partly imaginative, partly strictly factual account of the experiences of the first groups of Finns who landed on or near the site of the present city of Philadelphia in 1640 and subsequent years. Mr. Rauanheimo later rewrote the book in English under the title of *Before William Penn* (1929). He considered his principal work to be *Canadan kirja* (1930), a volume regarding the Finns in Canada.

Humour apparently has not been an especially favored *métier* of the Finnish writers. However, Kalle Potti seasoned his home-spun stories with considerable robust humour. Trenchant political essays have been published by some of our Left Wing writers [Kurikka (1863–1915), Mäkelä (1862–c. 1932), Hahl (1879–1928), Alanne (b. 1879), Laukki (b. 1880), Nuorteva (c. 1880–c. 1929), Tainio], although most of their products are serious political and sociological dissertations [John Kock (1861–1915), Tokoi (b. 1873), Syrjälä (1880–1931), J. A. Mustonen].

Whether due to their inheritance of the traditions of the *Kalevala* or not, the Finnish writers have been especially prolific in producing poetry. Such poets as Eetu Aaltio (1873–c. 1926), Eenokki Pohja (c. 1858–1930), J. A. Antila (1861–1920, who published his first volume of poems in 1890), Evert Määttälä (1876–1936), Aku Päiviö (b. 1880), Matti Antila (b. 1881), Aku and Kalle Rissanen (b. 1881), Antti Lepistö (b. 1883), Adolf Lundqvist (b. 1886), Hugo Hillilä (b. 1888), Kalle Haapakoski (first volume published in 1892), Matti

Johnson, Eemeli Parras, and a score of others have had their poems published in book form, while a far greater number have contributed verses to newspapers and magazines. (There are some fifteen Finnish-language newspapers being published in the United States, four dailies and the rest tri-weeklies, bi-weeklies and weeklies; and two in Canada.)

Among poets, Emil Tolonen (b. 1885) deserves special mention inasmuch as he has used the English language as his medium with remarkable results (*Daybreak and other poems*, Helsinki, Finland, 1929; *Sylvia*, 1930).

Another writer who has made a successful *début* into literary fields in English is Elizabeth Eastman (b. 1905), a second-generation American Finn, whose *Sun on their shoulders* (1934) had an unusually favourable reception from the American press. As a pioneer in the use of English in a novel she was preceded by Carl Wilhelmson with his *Midsummernight* (1930).

In the field of research and educational literature the Finns in America have made a promising beginning. Of the works written in Finnish, Salomon Ilmonen (b. 1871), a clergyman of Fort Bragg, California, deserves precedence with his *Amerikan suomalaisten historia* (History of the Finns in America, I–III, 1917–23) and *Amerikan suomalaisten sivistyshistoria* (History of Finnish-American culture, I–II, 1929–31) and other books of historical nature. Evert Alexander Louhi's *The Delaware Finns* (in English, 1925) is almost entirely based on the works of the Rev. Ilmonen and Akseli Rauanheimo. Juuso Hirvonen (d. about 1926) has written a historical sketch of the Finns in the North-west, *Michiganin Kuparialueen suomalaisten historia* (1920).

Viljami Rautanen (b. 1882), another clergyman, of Warren, Ohio, has written the history of the Finnish-American Church, *Amerikan suomalainen kirkko* (1911), perhaps his chief contribution to Finnish-American literature. Important also is his *Itämailla* (1927), an account of his travels in the Orient, which evidences a remarkably penetrating eye and interpretative power.

F. J. Syrjälä (1880–1931) wrote the history of the Labor movement among the Finns in America, *Amerikan suomalaisen työväenliikkeen historia* (1924), and a number of other writers have made sundry attempts to chronicle Finnish-American life in its various manifestations.

One of the most noteworthy books in this category is Dr. John H. Wuorinen's (b. 1897) *Nationalism in modern Finland* (in English, 1931). This scholarly narrative, by a member of the faculty of Columbia University, is written with such impartial objectivity and provided with such a wealth of facts that it would make an excellent text-book for anyone desiring a comprehensive introduction to the cultural events in Finland during the past century. (The book was rewritten in Finnish by Dr. Wuorinen and published in Finland in 1935.)

Another scholarly work is *The Americanization of the Finns* (1924), by Dr. John Wargelin (b. 1881), president of Suomi College, Hancock, Michigan. This volume is an inclusive investigation throwing light on many phases of Finnish immigration: the economic factors involved, the cultural background of the Finns, the effect that their sojourn in the United States has had upon them, their mental development and their reaction to the new conditions under which they live in this country.

The output of religious literature among Finnish-Americans probably exceeds all other classifications. Most of it takes the form of pamphlets, tracts, year-books, quarterlies, almanacs, prayer-books, hymn-books, etc., but among these are some more ambitious works, such as *Suuri uskonpuhdistaja* (1915) by Dr. J. K. Nikander (1855–1919), *Herran tulen kantaja* (1919) by Evert Määttälä, *Luterilainen kotilähetys* (1919) by Alvar Rautalahti (b. 1882), *Salainen voima* (1927, spiritualistic) by Immanuel Salminen (b. 1877), *Kristillinen Hyväntekeväisyys* (1927) by Dr. J. Wargelin and *Onko Jesus todella noussut ylös?* (1931) by A. Könönen (b. 1876).

In the opposite direction, *i. e.,* on the Left, the pamphleteers are equally prolific producers.

As a peculiar yet quite important form of "literature" we should not omit our numerous Finnish-English and English-Finnish dictionaries. Among the lexicographers there have been the following: Matti Fredd (1845–1922), Aatu Rekonen (1853–c. 1925), Dr. Karl Vilhelm Arminen (b. 1874), Santeri Nuorteva, Evert Määttälä, Severi Alanne and, in a class by himself, Clemens Niemi, who wrote a Finnish grammar as a text-book for non-Finnish students of the language.

Finnish-American literature, on the whole, is not pretentious. And on account of the stringent immigration laws there is little prospect of its further extensive growth. It probably means very little or nothing to Americans to whom only the few works written in English are comprehensible. But to Finns in America their own literature has meant a great deal. And perhaps it will, in the future, serve as an incentive to some gifted descendant of theirs who realizes that even the loneliest settlements of the most remote sections of the country may contain a sufficient microcosm for all purposes of literary artistry.

THE END

SELECTED BIBLIOGRAPHIES

of Books and Articles, especially in English, comprising the Standard Works of Literary History, Criticism, and Comment, and Translations into English of the Major Works.

SELECTED BIBLIOGRAPHIES

I

BIBLIOGRAPHIES OF BOOKS IN ENGLISH

AND OTHER BIBLIOGRAPHIES AND SCANDINAVIAN COL-
LECTIONS AVAILABLE IN AMERICA
by
FREDERIKA BLANKNER, LITT.D.

Western Reserve University

The American student of Scandinavian literatures has
at his service the Information Bureau of the American-
Scandinavian Foundation (116 East 64th Street, New
York City).

For material available in English the reader is referred
to the Foundation's various lists compiled from time to
time and distributed gratis, among which the most important is its booklet, *A list of five hundred books by
Scandinavians and about Scandinavia*, selected for the
American-Scandinavian Foundation (second edition,
1923), which is "a compact list of authoritative works
on the Northern countries and a selected bibliography
of English translations of books by Scandinavian authors . . . for the use of Americans and American
libraries."

The five hundred books listed concern the following
material: "SCANDINAVIA—Bibliography; Periodicals and
other serial publications; Dictionaries and grammars;

Old Norse literature and mythology; Old Norse history and antiquities; History and politics; Description, travel, social life and customs; Folk-lore; Biography; Scandinavians in America; Literary history and criticism; Collections; Other works relating to Scandinavia; WRITINGS OF INDIVIDUAL AUTHORS—Danish, Icelandic, Norwegian, Swedish; and SCANDINAVIAN AUTHORS ON NON-SCANDINAVIAN SUBJECTS."

The bibliography gives also a partial list of the publications of the American-Scandinavian Foundation, comprising the Scandinavian Monographs and its translations of the Scandinavian Classics. The complete bibliography of the Foundation's publications with descriptive comment may be had in a separate booklet.

Of the newer books a number are listed in their "Outline of Scandinavian literature" (mimeographed sheets), which comprises translations, criticism, and general works. Recently published books are included also in the volume *Scandinavian literature from Brandes to the present day* by Helge Gottlieb Topsöe-Jensen (New York, American-Scandinavian Foundation, W. W. Norton Company, 1929), which carries a five-page "Selected list of Scandinavian books in English translation" limited to modern authors; and in *Scandinavian literature* by Hanna Astrup Larsen (Chicago, American Library Association, in the "Reading with a purpose" series, 1930), offering a three-page general list of recommended books.

For the convenience of the reader we repeat here the list of other bibliographies with which the *List of five hundred books,* just referred to, opens:

BAY, JENS CHRISTIAN. *Denmark in English and American literature; a bibliography.* Chicago, Danish Amer. Assoc., 1915. 96 pp.

CORNELL UNIVERSITY LIBRARY. *Catalogue of the Icelandic collection bequeathed by Willard Fiske.*

Comp. by Halldór Hermannsson. Ithaca, N. Y., 1914. 755 pp.; addition 1927.

FLOM, GEORGE TOBIAS. *A history of Scandinavian studies in American universities, with a bibliography.* Iowa City, State Univ. of Iowa, 1907. 66 pp. (*Iowa studies in language and literature*, II.)

GRISWOLD, WILLIAM MCCRILLIS. *A descriptive list of novels and tales dealing with life in Norway.* Cambridge, Mass., Griswold, 1892. 20 pp.

KNAPP, WINIFRED. *Select list of books in English about Scandinavia or by Scandinavians.* ("Bulletin of bibliography," Boston, 1915, Vol. VIII, pp. 187–192.)

SOLBERG, THORVALD. *Bibliography of Scandinavia. A catalogue of the important books in the English language.* (Horn, F. W., *History of the literature of the Scandinavian North*, Chicago, Griggs, 1884, pp. 413–500.)

The last-mentioned list, by Solberg, is extensive, occupying almost one hundred pages. Additional bibliographies with special reference to Norwegian literature appear in *Norwegian life and literature—English accounts and views especially in the nineteenth century* by Carl John Birch Burchardt (London, Oxford University Press, 1920), which lists English books of travel on Norway in the nineteenth century, certain English novels dealing with life in Norway, some articles in English periodicals (1820–1900) dealing with ancient Scandinavian subjects, and material on Ibsen in England, including theatrical performances as well as translations. Other bibliographies on Norwegian literature appear in *Chapters on Norwegian literature* by Illit Gröndahl and Ola Raknes (London, Gyldendal, 1923), which gives a list of English translations; and in *History of Norwegian literature* by Theodore Jorgenson (New

York, Macmillan, 1933), which lists at the end of each section the relevant books in the Scandinavian languages as well as in English.

For Swedish literature there is the recently published "Bibliographical list of books in English on Sweden and literary works translated into English from Swedish" to be found in the *Sweden year-book,* 1936 (Uppsala, Almquist and Wiksell).

An annotated *Catalogue of Scandinavian books translated into English,* a commercial but very helpful list of the leading translations and other material available in English, as well as of text-books (readers, grammars, and dictionaries), is issued regularly by the Albert Bonnier Publishing House, importers of Scandinavian literature (561 Third Avenue, New York City). This same house also issues numerous catalogues of books in the original Scandinavian languages, some of them illustrated. The catalogues are furnished gratis on request.

For the guidance of the student desiring to do extensive work in the field the Harvard College Library has compiled the "Union catalogue" of Scandinavian books found in the most important American libraries, with a card index of over 55,000 entries,—an author catalogue, available only at Harvard.

For the student interested in Icelandic literature there is the famous Icelandic collection at Cornell University Library, of which there is a catalogue by Halldór Hermannsson mentioned above, with supplement. Harvard College Library also has an Icelandic collection of prime importance, rich in sagas and other mediaeval literature, with excellent periodical material, comprising the recently added Schofield Memorial Collection. Descriptions of this collection are available in articles by Gudrun Barnason in *Harvard Library Notes,* Number 23, for July, 1931, and by F. Stanton Cawley in the *Harvard Alumni Bulletin,* for June 11, 1931.

SELECTED BIBLIOGRAPHIES

The Yale University Library collection of Scandinavian items is described in part in an article by Adolph B. Benson published in *The Yale University Library Gazette*, July, 1933. This collection contains practically all the five thousand five hundred volumes mentioned in the *Catalogue de la bibliothèque de feu M. le comte Riant de l'Institut, rédigé par L. de Germon et L. Polain: première partie, livres concernant la Scandinavie* (Paris, Picard et Fils, 1896), and in addition all the prominent modern authors, the reports of the Swedish Academy of Belles-lettres, the reports of the Swedish Academy of Sciences, and many other such serial works, as well as 22,000 Swedish dissertations. The Yale collection includes also some incunabula and about fifty manuscripts.

The *Marsh Library catalogue* of the University of Vermont (Burlington, Vermont, 1892) lists a large number of Scandinavian works.

Reviews of current books are published by the American-Scandinavian Foundation in the *American-Scandinavian Review* edited by Hanna Astrup Larsen, and occasionally in the quarterly *Books Abroad* edited by Roy Temple House of the University of Oklahoma (in the department "Books in various languages").

Current Scandinavian books of a more scholarly and specialistic nature are reviewed in the quarterly *Scandinavian Studies and Notes*, at present edited by A. M. Sturtevant of the University of Kansas, and published by the Society for the Advancement of Scandinavian Study. This organization, devoted to scholarship in the Scandinavian field, holds annual meetings in May for the reading of papers and for discussions. Also at the annual meetings of the Modern Language Association of America a section is devoted to Scandinavian languages and literatures.

Suggested lists of first selected readings in the various national divisions of the field follow, each compiled by a specialist and each organized as the author has found advisable for the material on hand. These bibliographies are preceded by an introductory list of recommended comprehensive works for the assistance of those whose interest in the subject may be more general.

When a book happens to be suitable for inclusion in more than one bibliography, the repetition has been allowed in the thought that each list will be of most service if it is a unit in itself.

II

COMPREHENSIVE WORKS

HORN, FREDERIK WINKEL. *Geschichte der Literatur des skandinavischen Nordens von den ältesten Zeiten bis auf die Gegenwart.* Leipzig, 1880.

HORN, FREDERIK WINKEL. *History of the literature of the Scandinavian North from the most ancient times to the present.* Revised by the author and translated by Rasmus B. Anderson. Chicago, 1884.

HOWITT, WILLIAM and MARY. *The literature and romance of northern Europe.* I–II, London, 1852.

ROSENBERG, C. *Nordboernes Aandsliv fra Oldtiden til vore Dage.* I–III, Köbenhavn, 1878–85. Left unfinished because of the author's death.

SCHWEITZER, PH. *Geschichte der skandinavischen Litteratur von ihren Aufängen bis auf die neueste Zeit.* I–III, Berlin, 1886–88.

SKOVRUP, EJNAR. *Hovedtraek af nordisk Digtning i Nytiden.* I–II, Köbenhavn, 1920–21.

TOPSÖE-JENSEN, H. G. *Scandinavian literature from Brandes to our day.* Translated from the Danish by Isaac Andersen. New York, 1929.

WOLLHEIM DA FONSECA, A. E. *Die National-Literatur der Skandinavier; eine prosaische und poetische Anthologie aus den besten nordischer Schriftstellern, mit erläuternden, kritischen und biographischen Notizen.* I–III, Berlin, 1875–77.

III

NORWEGIAN LITERATURE
by
EINAR I. HAUGEN, PH.D.

*Chairman of the Department of Scandinavian,
University of Wisconsin*

The following titles have been chosen with an eye to the American student. For this reason works in English have been favored, even if they are not always as significant as the contributions of native scholars. But nothing has been included that the writer does not consider at least reasonably competent. The Norwegian titles represent something like a minimum equipment toward the scholarly study of Norwegian literature. For each author an attempt has been made to select the best that is available, subject to limitations of space. English translations of literary works have been given only for authors who are represented by relatively few translations.

I. GENERAL WORKS

GATHORNE-HARDY, G. M. *Norway.* New York, 1925. (Series: *The modern world.*) A good survey.

FISCHER, KARL, ed. *Norway to-day.* Oslo, 1933. Beautifully illustrated.

BURCHARDT, CARL J. B. *Norwegian life and literature; English accounts and views, especially in the 19th century.* London, 1920.

[328]

II. BIBLIOGRAPHY AND REFERENCE

Five hundred books by Scandinavians and about Scandinavia. Selected for the American-Scandinavian Foundation. New York, 1921; second edition, 1923.

LARSEN, HANNA ASTRUP. *Scandinavian literature.* A.L.A., Chicago, 1930. (*Reading with a purpose.* No. 54.)

PETTERSEN, HJALMAR. *Bibliotheca norvegica. Norsk boglexikon, 1643–1813.* 4 vols., Christiania, 1899–1924.

Norsk biografisk leksikon. Editors: Edv. Bull, Anders Krogvig, Gerhard Gran. Christiania, 1923 ff. Has reached the letter K.

Norsk bogfortegnelse, 1814–1930. 10 vols., Christiania, 1848–1932. Book list.

HALVORSEN, JENS B. *Norsk forfatter-lexikon, 1814–1880.* 6 vols., Christiania, 1885 ff. Indispensable reference work.

Norsk tidsskriftindex. Christiania, 1918–date. Annual magazine index.

AURE, ANTON, ed. *Nynorsk boklista; skrifter i bokform på norsk bygdemål og landsmål.* 3 vols., Christiania, 1916, 1921, 1926. Bibliography of writings in New Norse.

III. PERIODICALS

The American-Scandinavian Review. New York, 1913–date. Very ably edited.

Edda. Christiania, 1909–date. Literary research.

Mål og Minne. Christiania, 1909–date. Philological.

Samtiden. Bergen, 1890–date. General periodical.

Syn og Segn. Christiania, 1895–date. Organ of the New Norse Movement.

IV. HISTORIES AND ANTHOLOGIES OF LITERATURE

BEYER, HARALD. *Norwegische Literatur.* Breslau, 1927. By a Norwegian scholar.

BORELIUS, HILMA. *Die nordischen Literaturen.* Potsdam, 1931. Judgments may sometimes be questioned.

BURGUN, ACHILLE. *Le développement linguistique en Norvège au 19ᵉ siècle.* Christiania, 1919–21. Only existing survey of Norwegian language in the 19th century.

BULL, EDVARD; KEILHAU, WILHELM; SHETELIG, HAAKON; STEEN, SVERRE. *Det norske folks liv og historie gjennem tidene.* Oslo, 1931. Latest history of Norway.

BULL, FRANCIS and PAASCHE, FREDRIK. *Norsk litteraturhistorie.* 5 vols. (4 and 5 in preparation), Christiania, 1924 ff. Brilliant and authoritative, the standard work.

ELSTER, KRISTIAN d. y. *Illustreret norsk litteraturhistorie.* 2 vols., Christiania, 1924. Primarily aesthetic in point of view.

GRAN, GERHARD, ed. *Nordmaend i det 19de aarhundrede.* 3 vols., Christiania, 1914. An important reference work, by various writers.

GRAN, GERHARD. *Norsk aandsliv i hundrede aar; spredte traek.* 3 vols., Christiania, 1915–19. Essays by a keen commentator on literature.

GRÖNDAHL, ILLIT and RAKNES, OLA. *Chapters in Norwegian literature.* London, 1923. Covers period since Reformation; readable, informative.

JORGENSON, THEODORE. *History of Norwegian literature.* New York, 1933. From earliest times to the present; it is the most detailed and informative history in English.

TOPSÖE-JENSEN, H. G. *Scandinavian literature from Brandes to our day.* New York, 1929. Sketchy.

SELECTED BIBLIOGRAPHIES

GOSSE, EDMUND and CRAIGIE, W. A., eds. *Oxford book of Scandinavian verse.* 1925. Not wholly representative.

KENT, CHARLES, ed. *Norsk lyrikk gjennem tusen år.* Oslo, 1929. Chiefly valuable for selection from modern poets.

KNUDSEN, D. F., ed. *Norsk prosa i utvalg.* Oslo. School text.

LARSEN, HANNA A., ed. *Told in Norway.* New York, 1927. Short stories.

V. LITERATURE BEFORE 1814

OLSEN, MAGNUS. *Farms and fanes of ancient Norway.* Oslo, 1928. Cultural, linguistic.

LEACH, HENRY G. *Angevin Britain and Scandinavia.* Cambridge, 1921. Mediaeval literary influences.

LARSON, LAURENCE MARCELLUS. *The King's mirror.* New York, 1917. The most important non-Icelandic literary work of mediaeval Norway.

LIESTÖL, KNUT, ed. *Folkvisor och folksägner.* Stockholm, 1931. (*Nordisk kultur,* 9.) Standard, authoritative.

HOLBERG, LUDVIG. *Three comedies.* Translated by Oscar J. Campbell and Frederic Schenck. New York, 1914.

CAMPBELL, OSCAR. *The comedies of Holberg.* Cambridge, Mass., 1914. A helpful discussion.

There is a mass of Holberg literature, from which it is hard to make a selection. The results of Professor Francis Bull's researches are embodied in his brilliant chapters on Holberg in the *Litteraturhistorie* cited above. He is also co-editor with Carl S. Petersen of the *Holberg aarbog,* published 1920–25. An exhaustive account can also be found in *Illustreret dansk Litteraturhistorie,* Vol. II, by Vilhelm Andersen (Copenhagen, 1934).

WINSNES, A. H. *Det norske selskab*. Christiania, 1924. Norwegian students at the University of Copenhagen in the 18th century.

WINSNES, A. H. *Johan Nordahl Brun*. Christiania, 1919.

VI. THE NATIONAL AWAKENING (1814–54)

FALNES, OSCAR. *Norwegian national romanticism*. New York, 1933. An excellent survey of romantic scholarship, 1840–70.

WERGELAND, HENRIK. *Poems*. Oslo-London, 1929. Capable translations by G. Gathorne-Hardy and others.

WERGELAND, HENRIK. *Samlede skrifter*. Ed. by H. Jaeger and D. A. Seip. Christiania, 1918 ff. The standard collected edition.

KOHT, HALVDAN. *Henrik Wergeland; ei folkeskrift*. Christiania, 1908.

LÖCHEN, A. *J. S. Welhaven; liv og skrifter*. 2 vols., Christiania, 1898–1900.

GRAN, GERHARD. *Norges daemring; en litteraturhistorisk indledning*. Bergen, 1899. The Welhaven-Wergeland controversy.

HANSEN, HANS. *P. Chr. Asbjörnsen; biografi og karakteristikk; med supplerende oplysninger om hans samtidige*. Oslo, 1932.

KROGVIG, ANDERS, ed. *Fra det nationale gjennembruds tid; breve til P. Chr. Asbjörnsen og andre*. Christiania, 1915. Letters from Jörgen Moe.

The fairy-tales of Asbjörnsen and Moe have been repeatedly translated:

Dasent. *Popular tales from the North*. Edinburgh and London, 1891 ff.

Braekstad. *Tales from the far North*. London, 1897.

Gade. *Norwegian fairy-tales*. New York, 1924.

KOHT, HALVDAN; GARBORG, ARNE; HOVDEN, ANDERS. *Ivar Aasen, granskaren, maalreisaren, diktaren.* Christiania, 1913. Koht's biography is the most thorough study of Aasen's life.

VII. REALISM (1854–90)

BRANDES, GEORGE. *Ibsen and Björnson.* New York, 1899.

KAHLE, BERNHARD. *Henrik Ibsen, Björnstjerne Björnson, und ihre Zeitgenossen.* Leipzig, 1908. (Series: *Aus Natur und Geisteswelt.*)

NECKEL, GUSTAV. *Ibsen and Björnson.* Leipzig, 1927. (Series: *Aus Natur und Geisteswelt.*)

TISSOT, ERNEST. *Le drame norvégien.* Paris, 1893.

BJÖRNSON, BJÖRNSTJERNE:

BULL, FRANCIS. Björnson-biography in *Norsk Biogr. Leks.* Introductions to Björnson's *Samlede verker; standard-utgave*, 1919. *Björnson-bibliografi*, Oslo, 1933. (Series: *Les med plan*, III.) The best that has been written on Björnson's life and works.

COLLIN, CHRISTEN. *Björnstjerne Björnson; hans barndom og ungdom.* 2 vols., 2nd ed., Christiania, 1923. An unfinished biography.

GIERLÖFF, CHRISTIAN. *Björnstjerne Björnson.* Oslo, 1932. Overpopularized.

GRAN, GERHARD. *Björnstjerne Björnson.* Copenhagen, 1916. (Series: *Mennesker.*) Critical, analytic.

KOHT, HALVDAN, ed. (with valuable introductions). *Björnson's letters: Vols. 1–2 Gro-tid; vols. 3–4 Brytnings-aar; vols. 5–6 Kamp-liv.* Christiania, 1912–32.

LESCOFFIER, JEAN. *Björnstjerne Björnson; la seconde jeunesse.* Paris, 1932. Thorough, important study.

PAYNE, W. MORTON. *Björnstjerne Björnson.* Chicago, 1910. Insignificant.

GARBORG, ARNE:

LIE, ERIK. *Arne Garborg; en livsskildring.* Christiania, 1914. Undistinguished.

THESEN, ROLV. *Arne Garborg; frå jaerbu til europear.* Oslo, 1933. *Europearen,* Oslo. 1936.

Two of Arne Garborg's works have been translated: *The lost father.* Boston, 1920.

Peace. New York, 1929.

IBSEN, HENRIK:

FIRKINS, INA TEN EYCK. *An Ibsen bibliography.* New York, 1921. Fairly complete on English and American material.

IBSEN, HENRIK. *Samlede verker; hundreårsutgave.* 20 vols., Oslo, 1928 ff. With valuable introductions by Halvdan Koht and Francis Bull.

LOGEMAN, HENRI. *A commentary on Peer Gynt.* Hague, 1917. Line by line comment.

Letters of Ibsen. New York, London, 1905. A pirated translation of the original edition by Koht and Elias.

Speeches and new letters. Edited by Arne Kildal, with bibliography. Boston, 1910.

HELLER, OTTO. *Henrik Ibsen; plays and problems.* Boston, 1912. Contains bibliography.

KOHT, HALVDAN. *Life of Ibsen.* 2 vols., New York, 1931. Most complete and authoritative.

MÖHRING, WERNER. *Ibsen und Kierkegaard.* Leipzig, 1928.

SHAW, GEORGE B. *The quintessence of Ibsenism . . . now completed to the death of Ibsen.* New York, 1913. More Shavianism than Ibsenism.

WEIGAND, HERMAN J. *The modern Ibsen; a reconsideration.* New York, 1925. Brilliant, provocative interpretation.

WÖRNER, ROMAN. *Henrik Ibsen.* 2 vols., Munich, 1900–10. Thorough criticism and analysis.

ZUCKER, ADOLPH E. *Ibsen, the master-builder.* New York, 1929. Anecdotal, interesting. With a bibliography.

KIELLAND, ALEXANDER:

GRAN, GERHARD. *Alexander Kielland og hans samtid.* Christiania, 1922.

Several of Kielland's books have been translated, but are out of print and difficult to secure:

Elsie (1894). *Garman and Worse* (1885). *Norse tales* (1897). *Professor Lövdahl* (1904). *Skipper Worse* (1885). *Tales of two countries* (1891).

LIE, JONAS:

GARBORG, ARNE. *Jonas Lie; en udviklingshistorie.* Christiania, 1893. A brilliant and sympathetic analysis.

WIEHR, JOSEPH. "The women characters of Jonas Lie," *Journal of English and Germanic Philology,* 28:41–71, 244–62 (1929).

Jonas Lie was extensively translated in earlier years; the only translation now easily available is *The family at Gilje,* New York, 1920.

VINJE, A. O.:

VISLIE, VETLE. *Aasmund Vinje; liv og dikting.* Oslo, 1929. A thorough study of a strange and fascinating writer.

VIII. MODERN CURRENTS (From 1890)

BUKDAHL, JÖRGEN. *Norsk national kunst; litteraere essays.* Copenhagen, 1924. A young Danish critic views Norwegian literature.

BOJER, JOHAN:

LA CHESNAIS, P. G. *Johan Bojer.* Oslo, 1932. Translated into Norwegian from French. Paris, 1930.

GAD, CARL. *Johan Bojer; the man and his works.* New York, 1920.

DUUN, OLAV:

ÖVERLAND, ARNULF. *Olav Duun*. Oslo, 1926.

Olav Duun's masterpiece has appeared in English as *The People of Juvik* (1930–35). Previously (1928) *Good conscience* was translated.

EGGE, PETER:

WOEL, CAI M. *Peter Egge*. Copenhagen, 1929.

One of Egge's books has been translated: *Hansine Solstad*, 1929.

HAMSUN, KNUT:

LARSEN, HANNA ASTRUP. *Knut Hamsun*. New York, 1922. A valuable contribution.

SKAVLAN, EINAR. *Knut Hamsun*. Oslo, 1929. Most recent biography.

WIEHR, JOSEPH. *Knut Hamsun; his personality and outlook upon life*. Northampton, 1922. (*Smith College studies*, vol. 3.)

KINCK, HANS E.:

GIERLÖFF, CHRISTIAN. *Kinck*. Christiania, 1923. Breezy.

HARBITZ, ALF, ed. *Et eftermaele*. Oslo, 1927. Collection of articles about Kinck, with an excellent bibliography of his works.

The only Kinck book translated is *A young people*, 1929. Many of his short stories have appeared in *The American-Scandinavian Review*.

OBSTFELDER, SIGBJÖRN:

CLAUSSEN, CHRISTIAN. *Sigbjörn Obstfelder i hans diktning og breve; en psykologisk studie*. Christiania, 1924.

OBSTFELDER, SIGBJÖRN. *Poems from the Norwegian*. Oxford, 1920. A small selection of his poems, with Norwegian text and English translation.

UNDSET, SIGRID:

VINDE, VICTOR. *Sigrid Undset, a Nordic moralist*. Seattle, Wash., 1930.

SELECTED BIBLIOGRAPHIES

LARSEN, HANNA ASTRUP. "Sigrid Undset," *American-Scandinavian Review*, 17:344–52, 406–414 (June–July, 1929). The best in English about the great author of *Kristin Lavransdatter*.

BING, JUST. *Sigrid Undset*. Christiania, 1924. Poor.

The earliest of Mrs. Undset's books that has been translated is *Jenny* (N. Y., 1921); several of her earlier writings are still awaiting translation.

Among other writers who have appeared in English are FALKBERGET, JOHAN: *Lisbeth of Jarnfjeld* (1930); GRIEG, NORDAHL: *The ship sails on* (1927); WIERS-JENSEN, H.: *Anne Pedersdotter* (1917); FANGEN, RONALD: *Duel* (1934); FÖNHUS, MIKKJEL; HAUKLAND, ANDREAS; and KRAEMMER, ELIAS. A volume of HERMAN WILDENVEY's poetry has been translated by Joseph Auslander (1935).

NORWEGIAN-AMERICAN LITERATURE

by

RICHARD BECK, PH.D.

Professor and Head of the Department of
Scandinavian Languages and Literatures
in the
University of North Dakota

AGER, WALDEMAR. "Norsk-Amerikansk skjönlittera-tur." In *Norsk-Amerikanernes festskrift.* Decorah, Iowa, 1914, pp. 291–306.

HOIDAHL, AAGOT, D. "Norwegian-American fiction since 1880." In *Norwegian-American studies and records,* Northfield, Minn., 1930, Vol. V, pp. 61–83.

JOSEPHSEN, EINAR. "An outline of Norwegian-American literature." In *Scandinavia,* Grand Forks, N. Dak., 1924, Vol. I, no. 4, pp. 50–55.

LIMA, LUDVIG. *Norsk-Amerikanske digte.* Minneapolis, 1903.

NORLIE, O. M. *History of the Norwegian people in America.* Minneapolis, 1925.

OLSON, JULIUS E. "Literature and the press." In *Norwegian immigrant contributions to America's making.* New York, 1921, pp. 125–138.

Skandinavens almanak-kalender for 1931 and 1932. 10th and 11th year, Chicago, 1930 and 1931.

Symra, an annual edited by Kristian Prestgard and J. B. Wist. Decorah, Iowa, 1905–1914. Contains many valuable articles on Norwegian-American literature.

SELECTED BIBLIOGRAPHIES

RÖLVAAG, O. E.:

BECK, RICHARD. "Penetrating novel." In *University of North Dakota Quarterly Journal*, Grand Forks, N. Dak., summer number, 1932, pp. 389–92.

COLCORD, LINCOLN. Introduction to *Giants in the earth*. New York, 1927, and following editions.

HAUGEN, EINAR I. "O. E. Rölvaag; Norwegian-American." In *Norwegian-American studies and records*, Northfield, Minn., 1933, Vol. VII, pp. 53–73.

HAUGEN, EINAR I. "O. E. Rölvaag." In *Dictionary of American biography*. New York, 1935.

LARSEN, H. A. "Ole Edvart Rölvaag." In *American-Scandinavian Review*, Jan., 1932, pp. 7–9.

OLSON, JULIUS E. "Ole Edvart Rölvaag, 1876–1931." In *Norwegian-American studies and records*, Northfield, Minn., Vol. VII, pp. 121–130.

PARRINGTON, V. L. Introduction to *Giants in the earth*. New York, 1929. (*Harper's modern classics*.)

RÖNNING, N. N. "O. E. Rölvaag." In *The Friend*, Minneapolis, December, 1931.

IV

SWEDISH LITERATURE

compiled by
JOSEPH H. MÜLLER, B.A.
University of Pennsylvania
under the supervision of
AXEL J. UPPVALL, PH.D.
*Professor and Head of the Department of
Scandinavian Languages and Literatures
in the
University of Pennsylvania*

I. ANTIQUITIES

MONTELIUS, OSCAR. *The civilization of Sweden in heathen times.* Translated by F. H. Woods. New York, Macmillan, 1888.

NILSSON, SVEN. *The primitive inhabitants of Scandinavia.* Third edition. London, Longmans, Green, 1868.

NORDÉN, ARTHUR. *Östergötlands bronsålder.* Linköping (Sweden), Henric Carlson, 1925.

WILLIAMS, MARY W. *Social Scandinavia in the viking age.* New York, Macmillan, 1920.

II. HISTORY (GENERAL)

BAIN, ROBERT N. *Charles XII and the collapse of the Swedish empire, 1682–1719.* New York, Putnam, 1895.

BAIN, ROBERT N. *Gustavus III and his contemporaries, 1746–92.* I–II, London, Paul, 1894.

BAIN, ROBERT N. *Scandinavia; a political history, 1513–1900.* Cambridge University Press, 1905. (*Cambridge historical series.*)

GEIJER, ERIK GUSTAF. *History of the Swedes.* Translated by J. H. Turner. First part only, to 1654. London, Whittaker and Co., 1845.

HALLENDORF, CARL, and SCHÜCK, ADOLF. *A history of Sweden.* Translated by Lajla Yapp. Stockholm, C. E. Fritze, Ltd., 1929.

MACKENZIE, FAITH COMPTON. *Sibyl of the North; the tale of Christina, Queen of Sweden.* London, Cassell, 1931.

STOMBERG, A. A. *A history of Sweden.* New York, Macmillan, 1931.

STURLUSON, SNORRI. *Heimskringla: the history of the old Scandinavian kings down to 1170.* Translated and edited by Monsen and Smith. New York, Appleton, 1932.

SVANSTRÖM, RAGNAR, and PALMSTIERNA, CARL. *A short history of Sweden.* Oxford University Press, 1934.

III. LANGUAGE

BJÖRKHAGEN, IMMANUEL. *A modern Swedish grammar.* I–II, Stockholm, Norstedt, 1923. Obtainable at the Bonnier Publishing House, 561 Third Ave., New York City, N. Y.

BERGER, V. *Svensk-amerikanska språket; ett bidrag till kännedomen om engelska språkets inflytande på svenska språket i Amerika.* Nordstjernans redaktion, 108 Park Row, New York City, 1934.

BORGSTRÖM, M. *Svenska språkets historia.* Uppsala, J. L. Lindblad, 1921.

ELMQUIST, LOUIS A. *Elementary Swedish grammar.* Rock Island, Ill., Augustana Book Concern, 1914.

FRIESEN, OTTO VON. *Runorna.* Stockholm, Bonnier, 1933. (*Nordisk kultur.*)

HARDING, ERIK. *Urnordisk grammatik.* I–II, Lund, Gleerup, 1932.

HELLQUIST, ELOF. *Svensk etymologisk ordbok.* Lund, Gleerup, 1922.

NOREEN, A. *De nordiska språken.* Stockholm, Norstedt, 1921.

NOREEN, A. *Geschichte der nordischen Sprachen.* Strassburg, Trübner, 1913.

NOREEN, A. *Vårt språk; Nysvensk grammatik.* I–XXXIII, Lund, Gleerup, 1903–24.

Ordlista över svenska språket. Utgiven av Svenska Akademien. Stockholm, Norstedt, 1930.

VICKNER, EDW. J. *Simplified Swedish grammar.* Rock Island, Ill., Augustana Book Concern, 1934.

WENSTRÖM and HARLOCK. *Svensk-engelsk ordbok.* Reformed spelling edition. Stockholm, Norstedt, 1929.

WENSTRÖM-LINDGREN. *English-Swedish dictionary.* Stockholm, Norstedt, 1930.

IV. LITERATURE, CRITICISM, AND LITERARY HISTORY

BENSON, ADOLPH B. *The Old Norse element in Swedish romanticism.* New York, Columbia University Press, 1914.

BERENDSOHN, W. A. *Selma Lagerlöf; her life and work.* Garden City, N. Y., Doubleday, Doran, 1932.

BERG, RUBEN G:SON. *C. J. L. Almquist i landsflykten.* Stockholm, Bonnier, 1928.

BJÖRKMAN, EDWIN. *Voices of tomorrow.* New York, Kennerly, 1913. Contains essays on Strindberg and Lagerlöf.

BOYESEN, HJALMAR HJORTH. *Essays on Scandinavian literature.* New York, Scribner, 1895. Contains essay on Tegnér.

CAMPBELL, G. A. *Strindberg.* London, Duckworth, 1933. (*Great lives series.*)

CRAIGIE, WILLIAM A. *Scandinavian folk-lore.* Paisley, Gardner, 1896.

DAHLSTRÖM, C. E. W. *Strindberg's dramatic expressionism.* University of Michigan, 1930.

GOSSE, EDMUND WILLIAM. *Northern studies.* London, Scott, 1890. Contains essay on Runeberg.

HALLSTRÖM, PER. *Minne av Carl Snoilsky.* Stockholm, Norstedt, 1933.

HORN, FREDERICK WINKEL. *History of the literature of the Scandinavian North.* Revised by the author and translated by R. B. Anderson, with a bibliography of the important books in English concerning Scandinavia, prepared by Thorvald Solberg. Chicago, Griggs, 1884.

HOWITT, W. and M. *The literature and romance of Northern Europe.* I–II, London, Colburn, 1852.

LARSEN, HANNA ASTRUP. *Scandinavian literature.* Chicago, American Language Association, 1930.

Selma Lagerlöf. Garden City, N. Y., Doubleday, Doran, 1936.

LIND AF HAGEBY, LIZZY. *August Strindberg, the spirit of revolt.* New York, Appleton, 1913.

MCGILL, V. J. *The bedevilled viking; a biography of Strindberg.* New York, Coward McCann, 1930.

MJÖBERG, JOSUA. *Svensk litteraturhistoria för den högre undervisningen.* Lund, Gleerup, 1927.

MJÖBERG and WAHLGREN. *Kort svensk litteraturhistoria.* Lund, Gleerup, 1921.

SCHÜCK, HENRIK. *Histoire de la littérature suédoise.* Paris, Leroux, 1923.

SCHÜCK, HENRIK, and WARBURG, KARL JOHAN. *Illus-*

trerad svensk litteraturhistoria. Third edition. I–VII, Stockholm, Hugo Gebers, 1926–32.

Songs of Sweden; 87 Swedish folk- and popular songs. Collected and edited by Gustaf Hägg. With Swedish and English text and piano music. New York, Schirmer, 1909.

STRINDBERG, FRIDA. *Strindberg och hans andra hustru.* I–II, Stockholm, Bonnier, 1933–34.

STORK, CHARLES WHARTON. "The poetry of Viktor Rydberg." In *Schelling anniversary papers.* pp. 287–299. Edited by A. C. Baugh. New York, Century, 1923.

Svenska författare. Utgivna av svenska vitterhetssamfundet. Stockholm, Bonnier, 1910–date.

A list of works of Swedish authors important in the study of Swedish literature. The titles follow:

Dalin, Olof von	*Den svenska Argus*
Leopold, C. G. af	*Samlade skrifter*
Stagnelius, C. J.	" "
Lucidor	" "
Bellman, C. M.	*Dikter*
Lenngren, A. M.	*Samlade skrifter*
Dahlstierna, G. A.	" *dikter*
Stiernhielm	*Skrifter*
Ehrensvärd, C. A.	"
Kellgren, J. H.	*Samlade skrifter*
Nordenflycht, H. C.	" "
Sjöberg, E.	" "
Thorild, T.	" "
Runeberg, J. L.	" "
Runius, J.	" "
Lidner, B.	" "
Wallenberg, J.	" "

Sveriges national-litteratur, 1500–1920. I–XXX, Stockholm, Bonnier, 1921–22.

SYLWAN, OTTO, ed. *Svenska litteraturens historia.* I–III, Stockholm, Norstedt, 1923.

TOPSÖE-JENSEN, HELGE GOTTLIEB. *Scandinavian literature from Brandes to our day.* New York, American-Scandinavian Foundation, 1929. (*Scandinavian classics,* Vol. XXXII.)

UDDGREN, GUSTAF. *Strindberg the man.* Translated by A. J. Uppvall. Boston, The Four Seas Co., 1919.

UPPVALL, AXEL JOHAN. "The poetry of Erik Axel Karlfeldt." In *Germanic Review,* Vol. II, no. 3, July, 1927, pp. 244–61.

UPPVALL, AXEL JOHAN. *Hösthorn; dikter av Erik Axel Karlfeldt.* Review. In *Scandinavian Studies and Notes,* Vol. X, no. 1, February, 1928, pp. 31–35.

UPPVALL, AXEL JOHAN. *August Strindberg, a psychoanalytic study with special reference to the Oedipus complex.* Boston, The Gorham Press, 1920. Contains bibliography.

V. ANTHOLOGIES

AHLÉEN, REINHOLD. *Swedish poets of the seventeenth century; some gleanings from the Swedish Parnassus.* San Francisco, Parker Printing Co., 1933. Contains bibliographical notes.

BORROW, GEORGE. *The songs of Scandinavia and other poems and ballads.* (Swedish—Vol. II, pp. 109–122.) New York, Gabriel Wells; London, Constable, 1923.

DJURKLOU, GABRIEL. *Fairy tales from the Swedish.* Translated by H. L. Braekstad. New York, Stokes, 1901.

FOSS, CLAUDE WILLIAM. *Masterpieces from Swedish literature.* I–II, Rock Island, Ill., Augustana Book Concern, 1909.

GOSSE, SIR EDMUND and CRAIGIE, W. A. *The Oxford book of Scandinavian verse.* Oxford, 1925. "The Poetry of Sweden," pp. 197–330.

LARSEN, HANNA ASTRUP, ed. *Sweden's best stories; an introduction to modern Swedish fiction.* Translated by Charles W. Stork. New York, American-Scandinavian Foundation, 1928. (*Scandinavian classics,* Vol. XXX.)

LOCOCK, C. D., tr. *A selection from modern Swedish poetry.* (Includes Heidenstam, Levertin, Karlfeldt, Vetterlund, Bergman, Siwertz, Österling and others.) New York, Macmillan, 1930.

LONGFELLOW, HENRY W. *The poets and poetry of Europe* (pp. 126–179). Philadelphia, Carry and Hart, 1845.

MJÖBERG, JOSUA. *Svensk litteratur från Bellman till våra dagar; i urval för den högre undervisningen: I, Från Dalin t.o.m. Almquist; II, Från Fredrika Bremer t.o.m. Karlfeldt.* Lund, Gleerup, 1922.

STORK, CHARLES WHARTON, ed. and tr. *Anthology of Swedish lyrics from 1750 to 1915.* New York, American-Scandinavian Foundation, 1917. (*Scandinavian classics,* Vol. IX.)

STORK, CHARLES WHARTON, ed. and tr. *Modern Swedish masterpieces.* New York, Dutton, 1923.

VI. INDIVIDUAL AUTHORS IN ENGLISH TRANSLATION

ALMQUIST, CARL JONAS LOVE. *Sara Videbeck* and *The chapel.* Translated by Adolph B. Benson. New York, American-Scandinavian Foundation, 1919. (*Scandinavian classics,* Vol. XII.)

BERG, BENGT. *The motherless.* Translated by Charles W. Stork. Garden City, N. Y., Doubleday, Doran, 1924.

BERGMAN, HJALMAR. *God's orchid.* Translated by E. Classen. New York, Knopf, 1924.

BREMER, FREDRIKA. *Works.* Translated by Mary Howitt. I–IV, London, Bell, 1892–1909. (*Bohn's library.*)

America of the fifties. Translated by A. B. Benson. New York, American-Scandinavian Foundation, 1924. (*Scandinavian classics*, Vol. XXII.)

Numerous other American and English translations.

CARLÉN, EMILIA FLYGARE. *The smugglers of the Swedish coast,* or *The rose of Thistle Island.* Translated by G. C. Hebbe and H. C. Deming. New York, Winchester, 1844.

ELKAN, MRS. SOFIE. *An exiled king, Gustaf IV Adolf of Sweden.* Translated by M. Eugenie Koch. I–II, London, Hutchinson, 1913.

FRÖDING, GUSTAF. *Selected poems.* Translated and with an introduction by Charles W. Stork. New York, Macmillan, 1916.

Guitar and concertina: a century of poems. Translated by C. D. Locock. Allen, London, 1930.

GEIJERSTAM, GUSTAF AF. *The book about little brother.* Translated and with an introduction by Edwin Björkman. New York, American-Scandinavian Foundation, 1921. (*Scandinavian classics*, Vol. XVIII.) Knopf, 1925. Contains a chronological list of Geijerstam's principal works.

Woman power. Translated and with an introduction by Esther Rapp. New York, American-Scandinavian Foundation, 1927. (*Scandinavian classics*, Vol. XXVIII.)

HALLSTRÖM, PER. *Selected short stories.* Translated by F. J. Fielden. New York, American-Scandinavian Foundation, 1922. (*Scandinavian classics*, Vol. XX.) Contains ten stories and a list of Hallström's principal writings.

HEIDENSTAM, VERNER VON. *Sweden's laureate: selected poems.* Translated and with an introduction by Charles W. Stork. New Haven, Yale University Press, 1919.

The Charles men. Translated by Charles W. Stork.

New York, American-Scandinavian Foundation, 1920. (*Scandinavian classics*, Vols. XV–XVI.)

The tree of the folkungs. Translated by Arthur G. Chater. New York, Knopf, 1925.

The Swedes and their chieftains. Translated by Charles W. Stork. New York, American-Scandinavian Foundation, 1925. (*Scandinavian classics*, Vol. XXV.)

JANSON, GUSTAF. *Pride of war.* (*Lögnerna.*) Boston, Little, Brown, 1912.

KEY, ELLEN. *Love and marriage.* Translated by Arthur B. Chater. New York, Putnam, 1911.

LAGERLÖF, SELMA. *Gösta Berling's saga.* Translated by Lillie Tudeer. New York, American-Scandinavian Foundation, 1918. (*Scandinavian classics*, Vols. X–XI.)

Invisible links. Translated by Pauline B. Flach. Garden City, N. Y., Doubleday, Doran, 1917.

Miracles of Antichrist. Translated by Pauline B. Flach. Boston, Little, Brown, 1915.

From a Swedish homestead. Translated by Jessie Brochner. Garden City, N. Y., Doubleday, Doran, 1916.

Queens of Kungahälla. Translated by Claude Field. London, Laurie, 1930.

Jerusalem. Translated by V. S. Howard; introduction by Henry Goddard Leach. Garden City, N. Y., Doubleday, Doran, 1915.

The Holy City (*Jerusalem, II*). Translated by V. S. Howard. Garden City, N. Y., Doubleday, Doran, 1918.

Christ legends. Translated by V. S. Howard. New York, Holt, 1930.

The treasure. Translated by Arthur G. Chater. Garden City, N. Y., Doubleday, Doran, 1925.

Liliecrona's home. Translated by Anna Barwell. New York, Dutton, 1926.

The Emperor of Portugallia. Garden City, N. Y., Doubleday, Doran, 1916.

The ring of the Löwenskölds. Containing *The General's ring,* translated by Francesca Martin; *Charlotte Löwensköld* and *Anna Svärd,* translated by Velma Swanston Howard. Garden City, N. Y., Doubleday, Doran, 1931.

Mårbacka. Translated by V. S. Howard. Garden City, N. Y., Doubleday, Doran, 1926. Autobiographical.

Memories of my childhood; further years at Mårbacka. Garden City, N. Y., Doubleday, Doran, 1934. Autobiographical.

The diary of Selma Lagerlöf. Translated by Velma Swanston Howard. Garden City, N. Y., Doubleday, Doran, 1936.

Harvest. Translated by Florence and Naboth Hedin. Garden City, N. Y., Doubleday, Doran, 1935. Autobiographical.

Almost all of Selma Lagerlöf's works are translated into English.

LUNDEGÅRD, AXEL. *The storm bird.* Translated by A. Kilgour. London, Hodder, 1895.

MALLING, FRU MATHILDA. *The Governor's wife; pictures from the imperial court of France, 1806–07.* Translated by H. L. St. John. New York, St. John, 1904.

NYBLOM, FRU HELENA AUGUSTA. *Jolly Calle and other Swedish fairy tales.* New York, Dutton, 1912.

RUNEBERG, JOHAN LUDVIG. *The songs of Ensign Stål.* Translated by C. B. Shaw. New York, Stechert, 1925.

King Fialar, a poem. Translated by E. Magnússon. London, Dent, 1912.

Lyrical songs, idylls, and epigrams. Translated by E. Magnússon and E. H. Palmer. London, Paul, 1878.

RYDBERG, VIKTOR. *Singoalla.* Translated by Axel

Josephsson; illustrated by Carl Larson. New York, Grafton Press, 1903.

The freebooter of the Baltic. Translated by C. L. Broomall. Media, Pa., Cooper and Vernon, 1891.

The last Athenian. Translated by W. W. Thomas, Jr. Philadelphia, Peterson, 1879.

SCHWARTZ, MARIE SOPHIE. *The man of birth and the woman of the people.* London, Strahan, 1873.

Numerous other American and English translations.

SIWERTZ, SIGFRID. *Downstream.* Translated by E. Classen. New York, Knopf, 1923.

Goldman's. Translated by E. G. Nash. New York, Cosmopolitan, 1930.

SÖDERBERG, HJALMAR. *Martin Birck's youth.* Translated by Charles W. Stork. New York, Harper, 1930.

SÖDERBERG, HJALMAR. *Selected short stories.* Translated by Charles Wharton Stork, Princeton University Press and American-Scandinavian Foundation, 1935.

STRINDBERG, AUGUST. *The red room.* Translated by Ellie Schleussner. New York, Putnam, 1913.

Married. New York, Boni, Liveright, 1917. (*Modern library.*)

The son of a servant. Translated by Claude Field. London, Rider, 1913.

Confession of a fool. Translated by Ellie Schleussner with preface by Ernest Boyd. New York, Viking Press, 1925.

The German lieutenant and other stories. (*The German lieutenant, Over-refinement, Unwelcome, Higher aims, Paul and Peter, The funeral, The last shot.*) Chicago, McClurg, 1915.

On the seaboard; a novel of the Baltic. Translated by E. C. Westergren. Cincinnati, Stewart, 1913.

Inferno. Translated by Claude Field. London, Rider, 1912.

Legends; autobiographical sketches. London, Melrose, 1912.

Plays. Series 1–5. Translated by Edwin Björkman. New York, Scribner, 1912–17.

Plays. Series 1–3. Translated by Edith and Warner Oland. Boston, Luce, 1912–14.

Plays. New York, Peter Smith, 1929–32. As follows:
Vol. I: *Easter,* tr. E. Classen; *The dance of death,* tr. C. D. Locock; *The ghost sonata,* tr. E. Palmstierna and J. B. Fagan; *A dream play,* tr. C. D. Locock. 1929.

Vol. II: *Lucky Peter's travels,* tr. E. Classen; *The father,* tr. C. D. Locock; *Lady Julie,* tr. C. D. Locock; *Playing with fire,* tr. E. Classen; *The bond,* tr. Elisabeth Sprigge and C. Napier. 1932.

Vol. III: *Master Olof,* tr. C. D. Locock; *Gustav Vasa,* tr. C. D. Locock; *Eric XIV,* tr. Joan Bulman; *The saga of the Folkungs,* tr. C. D. Locock. 1932.

SWEDENBORG, EMANUEL. *Works.* I–XXV, New York, New Church Society, 1905–09.

TEGNÉR, ESAIAS. *Poems: The children of the Lord's Supper,* translated by Henry W. Longfellow; and *Frithiof's saga,* translated by W. L. Blackley; introduction by Paul R. Lieder. New York, American-Scandinavian Foundation, 1914. (*Scandinavian classics,* Vol. II.)

Axel. Translated by Magnus Bernhard. Revised edition. Buffalo, N. Y., Burow's Sons, 1915.

TOPELIUS, ZACHRIS. *The surgeon's stories; Swedish historical romance in six cycles.* Chicago, Jansen, McClurg, 1884.

Snowdrops; Finland idylls for children. Translated by Albert Alberg. London, Allen, 1881.

Four fairy plays. Translated by E. J. Macintyre. *Poet Lore,* Boston, 1917, Vol. XXVIII, no. v, pp. 567–599.

WALLIN, JOHAN OLOF. *The angel of death.* Translated by C. B. Shaw. Chicago, Engberg-Holmberg, 1910.

ÖSTLUND, HILDING. *We poor miserable devils.* Translated by I. Modin. London, Cassell, 1934.

VII. TRAVEL AND DESCRIPTION

BLOMSTEDT, M., and BOOK, F., eds. *Sweden of today; a survey of its intellectual and material culture.* Stockholm, Tullberg, 1930.

GUINCHARD, J., ed. *Historical and statistical handbook.* Stockholm, Government Printing Office, 1914.

HEIDENSTAM, OSCAR GUSTAF VON. *Swedish life in town and country.* New York, Putnam, 1904. (*Our European neighbors,* Vol. XII.)

LEACH, HENRY GODDARD. *Scandinavia of the Scandinavians.* New York, Scribner, 1916.

LUNDBORG, H., M.D., and RUNNSTRÖM, J., PH.D. *The Swedish nation: in word and picture.* A jubilee book . . . published by the Swedish Society for Race Hygiene. Stockholm, Tullberg and Co. Ltd., 1921.

MEDILL, ROBERT (ROBERT MEDILL McBRIDE). *Sweden and its people.* New York, McBride, 1924.

ROTHERY, AGNES. *Sweden, the land and the people.* New York, Viking Press, 1934. Contains a good bibliography on Sweden, in English.

Sweden illustrated; 94 illustrations from photographs with text in Swedish and English. New York, Bonnier distributors, 1929.

The Sweden year-book, 1921–36. Stockholm; edited and published with the assistance of public authorities, none issued for certain years, e. g., 1927. Some years, i. e., 1921, 1922, 1923–24 have for title *The Swedish year-book.* The 1936 edition contains an up-to-date *Bibliographical list of books in English on Sweden and*

literary works translated into English from Swedish,
which list is obtainable also separately.

WHYTE, FREDERIC. *A wayfarer in Sweden*. Boston and
New York, Houghton, Mifflin, 1927.

ÅSBRINK, G. E. *A book about Sweden; a short survey of
the country, its people, history, culture, industrial
life, and tourist resorts*. Third edition. Stockholm,
C. E. Fritze, 1928.

VIII. PERIODICALS

Allsvensk Samling. Organ of *Riksföreningen för svensk-
hetens bevarande i utlandet*. Göteborg, 1913– .

American-Scandinavian Review. Ed., Hanna Astrup
Larsen. New York, American-Scandinavian Foundation, 1913– . Bi-monthly; now quarterly. Contains
a large number of translations (prose and poetry) not
listed separately in this bibliography.

The American Swedish Monthly. Ed., Victor O. Free-
burg. Published monthly by the Swedish Chamber
of Commerce of the U. S. A., 630 Fifth Ave., New
York City, 1917– .

Books Abroad. Ed., Roy Temple House. University of
Oklahoma, 1927– . A quarterly devoted to comment on foreign books.

*Fornvännen; meddelanden från k. vitterhets historie
och antikvitets akademien*. Ed., Sigurd Curman.
Stockholm, Wahlström och Widstrand, 1906– .

Hvar 8 Dag; illustrerat magasin. Göteborg, 1899– .
Now defunct.

Idun; illustrerad tidning för kvinnan och hemmet.
Stockholm, 1888– .

Ord och Bild; illustrerad månadsskrift. Ed., Karl Wåhlin.
Stockholm, Wahlström och Widstrand, 1892– .

Samlaren. Uppsala, Svenska litteratursällskapets arbets-
utskott. 1880–1919. Ny följd, 1920–

THE SCANDINAVIAN LITERATURES

Scandinavian Studies and Notes. Ed., A. M. Sturtevant. University of Kansas, Lawrence, Kan., 1911– . Quarterly.

Svenska Turistföreningens Årsskrift. Stockholm, Wahlström and Widstrand. 1885– .

IX. WORKS OF REFERENCE

HOFBERG, HERMAN. *Svenskt biografiskt handlexikon.* I–II, Stockholm, Bonnier, 1906.

Nordisk familjebok; encyklopedi och konversationslexikon. 3 väsentl. omarb. och koncentrerade uppl. Editor-in-chief, Yngve Lorents. I–XX, Stockholm, Aktiebolaget familjebokens förlag, 1923–34.

Svenskt biografiskt lexikon. Ed., Bertil Boetius. Vols. I– , Stockholm, Bonnier, 1918– . In process of publication. To date Vol. I–X have appeared.

Svensk uppslagsbok. Editor-in-chief, J. Carlquist. To be complete in 28 volumes, of which 16 have already appeared. Malmö, Baltiska förlaget a.–b., 1930– .

NOTE: For further information about Swedish literature, or the literature of the Scandinavian countries as a whole, or for Scandinavian periodicals and newspapers, address: Albert Bonnier Publishing House, 561 Third Avenue, New York City, N. Y.

SWEDISH-AMERICAN LITERATURE

by

ADOLPH B. BENSON, PH.D.

Professor of German and Scandinavian

in

Yale University

ALEXIS, JOSEPH E. A. *La littérature suédoise d'Amérique.*
Paris, 1930.

BONGGREN, JAKOB. "Swedish-American literature." In
The Swedish element in America. Chicago, 1931, Vol.
II, pp. 313–23.

LINDER, OLIVER A. "Svensk-amerikanska litteraturen."
In *Svenskarna i Amerika.* Stockholm, 1925, Vol. II,
pp. 193–213.

SKARSTEDT, ERNST. *Pennfäktare. Ny omarbetad och
tillökad upplaga.* Stockholm, 1930. The previous edition of 1897 was entitled *Våra pennfäktare.*

SWAN, G. N. "Svensk-amerikanska bilder och minnen."
In *Svenska Amerikanaren,* Chicago. Dr. Swan has
contributed articles on the subject to this journal for
several years. Consult the newspaper.*

* The following recent title should be added:
BENSON, ADOLPH B., ed. *The America of 1750: Peter Kalm's travels in
North America; the English version of 1770.* Revised from the original
Swedish and edited with a translation of new material from Kalm's diary
notes. I–II, New York, 1937.—Ed.

V

DANISH LITERATURE

by

JOHANNES KNUDSEN, cand. mag.
Professor of Danish and Scandinavian Literature
in
Grand View College
assisted by
ELVA L. KROGH, A.M.
Cataloguer, University of Illinois Library.

I. LITERARY HISTORY AND CRITICISM

ANDERSEN, VILHELM. *Tider og Typer af dansk Aands Historie.* I–IV, Köbenhavn, 1907–16.

BOMHOLT, JUL. *Dansk Digtning fra den industrielle Revolution til vore Dage.* Köbenhavn, 1930.

BOMHOLT, JUL. *Moderne Skribenter.* Köbenhavn, 1933.

BRANDES, GEORG. *Det moderne Gennembruds Maend.* Köbenhavn, 1883.

BRANDES, GEORG. *Samlede Skrifter.* I–III, Köbenhavn, 1899 (1919).

BRIX, HANS. *Danmarks Digtere.* Köbenhavn, 1925.

BUKDAHL, JÖRGEN. *Dansk national Kunst.* Köbenhavn, 1929.

BUKDAHL, JÖRGEN. *Det moderne Danmark.* Köbenhavn, 1931.

ELFELT, KJELD. *Litteraturen idag.* Köbenhavn, 1926.

GAD, CARL. *Omkring Kulturkrisen.* Köbenhavn, 1929.

GOSSE, E. W. *Northern studies.* (Includes four Danish poets: Grundtvig, Bödtcher, Andersen, Paludan-Müller.) London, 1890.

SELECTED BIBLIOGRAPHIES

GUNDEL, SVEN. *Dansk Digtning fra Halvfjerdserne til Nutiden; Naturalismens Historie i Omrids.* Köbenhavn, 1933.

HANSEN, PETER. *Illustreret dansk Litteraturhistorie.* I–III. Köbenhavn, 1902.

HESSELAA, PETER. *Vor Tids Digtere.* Köbenhavn, 1926.

KEHLER, HENNING. *Kronik og Kritik.* I–III, Köbenhavn, 1922–23.

LARSEN, HANNA ASTRUP. *Scandinavian literature.* Chicago, 1930.

MORTENSEN, KARL. *Dansk Litteraturhistorie.* Köbenhavn, 1918.

NIELSEN, HARALD. *Moderne Litteratur.* I–II, Köbenhavn, 1904–23.

PALUDAN, JULIUS. *Danmarks Litteratur i Middelalderen.* Köbenhavn, 1896.

PALUDAN, JULIUS. *Danmarks Litteratur mellem Reformationen og Holberg.* Köbenhavn, 1896.

PETERSEN, CARL SOPHUS, and ANDERSEN, VILHELM. *Illustreret dansk Litteraturhistorie.* I–IV, Köbenhavn, 1924–34.

PETERSEN, NIELS MATTHIAS. *Bidrag til den danske Literaturs Historie.* I–V, Köbenhavn, 1853–64; second edition, 1867–72.

RIMESTAD, CHRISTIAN. *Fra Stuckenberg til Seedorf; den lyriske Renaessance i Danmark.* I–II, Köbenhavn, 1922.

SKOVRUP, EINAR, compiler. *Hovedtraek af Nordisk Digtning i Nytiden.* (*Danmark*). Köbenhavn, 1920.

STANGERUP, HAKON. *Den unge Litteratur.* Köbenhavn, 1928.

TOPSÖE-JENSEN, HELGE GOTTLIEB. *Den skandinaviske Litteratur fra 1870 til vore Dage.* Köbenhavn, 1928.

TOPSÖE-JENSEN, HELGE GOTTLIEB. *Scandinavian literature from Brandes to our day.* Translated by Isaac Anderson. New York, 1930.

VEDEL, VALDEMAR. *Firsernes Förere*. Köbenhavn, 1923.

VEDEL, VALDEMAR. *Studier over Guldalderen i dansk Digtning*. Köbenhavn, 1890.

WINKEL HORN, FREDERIK. *History of the literature of the Scandinavian North from the most ancient times to the present*. Translated by Rasmus B. Anderson. Chicago, 1884.

ÖSTERGAARD, VILHELM. *Illustreret dansk Litteraturhistorie; danske Digtere i det 19de Aarhundrede, med en kort Oversigt over aeldre dansk Literatur*. Köbenhavn, 1907.

II. BIOGRAPHY

BRICKA, C. F., *Dansk biografisk Leksikon*. I–XIX, Köbenhavn, 1887–1905. An enlarged ed. in progress, 1933– .

DAHL, SVEND and ENGELSTOFT, P. *Dansk biografisk Haandleksikon*. I–II, Köbenhavn, 1920–26.

EHRENCRON-MÜLLER. *Forfatterlexikon omfattende Danmark, Norge og Island indtil 1814*. I–XII, Köbenhavn, 1924–35.

III. EARLY LITERATURE

SAXO GRAMMATICUS. *The first nine books of the Danish history of Saxo Grammaticus*. Translated by Oliver Elton, with notes by Frederic York-Powell. London, 1894.

OLRIK, AXEL. *The heroic legends of Denmark*. Translated and revised in collaboration with the author by Lee M. Hollander. New York, 1919.

OLRIK, AXEL. *Viking civilization*. Revised after the author's death by Hans Ellekilde; translated by Jacob Wittmer Hartmann and Hanna Astrup Larsen. New York, 1930.

Ancient Danish ballads. Translated from the originals by R. C. Alexander Prior. I–III, London, 1860.

SELECTED BIBLIOGRAPHIES

Ballads from the Danish and original verses. Translated and written by E. M. Smith-Dampier. London, 1910.

More ballads from the Danish and original verses. Translated and written by E. M. Smith-Dampier. London, 1914.

Danish ballads. Translated by E. M. Smith-Dampier. New York, 1920.

BORROW, GEORGE HENRY. *Romantic ballads, translated from the Danish; and miscellaneous pieces.* New York, 1913.

The Norse King's bridal. Translated from the Danish and Old Norse, with original ballads, by E. M. Smith-Dampier. London, 1912.

HUSTVEDT, SIGURD BERNHARD. *Ballad criticism in Scandinavia and Great Britain during the eighteenth century.* New York, 1916.

HUSTVEDT, SIGURD BERNHARD. *Ballad books and ballad men; raids and rescues in Britain, America, and the Scandinavian North since 1800.* Cambridge, Mass., 1930.

STEENSTRUP, JOHANNES C. H. R. *The mediaeval popular ballad.* Translated by Edward Godfrey Cox. Boston, New York, Chicago and London, 1914.

IV. ANTHOLOGIES

LARSEN, HANNA ASTRUP. *Denmark's best stories; an introduction to Danish fiction.* New York, 1928.

A book of Danish verse. Translated by S. Foster Damon and Robert Hillyer; selected and annotated by Oluf Friis. New York, 1922.

V. INDIVIDUAL AUTHORS

ANDERSEN, HANS CHRISTIAN:
Andersen's fairy tales. Edited by Margherita O. Os-

borne; illustrated by Ben Kutcher. Philadelphia, 1930.

Fairy tales and other stories. Revised and in part newly translated by W. A. and J. K. Craigie. London, New York, 1914.

Fairy tales and stories. Translated by H. L. Braekstad. New York, 1900.

Fairy tales. Illustrated by Kay Nielsen. Garden City, N. Y., 1932.

Fairy tales. Illustrated by Arthur Rackham. Philadelphia, 1932.

Forty stories. Newly translated from the Danish by M. R. James. London, 1930.

Stories from Hans Andersen. Illustrated by Edmund Dulac. New York, 1922.

The improvisatore. Translated by Mary Howitt. New York, 1845; London, 1847; Boston, 1890.

The real princess. Illustrated by Hedvig Collin. Chicago, 1932.

The story of a mother. Art edition, commemorating the one hundred and twenty-fifth anniversary of his birth. Illustrated by Fritz Syberg. Cincinnati, Ohio, 1929.

The true story of my life. Translated by Mary Howitt. New York, 1926.

BAIN, R. NISBET. *Hans Christian Andersen; a biography.* New York, London, 1895.

REUMERT, ELITH. *Hans Andersen, the man.* Translated by Jessie Bröchner. London, 1927.

RUSSELL, CHARLES. *Ugly duckling.* London, 1934. A biography of Andersen.

TOKSVIG, SIGNE. *The life of Hans Christian Andersen.* New York, 1934.

ANDERSEN, KNUD:

The brand of the sea. Translated by Grace Isabel Colbron. New York, 1929.

Surf. Translated by Grace Isabel Colbron. New York, 1931.

ANDERSEN-NEXO, MARTIN:

Pelle the Conqueror. Translated by Jessie Muir and Bernhard Miall. I–IV, New York, 1917.

Ditte, girl alive! New York, 1920.

Ditte, daughter of man. Translated by A. G. Chater and Richard Thrisk. New York, 1921.

Ditte, towards the stars. Translated by Asta and Rowland Kenney. New York, 1922.

In God's land. Translated by Thomas Seltzer. Viking Press, 1933.

ANKER-LARSEN, JOHANNES:

A stranger in paradise. Translated by Ruth Castberg Jordan. New York, 1929.

Martha and Mary. Translated by Arthur G. Chater. New York, 1926.

The philosopher's stone. Translated by Arthur G. Chater. New York, 1926.

BANG, HERMAN:

Denied a country. Translated by Marie Busch and A. G. Chater. New York, 1927.

Four devils. Novelized by Guy Fowler from the Fox picture produced by F. W. Murman. New York, 1928.

Ida Brandt. Translated by Arthur G. Chater. New York, 1928.

BRANDES, GEORG:

Eminent authors of the nineteenth century. Translated by Rasmus B. Anderson. New York, 1886.

Main currents in nineteenth century literature. Translated by Diana White and Mary Morison. London, 1901–05; New York, 1906.

Creative spirits of the nineteenth century. Translated by Rasmus B. Anderson. New York, 1923.

Ferdinand Lassalle. London, 1925.

Friedrich Nietzsche. Translated by Arthur G. Chater. New York, 1909.

Hellas; travels in Greece. Translated by Jacob W. Hartmann. New York, 1926.

Impressions of Russia. Translated by Samuel C. Eastman. New York, 1889.

Jesus, a myth. Translated by Edwin Björkman. New York, 1926.

Lord Beaconsfield. Translated by Mrs. George Sturge. New York, 1886.

Voltaire. Translated by Otto Kruger and Pierce Butler. New York, 1930.

William Shakespeare. Translated by William Archer, Mary Morison, and Diana White. New York, 1924.

Wolfgang Goethe. Translated by Allen W. Porterfield. New York, 1924.

On reading; an essay. New York, 1906; revised edition, 1923.

Reminiscences of my childhood and youth. London and New York, 1906.

MORITZEN, JULIUS. *Georg Brandes in life and letters;* with an introduction by Professor Robert H. Fife. Newark, New Jersey, 1922.

BREGENDAHL, MARIE:
A night of death. Translated by Margery Blanchard. New York, 1931.

DRACHMANN, HOLGER:
Nanna; a story of Danish love. Rewritten in English by Frances F. Browne. Chicago, 1901.

Renaissance. Translated by L. M. Hollander. *Poet Lore,* Vol. XIX, no. 4, 1908.

EWALD, CARL:
The four seasons. Translated by Alexander Teixeira de Mattos. New York, 1913.

The old room. Translated by Alexander Teixeira de Mattos. New York, 1908.

The pond and other stories. Translated by Alexander Teixeira de Mattos. London, 1909.

Two legs. Translated by Alexander Teixeira de Mattos. London, 1930.

A large number of Ewald's many other stories have been translated.

EWALD, JOHANNES:

The death of Balder. Translated by George Borrow. London, 1889.

GJELLERUP, KARL:

Minna. Translated by C. L. Nielsen. London, 1913.

The pilgrim Kaminite. Translated by John E. Logie. New York, 1912.

GRUNDTVIG, S. H.:

Fairy tales from afar. Translated by Jane Muller. New York, 1902.

Danish fairy tales. Translated by J. Grant Cramer. Boston, 1912.

HAUCH, JOHANNES CARSTEN:

Robert Fulton; an historical novel. Translated by Paul C. Sinding. New York, 1868.

HOLBERG, LUDVIG:

Comedies by Holberg: Jeppe of the hill, The political tinker, Erasmus Montanus. Translated by Oscar James Campbell, Jr., and Frederic Schenck, with an introduction by Oscar James Campbell. New York, 1914.

Three comedies. Translated by H. W. L. Hime. London, 1912.

Jeppe on the hill. Translated by W. C. Westergaard and M. B. Ruud. Grand Forks, N. D., 1906.

The blue apron statesman. Translated by T. Weber. Copenhagen, 1885.

A journey to the world underground by Nicholas Klimius. London, 1742.

Niels Klim's journey under the ground. Translated by John Gierlow. New York, 1845.

Memoirs. London, 1827.

CAMPBELL, OSCAR JAMES, JR. *The comedies of Holberg.* Cambridge, Mass., 1914.

INGEMANN, BERNHARD SEVERIN:

King Eric and the outlaws, or the throne, the church, and the people in the 13th century. Translated by J. F. Chapman. I–III, London, 1843.

The childhood of King Erik Menved. Translated by J. Kesson. London, 1846.

JACOBSEN, JENS PETER:

Marie Grubbe, a lady of the 17th century. Translated by Hanna Astrup Larsen. New York, 1917.

Mogens and others stories. Translated by Anna Grabow. New York, 1926.

Niels Lyhne. Translated by Hanna Astrup Larsen. New York, 1919.

Poems. Translated by P. Selver. New York, 1923.

JENSEN, JOHANNES VILHELM:

The long journey. Translated by A. G. Chater. I–III, New York, 1923–24.

The fall of the king. Translated by P. T. Federspiel and Patrick Kirwan. New York, 1923.

JÖRGENSEN, JOHANNES:

An autobiography. Translated by Ingeborg Lund. I–II, London, New York, 1928.

False witness. Authorized translation of "Klokke Roland." London, 1916.

Lourdes. Translated by Ingeborg Lund, New York, 1914.

Saint Francis of Assisi. Translated by T. O'Connor Sloane. New York, 1912.

SELECTED BIBLIOGRAPHIES

KIERKEGAARD, SÖREN AABYE:

Selections from the writings of Kierkegaard. Translated by L. M. Hollander. Austin, Texas, 1923.

Philosophical fragments; or a fragment of philosophy. Translated with introduction and notes by David F. Swenson. New York and Princeton, 1936.

LAUESEN, MARCUS:

Waiting for a ship. Translated by Arthur G. Chater. New York and London, 1933.

MICHAELIS, KARIN:

Andrea, the tribulations of a child. Translated by John Nielsen Laurvik. New York, 1904.

Bibi, a little Danish girl. Translated by Lida Siboni Hanson. Garden City, N. Y., 1927.

The dangerous age; letters and fragments from a woman's diary. New York, 1911.

Elsie Lindtner; a sequel to The dangerous age. Translated by Beatrice Marshall. New York, 1912.

The governor. Translated by Amy Skovgaard-Pedersen. New York, 1913.

Venture's end. Translated by Grace Isabel Colbron. New York, 1927.

OEHLENSCHLÄGER, ADAM:

Aladdin. Translated by Theodore Martin. London, 1863.

An English version of Oehlenschlaeger's Hakon Jarl. Translated by James Christian Lindberg. Lincoln, Neb., 1905. (*Nebraska University Studies*, Vol. V, no. 1, pp. 39–141.)

Axel and Valborg. Translated by F. S. Kolle. New York, 1906.

Hakon Jarl. Translated by F. S. Kolle. New York, 1911.

Palnatoke, a tragedy. Translated by John Chapman. London, 1855.

[365]

The gods of the North, an epic poem. Translated by W. E. Frye. London, 1845.

DEPPING, GEORG BERNHARD. *Wayland Smith, a dissertation of the Middle Ages, and the amplified legend by Oehlenschläger.* London, 1847.

PALUDAN, JACOB:

Birds around the light. Translated by Grace Isabel Colbron. New York, 1928.

PETERSEN, NIS:

The street of the sandalmakers. Translated by Elizabeth Sprigge and Claude Napier. New York, 1933.

RUNG, OTTO:

Shadows that pass. Translated by Grace Isabel Colbron. New York, 1924.

SÖIBERG, HARRY:

The sea king. Translated by Edwin Björkman. New York, 1928.

STUCKENBERG, VIGGO HENRIK FOG:

By the wayside; little tales and legends. Translated and illustrated by Una Hook. London, 1917.

ULFELDT, LEONORA CHRISTINA:

Memoirs of Leonora Christina, daughter of Christian IV of Denmark, written during her imprisonment in the Blue Tower at Copenhagen, 1663–1685. Translated by F. E. Bunnett. New York, 1929.

WIED, GUSTAV:

Autumn fires; a comedy. Translated by Benjamin F. Glazer. Cincinnati, 1920.

$2 \times 2 = 5$; *a comedy in four acts.* Translated by Ernest Boyd and Holger Koppel. New York, 1923.

DANISH-AMERICAN LITERATURE

by

JOHANNES KNUDSEN, cand. mag.
Professor of Danish and Scandinavian Literature
in
Grand View College

BAY, J. CHRISTIAN. *Denmark in English and American literature*. Chicago, 1915.

CHRISTENSEN, THOMAS P. *Dansk-amerikansk Histoire*. Cedar Falls, Ia., 1927.

HENIUS, MAX, compiler. *Den danskfödte Amerikaner*. Chicago, 1912.

VIG, P. S., and others. *Danske i Amerika*. Edited and published by C. Rasmussen. Minneapolis and Chicago, 1907.

BAY, J. CHRISTIAN. "Carl Hansens Levnet og Gerning." Introduction to *Fra Praerien* by Carl Hansen. Cedar Falls, Ia., 1916.

VI

ICELANDIC LITERATURE

by

RICHARD BECK, PH.D.
*Professor and Head of the Department of
Scandinavian Languages and Literatures
in the
University of North Dakota*

ANDRÉSSON, KRISTINN. "The Icelanders and their writers." Translated by Jón Stefánsson. In *Life and Letters Today*, Winter, 1936, Vol. XV, no. vi, pp. 50–55.

ASHDOWN, M. *English and Norse documents relating to the reign of Ethelred the Unready*. Cambridge, 1930.

BECK, RICHARD. *Icelandic lyrics*. Reykjavik, 1930.

CHADWICK, H. M. *The heroic age*. Cambridge, 1912.

CHAPMAN, OLIVE MURRAY. *Across Iceland*. London and New York, 1930.

CRAIGIE, W. A. *The Icelandic sagas*. Cambridge, 1913.

CRAIGIE, W. A. *The Oxford book of Scandinavian verse*. Oxford, 1926.

CRAIGIE, W. A. "The poetry of the skalds." In *The Scottish Review*, October, 1896, Vol. XXVIII, pp. 331–46.

CRAIGIE, W. A. *The religion of ancient Scandinavia*. London, 1906.

CRAIGIE, W. A. *Scandinavian folk-lore*. Paisley, 1896.

Egil's saga. Done into English out of the Icelandic by E. R. Eddison. Cambridge, 1931.

EINARSSON, INDRIDI. *Sword and crozier*. Translated by

Lee M. Hollander. In *Poet Lore*, Vol. XXIII, 1912.

The Elder or Poetic Edda. Edited and translated by Olive Bray. London, 1908.

FARADAY, WINIFRED. *The Edda: I. The divine mythology of the North. II. The heroic mythology of the North*. London, 1902.

GJERSET, KNUT. *History of Iceland*. New York, 1924.

GOLTHER, W. *Nordische Literaturgeschichte*. Vol. I, Leipzig, 1905.

GUDMUNDSSON, KRISTMANN. *The bridal gown*. Translated by O. F. Theis. New York, 1931.

GUDMUNDSSON, VALTÝR. *Island am Beginn des 20. Jahrhunderts*. Kattowitz, 1904.

GUNNARSSON, GUNNAR. *Guest the one-eyed*. London, 1920.

GUNNARSSON, GUNNAR. *Seven days' darkness*. Translated by Roberts Tapley. New York, 1930.

GUNNARSSON, GUNNAR. *The sworn brothers*. London, 1920.

HANSEN, OLAF. *Islandsk Renaessance*. Köbenhavn. 1907.

HANSEN, OLAF. *Ny-islandsk Lyrik*. Köbenhavn, 1901.

HANSEN, OLAF. *Udvalgte islandske digte*, etc. Köbenhavn-Kristiania, 1919.

The Hávamál. With selections from other poems of the *Edda*. Edited and translated by D. E. Martin Clarke. Cambridge, 1923.

HERRMANN, PAUL. *Island in Vergangenheit und Gegenwart*. Vols. I–III, Leipzig, 1907–10.

HERMANNSSON, H. *The periodical literature of Iceland*. Ithaca, 1918. (*Islandica*, Vol. XI.)

HERMANNSSON, H. *Icelandic authors of to-day*. Ithaca, 1913. (*Islandica*, Vol. VI.)

HERMANNSSON, H. *Icelandic manuscripts*. Ithaca, 1929. (*Islandica*, Vol. XIX.)

HERMANNSSON, H. *Old Icelandic literature*, Ithaca, 1933. (*Islandica*, Vol. XXIII.)

HOLLANDER, L. M. "The drama in Iceland, a sketch." In *Publications of the Society for the Advancement of Scandinavian Study*, Vol. I, 1912, pp. 99–106.

Icelandic legends. Collected by Jón Árnason. Translated by G. E. J. Powell and Eiríkr Magnússon. London, 1864. Second series. London, 1866.

JOHNSON, SVEINBJORN. *Pioneers of freedom*. Boston, 1930.

JÓNSSON, FINNUR. *Den oldnorske og oldislandske Litteraturs Historie*. Second edition. Vols. I–III, København, 1920–24.

JÓNSSON, FINNUR. *Den islandske Litteraturs Historie*. København, 1907.

KAMBAN, GUDMUNDUR. *Hadda Padda*. A drama in four acts translated by Sadie Luise Peller. New York, 1917. (*The Borzoi plays*, Vol. V.)

KER, W. P. *Collected essays*. Vol. II, London, 1925.

KER, W. P. *The dark ages*. New York, 1904.

KER, W. P. *Epic and romance*. London, 1908.

KERSHAW, N. *Anglo-Saxon and Norse poems*. Cambridge, 1922.

KIRKCONNELL, W. *The North American book of Icelandic verse*. New York and Montreal, 1930.

KIRKCONNELL, W. "Icelandic poetry today." In *Life and Letters Today*, Winter, 1936, Vol. XV, no. vi, pp. 42–49.

KOHT, H. *The Old Norse sagas*. New York, 1931.

KÜCHLER, K. *Geschichte der isländischen Dichtung der Neuzeit*. Vols. I–II, Leipzig, 1896–1902.

The Laxdaela saga. Translated from the Icelandic by Thorstein Veblen. New York, 1925.

LAXNESS, H. K. *Salka Valka*. Translated by F. H. Lyon, Boston, 1936.

LIESTÖL, KNUT. *The origin of the Icelandic family sagas*. Oslo, 1930.

The life and death of Kormac the Skald. Being the Icelandic *Kormaks saga* rendered into English by W. G. Collingwood and Jón Stefánsson. Ulverston, 1902.

Mogk, E. *Geschichte der norwegisch-isländischen Litteratur.* Second edition. Strassburg, 1904.

Nordal, S. *Íslensk lestrarbók.* Reykjavík, 1924.

Nordal, S. *Udsigt over Islands litteratur i det 19. og 20. aarhundrede.* Oslo, 1927.

Olrik, Axel. *Viking civilization.* London and New York, 1930.

Paasche, F. "Norges og Islands litteratur indtil utgangen av middelalderen." In Bull and Paasche, *Norsk litteraturhistorie.* Vol. I, Kristiania, 1924.

Phillpotts, B. S. *Edda and saga.* New York and London, 1931.

Pilcher, C. V. *Icelandic meditations on the passion.* New York and London, 1923.

Pilcher, C. V. *The passion-hymns of Iceland.* London, 1913.

Poestion, J. C. *Eislandsbluten; ein Sammelbuch neuisländischer Lyrik.* Leipzig and München, 1904.

Poestion, J. C. *Isländische Dichter der Neuzeit.* Leipzig, 1897.

Poestion, J. C. *Zur Geschichte des isländischen Dramas und Theaterwesens.* Wien, 1903.

The Poetic Edda. Translated by Henry Adams Bellows. New York, 1923. (*Scandinavian classics,* Vols. XXI-XXII.) Two volumes in one, Princeton University Press and American-Scandinavian Foundation, 1936.

The Poetic Edda. Translated by Lee M. Hollander. University of Texas, 1928.

The saga of Grettir the Strong. Translated by G. A. Hight. London and New York, 1914. (*Everyman's library.*)

The saga of the Volsungs; the saga of Ragnar Lodbrok. Translated by Margaret Schlauch. New York, 1930. (*Scandinavian classics,* Vol. XXV.)

The saga library. Edited by William Morris and Eiríkr Magnússon. Vols. I–IV, London, 1891–1905.

SCHAUCH, M. *Romance in Iceland.* New York, 1934.

SCHWEITZER, P. *Geschichte der skandinavischen Litteratur.* Leipzig, 1886–88.

SCHWEITZER, P. *Island, Land und Leute, Geschichte, Litteratur und Sprache.* Leipzig and Berlin, 1885.

SIGURJÓNSSON, JÓHANN. *Modern Icelandic plays.* Translated by Henninge Krohn Schanche. New York, 1929. (*Scandinavian classics,* Vol. VI.)

SKOVRUP, EJNAR. *Hovedtraek af nordisk Digtning i Nytiden.* Köbenhavn, 1920–21.

SÓLARLJÓÐ. *An Icelandic Divine Comedy.* Translated by C. V. Pilcher. In *The Canadian Journal of Religious Thought,* Vol. I, no. vi, 1924, pp. 499–508.

STEFÁNSSON, VILHJÁLMUR. "The newer literature of Iceland" and "Present-day literature of Iceland." In *Poet Lore,* Vol. XV, 1904, no. i, pp. 62–76; no. ii, pp. 126–38.

The Story of Burnt Njal. From the Icelandic of the *Niáls saga* by G. W. Dasent. Edinburgh, 1861, and London, 1906. London, 1911. (*Everyman's library.*)

STURLUSON, SNORRI. *The Heimskringla.* Translated from the Icelandic by Samuel Laing. Vols. I–III, London, 1844. Second edition, Vols. I–IV, London, 1899.

Separate edition: *The Olaf-sagas.* London and New York, 1914. (*Everyman's library.*)

The Norse King's sagas. London and New York, 1930. (*Everyman's library.*)

STURLUSON, SNORRI. *The Heimskringla.* Edited and translated by Erling Monsen. New York, 1932.

STURLUSON, SNORRI. *The Prose Edda.* Translated from the Icelandic by A. G. Brodeur. New York, 1916. (*Scandinavian classics,* Vols. XXI–XXII.)

THORGILSSON, ARI. *The Book of Icelanders (Íslend-*

ingabók). Edited and translated by Halldór Hermannsson. Ithaca, 1930. (*Islandica*, Vol. XX.)

THORODDSEN, JÓN. *Lad and lass*. Translated by Arthur M. Reeves. London, 1890.

THORSTEINSSON, TH. *Iceland*. Second edition, Reykjavík, 1930.

Three northern love stories and other tales. Translated from the Icelandic by Eiríkr Magnússon and William Morris. Second edition. London and New York, 1901.

WILLIAMS, M. W. *Social Scandinavia in the viking age*. New York, 1920.

WORSTER, W. "Four Icelandic poets." In *The Edinburgh Review*, Vol. CCXXXVIII, October, 1923, pp. 302–19, and in *The American-Scandinavian Review*, Vol. XII, June, 1924.

ADDENDA

BECK, RICHARD. "Einar H. Kvaran, an Icelandic novelist and dramatist." In *Poet Lore*, Vol. XLIII, 1936, no. i, pp. 56–63.

BECK, RICHARD. "Iceland's poet laureate." (Einar Benediktsson.) In *Books Abroad*, Vol. X, Summer, 1936, pp. 270–71.

GUDMUNDSSON, KRISTMANN. *The morning of life*. Translated by Elizabeth Sprigge and Claude Napier. Garden City, N. Y., 1936.

KAMBAN, GUDMUNDUR. *The virgin of Skalholt*. Translated by E. Ramsden. Boston, 1935.

KVARAN, EINAR H. *Governor Lenhard*. Translated by Jakobina Johnson. In *Poet Lore*, Vol. XLIII, 1936, no. i, pp. 3–55.

ICELANDIC-AMERICAN LITERATURE

by

RICHARD BECK, PH.D.

*Professor and Head of the Department of
Scandinavian Languages and Literatures
in the
University of North Dakota*

BECK, RICHARD. "An Icelandic poet-pioneer." In *The American-Scandinavian Review*, July, 1929, pp. 424–25.

BECK, RICHARD. "Bokmentaidja Islendinga i Vesturheimi." In *Eimreidin*, Vol. XXXIV, nos. i and iv, 1928, pp. 41–69, 321–40; and Vol. XXXV, no. i, pp. 49–62, 1929.

BECK, RICHARD. *Icelandic lyrics.* Reykjavik, 1930.

HERMANNSSON, HALLDÓR. "Icelandic-American periodicals." In *Publications of the Society for the Advancement of Scandinavian Study*, Vol. III, 1916.

HERMANNSSON, HALLDÓR. *Islaenderne i Amerika.* Copenhagen, 1922.

JOHNSON, JAKOBINA. "Stephan G. Stephansson." In *Scandinavia*, Vol. I, no. iv, April, 1924, pp. 38–43.

KIRCONNELL, W. *The North American book of Icelandic verse.* New York and Montreal, 1930.

KIRKCONNELL, W. "Icelandic-Canadian poetry." In the *Dalhousie Review*, October, 1934, pp. 331–44.

KIRKCONNELL, W. *Canadian Overtones.* Winnipeg, 1935.

Tímarit Thjódraeknisfelags Islendinga. Edited by Rögnvaldur Pétursson. Winnipeg, 1911– .

Vestan um haf. Edited by Einar H. Kvaran and Gudmundur Finnbogason. Reykjavik, 1930.

VII

FINNISH LITERATURE

by
RICHARD BECK, PH.D.
*Professor and Head of the Department of
Scandinavian Languages and Literatures
in the
University of North Dakota*

AHO, JUHANI. *Squire Hellman and other stories.* Translated by R. Nisbet Bain. London, 1893.

Anthology of Swedish lyrics. Translated in the original meters by Charles Wharton Stork. New York, 1930. (*Scandinavian classics,* Vol. IX.)

ASPELIN, E. "Den finskspråkiga litteraturen." In *Finland i XIX seklet.* Helsingfors, 1893.

BILLSON, C. J. *Popular poetry of the Finns.* London, 1900. Vol. V in series *Popular studies in mythology and folklore,* I–XV. London, 1899–1906.

BOTSFORD, F. *Folk songs of many peoples.* Vols. I–II, New York, 1921.

BRUHN, R. "Finlands svenska litteratur." In *Finland,* Vol. III, Stockholm, 1925; and in *Det Svenska Finland,* Vol. II:2, Stockholm, 1923.

CASTRÉN, G. "Den nyare finska litteraturen." In *Vår tid.* Årsbok utg. av Samfundet De Nio. IX, Stockholm, 1924.

COMPARETTI, D. *The traditional poetry of the Finns.* London, 1898.

CRAWFORD, J. C. *The Kalevala.* Vols. I–II, Cincinnati, 1887.

[375]

ESTLANDER, G. "Finlands svenska litteratur." In *Finland i XIX seklet*. Helsingfors, 1893.

Finsk tidskrift för vitterhet, vetenskap, konst och politik. Periodical. Helsingfors, 1876– .

GOSSE, E. *Studies in the literature of northern Europe*. London, 1879.

Granskaren; tidskrift för kultur, ekonomi, politik. Periodical. Åbo, 1929– .

HEDVALL, RUTH. *Finlands svenska litteratur*. Stockholm, 1917.

HERTZMAN-ERICSON, G. *Poetic profiles in Finland*. In *The American-Scandinavian Review*, Vol. XXI, August-September, 1933, pp. 423–28.

HOMÉN, L. O. *De nyare författarna*. Helsingfors, 1915.

KALLAS, AINO. *White ship*. Translated from the Finnish by Alex Matson. London and New York, 1924.

KALLAS, AINO. *Eros the slayer*. Translated from the Finnish by Alex Matson. New York and London, 1927.

KIVI, ALEXIS. *Seven brothers*. Translated from the Finnish by Alex Matson. New York, 1929.

LANDQUIST, JOHN. *Modern svensk litteratur i Finland*. Stockholm, 1929.

LINNANKOSKI, J. (PELTONEN, V.). *Song of the blood-red flower*. Translated from the Finnish by W. Worster. New York, 1921.

Nya Argus. Periodical. Helsingfors, 1907– .

READE, ARTHUR. *Finland and the Finns*. New York, 1917.

RUNEBERG, J. L. *King Fialar; a poem in five songs*. Translated by Eiríkr Magnússon. London, 1912.

RUNEBERG, J. L. *Lyrical songs, idylls and epigrams*. Translated by Eiríkr Magnússon and E. H. Palmer. London, 1878.

RUNEBERG, J. L. *Nadeschda, a poem*. From the Swedish by Mrs. J. Shipley. New York and London, 1890.

RUNEBERG, J. L. *Songs of Ensign Stål*. From the Swedish in original meters. Translated by Clement Burbank Shaw. New York, 1925.

SETÄLÄ, E. N. *Die finnische Literatur*. Leipzig, 1908. (*Kultur der Gegenwart*, I, 9.)

SILLANPÄÄ, F. E. *The maid Silja*. Translated from the Finnish by Alex Matson. New York, 1933.

SKOVRUP, EJNAR. *Hovedtraek af nordisk Digtning i Nytiden; Danmark, Island, Norge, Sverige, Finland*. Köbenhavn, 1920–21.

TARKIANEN, V., AND LAURILA, K. S. "Den finska litteraturen." In *Finland*. Vol. III, Stockholm, 1925.

TIANDER, K. "Finnische Dichtung." In *Deutsche Rundschau*, Vol. CCII, January, 1925, pp. 81–95.

TOPELIUS, Z. *Canute Whistlewinks and other stories*. Translated from the Swedish by C. W. Foss. New York, 1927.

TOPELIUS, Z. *King's ring; romance of the days of Gustavus Adolphus and the 30 years' war*. Translated from the Swedish by Sophie Ohrwall and Herbert Arnold. London, 1901.

TOPELIUS, Z. *Stories for children*. Translated from the Swedish by C. W. Foss. Rock Island, Illinois, 1911.

TOPELIUS, Z. *Two times two is four*. Adapted from the Swedish by Vera C. Himes. New York, 1931.

VAN CLEEF, E. *Finland—the republic farthest north*. Columbus, Ohio, 1929.

FINNISH-AMERICAN LITERATURE

by
GEORGE SJÖBLOM
Formerly Editor of Valvoja *and*
New Yorkin Uutiset

ILMONEN, SALOMON. "Katsaus kirjallisuuteen." In *Amerikan suomalaisten historia.* Hancock, Mich., 1923, Vol. III, pp. 114–126.

NIKANDER, WERNER. *Amerikan suomalaisia.* Hancock, Mich., 1927.

RAUTANEN, VILJAMI. *Amerikan suomalainen kirkko.* Hancock, Mich., 1917.

SYRJÄLÄ, F. J. *Amerikan suomalaisen työväenliikkeen historia.* Fitchburg, Mass., 1923.

WARGELIN, JOHN. *The Americanization of the Finns.* Hancock, Mich., 1923.

New Yorkin Uutiset (newspaper). Brooklyn, N. Y. Articles and book reviews. 1915–

INDEX

INDEX

AUTHORS

TITLES

INDEX

INDEX

INDEX

[384]

INDEX

INDEX

INDEX

INDEX

AUTHORS

TITLES

INDEX

INDEX

[390]

INDEX

INDEX

INDEX

AUTHORS

TITLES

INDEX

INDEX

INDEX

INDEX

INDEX

AUTHORS

TITLES

INDEX

AUTHORS

TITLES

INDEX

INDEX

[401]

INDEX

INDEX

INDEX

AUTHORS

Taine, 200
Tainio, 314
Talis Qualis, 120
Talvio, Maila, 299
Tausen, Hans, 167
Tavaststjerna, Karl August, 305-
06, 306
Tegengren, Jacob, 307-08
Tegnér, Esaias, 104, 105-09, 116,
119, 120, 201, 246, 260
Teigen, Knut M., 75
Tennyson, 152
Terkelsen, Sören, 172
Thaarup, Thomas, 178

TITLES

*Struggle between Norns and gods,
The*, 188
Stucco, 207
Sturlunga saga, 244-45
Sun on their shoulders, 315
Sunset, 61
Suomi, 294
Suomis sång, 305
Suuri uskonpuhdistaja, 317
Svend Grathe, 190
Svenska Amerikanaren, 152, 157
Svenska Amerikanska Posten, 152
Svenska bilder, 118-19
Svenska krönika, 90
Svenska Kuriren, 152
Svenska Tribunen-Nyheter, 152
Svensk Försäkringstidning, 122
Sverd og bagall, 275
Swanwhite, 130
Swedes and their chieftains, The,
134
Swedish-American literature, 144-
58
Swedish Argus, The, 95
Swedish destinies and adventures,
123
Swedish figures, 135
Swedish literature, 87-143
Swedish Mass, The, 90
Swedish people, The, 123
Sylvia, 315
Symra, 30, 83
Synnöve Solbakken, 43-44, 260

Taarnet, 211
Take all to Nebraska, 229
Talven maassa, 301
Talvikuva, 301
Temple of fame, 254
Tengdamamma, 270
Thanatos, 136
Their fathers' God, 81
Theodora, 66
Thousand and one nights, 194
Three friends, 67
Thrymskvida, 236
Thú vinvidur breini, 271
Tiberius, 190
Til Een, 194

[404]

INDEX

INDEX